ATLAS OF
AMERICAN
WARS

ATLAS OF AMERICAN WARS

Maps by

RICHARD NATKIEL

Text by

JOHN KIRK AND JOHN WESTWOOD

Arch Cape Press
A Division of Crown Publishers, Inc.

A Bison Book

Published 1986 by
Arch Cape Press, distributed by
Crown Publishers Inc.

Produced by Bison Books Corp.
17 Sherwood Place
Greenwich, CT 06830, USA

Printed in Hong Kong

ISBN 0-517-60468-X
h g f e d c b a

Richard Natkiel would like to thank his assistant David Burles for his help in preparing the maps.

Page 1: *Ulysses S Grant at Cold Harbor, June 1964.*
Pages 2–3: *Union troops during the Civil War.*
This page: *A US destroyer lays smoke off Leyte, October 1944.*

CONTENTS

INTRODUCTION

For a nation that has prided itself both on its essentially peaceful nature and on its success in avoiding 'foreign entanglements' America has fought a quite remarkable number of wars.

By the time the North American colonists were ready to declare their independence of Great Britain they had already been involved in four major wars with the French, two minor wars with the Dutch and Spanish and a long guerrilla struggle with the Indians was still in progress. Between 1776 and the time the United States – itself born of war – celebrated its Bicentennial, the nation had contrived to fight eight more wars against foreign enemies, a Civil War that dwarfed all but a handful of international wars, 114 more years of war against the Indians and a host of smaller actions in places as far-flung as Nicaragua, China, and the Philippines. Even in the relatively peaceful decade since 1976 the United States has committed its regular forces to some form of significant military action on an average of once every 24 months.

If, in the face of this record, Americans nevertheless still have some warrant for claiming to be a basically peaceful people, it may consist in the fact that for most of the wars on which she embarked America was singularly unprepared. For much of her history it was standard practice for the United States to maintain absurdly small (and often ill-funded, ill-trained and ill-equipped) peacetime military forces.

This traditional 'unfitness for war,' proudly proclaimed a certain Congressman Fisher in 1821, 'is the best feature of our government.' Perhaps, but it certainly did little to shorten the wars America regularly had to fight, and to what extent it may have invited some of those wars is at least moot. In essence, of course, this habitual unpreparedness was founded on an illusion, a popular willingness always to believe – despite the burden of historical evidence – that the war just fought would be the last. 'The war to end all wars' may have been a formulation peculiar to 1918, but it expressed a venerable American idea.

Of a piece with the traditional preference for believing that war would have no place in America's future was a certain reluctance to acknowledge that it had played an important role in America's past. Most standard American history textbooks paid (and to some extent still pay) scant attention to the details of the nations' wars. Military history was treated as a special subject, apart from the mainstream of historical study, the province of a limited number of military professionals and buffs. By the same token, on the rare occasion when a work of military history did manage to find a popular audience – as in the case of Alfred Thayer Mahan's *The Influence of Sea Power Upon History* – it was often treated as a sort of revelation, and the importance of its message exaggerated beyond the intention of its author.

It was during World War II that the way Americans traditionally thought about war first began to undergo significant change. Not every illusion was dispelled, of course. Such time-honored propensities as believing implicitly in the justice of the national cause and expecting nothing less than total victory were, if anything, reinforced by the war's peculiar morality-play scenario. But in some other important respects World War II fostered a greater realism in American attitudes. Obviously the initial disaster at Pearl Harbor administered a painful lesson about the high cost of military unpreparedness. Other dramatic lessons followed. And in a broader sense, simply because so many Americans either served in the war or, thanks to mass communication, were able to follow it in elaborate detail as it evolved, a whole generation in effect received a crash course in, if not classical military history, at least military history in-the-making.

By the early 1950s American publishers were for the first time beginning to find a mass market for books on military history. That market persisted even during the Vietnam era and the upsurge of anti-war sentiment in the late 1960s and early 1970s, and it now seems firmly established. The result is that today more Americans know more about their martial heritage than at any time past.

Although the new amateurs of American military history have been increasingly well provided with reference material in recent years, this has perhaps been least true of cartography. World War II has, to be sure, been extensively covered, especially in the several highly popular military atlases created by Richard Natkiel. But earlier American wars have been less well served in terms of comprehensive battle and campaign maps that are at once accurate and detailed, vivid and easy-to-read, accessible . . . and affordable. Less well served, that is, until now, for in this new *Atlas of American Wars* Richard Natkiel has provided precisely the cartographic reference work that has so long been missing

from the libraries of all but a handful of students of American military history. Here Mr Natkiel has skillfully combined scores of brand new maps with his own existing cartography to produce the first popularly-priced atlas that covers every major battle and campaign of every American war from the mid-18th century to the 1986 US air strike on Qadhafi's Tripoli. (Indeed, you will even find a map of that other – now almost forgotten – US assault on Tripoli that took place nearly two centuries ago.)

For the serious reader of military history a cartographic resource such as this is truly indispensable, for it presents a whole category of graphic information about the progress of battles and campaigns that can never be satisfactorily conveyed in words or pictures. And almost as important as what these maps show is what they imply. Beneath their dramatic surface displays – lightning campaigns of maneuver conducted by such masters as Jackson and Patton, grim slugging matches in which only dogged persistence and the unbreakable will of

commanders such as Grant or Pershing could confer victory, breathtaking strategic reversals such as those achieved by Washington at Yorktown and MacArthur at Inchon – beneath such surfaces lie equally fascinating subtexts. Texts that not only speak to us about what *kind* of wars these were and what kind of societies fought them, but that also remind us of continuities we may be tempted to forget.

For example, implicit in all the maps is the enduring interrelationship between war and technology. Nowadays, bemused by showers of such hi-tech marvels as laser-guided shells and nuclear-powered ballistic missile submarines, many people seem to imagine that our own time is one in which war is uniquely dominated by technological innovation. But to look at, say, Mr Natkiel's map of Grant's descent on Richmond in 1864–5, and to remember while doing so the staggering casualties sustained by both sides during that agonizing campaign, is to be reminded of what mid-nineteenth century advances in battlefield firepower meant to the participants in

the Civil War. As technical innovations go, percussion locks, rifled artillery and repeating pistols and carbines may seem small beer when compared to a modern stealth bomber, but they were evidently lethal enough to the fighting men of the Union and the Confederacy, more of whom were killed than were their American counterparts in World War II. The degree to which Civil War commanders were able to adjust their tactics to the capabilities of contemporary technology plainly had much to do with whether they won or lost. The same was true in World War I, World War II, Vietnam and, indeed, in every American war. (Consider, for example, the dramatic effect American innovations in naval architecture had on the outcome of the famous series of Anglo-American frigate duels fought in 1812.) The technological considerations that military planners have to take into account today may be very different in detail, but they are much the same in essence.

The maps suggest other continuities, as well. If, to give just one more example, Vietnam taught the current generation of Americans (as Afghanistan is still teaching the Russians) sharp lessons about the difficulties that sophisticated conventional military forces encounter when trying to fight a fluid guerrilla campaign with determined local irregulars, a good many of those lessons would probably have seemed all too familiar to the US Indian-fighting Army of the 1870s.

We have come a long way since the days when, on ideological grounds, most Americans preferred to believe that the study of their military past could yield few worthwhile practical results. Doubtless that is a good thing in these days when military considerations loom large in many of our public debates about fiscal policy and most of our debates about foreign policy. To be sure, we still have much to learn from the study of military history, as we do from the study of all history. But we can be grateful that we have books such as this one to help us on our way.

John Kirk

THE FRENCH AND INDIAN WARS

Colonial Warfare

'The French and Indian Wars' is the general name given to a series of four wars fought between English and French colonists in North America between 1689 and 1763. Insofar as the colonials were concerned, the concept of individual 'wars' was to some extent notional, since local armed hostilities tended to persist even during the intervals of 'peace' recognized by the mother countries. Geographically, there were two main theaters of conflict: the border between New England and New France, an ill-defined zone that ran, a little to the south of the St Lawrence River, northeast from Lake Erie to the Atlantic; and the disputed interior of the continent that lay west of the Appalachians. French strategy consisted in attempting to discourage English expansion north and west by means of incessant harassing raids conducted by French troops and their Indian allies along the peripheries of the English colonies. The English counter-strategy was to try to neutralize the key French bases: Montreal and Quebec on the St Lawrence, various port settlements in Nova Scotia and on Ile Royale (Cape Breton Island) and the chains of forts the French had built in the interior.

The final phase of this protracted struggle began in 1755 (one of the periods of formal 'peace') when British Major General Edward Braddock led a body of about 2000 regulars and Virginia militia in an assault on France's Fort Duquesne, situated at the confluence of the Allegheny and Monongahela Rivers. Braddock unwisely let his troops become strung

out during his advance, and on 9 July his forward force of 1200 was ambushed by 900 French regulars, Canadian militia and Indians. The result was a resounding British defeat: 914 English soldiers killed, including 63 officers, of whom Braddock was one. (Among the survivors was Braddock's aide-de-camp, Colonel George Washington.) Braddock's tactics in this battle – the attenuated force, the lack of forward scouting, the close-order formations used by the regular infantry – came to be regarded as virtually a textbook of how *not* to conduct wilderness warfare.

Above: *The mortally wounded General Braddock is carried away by his retreating army.*
Above right: *General Edward Braddock (1695–1755).*

MAP, top right: *Campaigns of the French and Indian Wars.*
Right: *Colonel George Washington giving orders to his men during Braddock's defeat.*

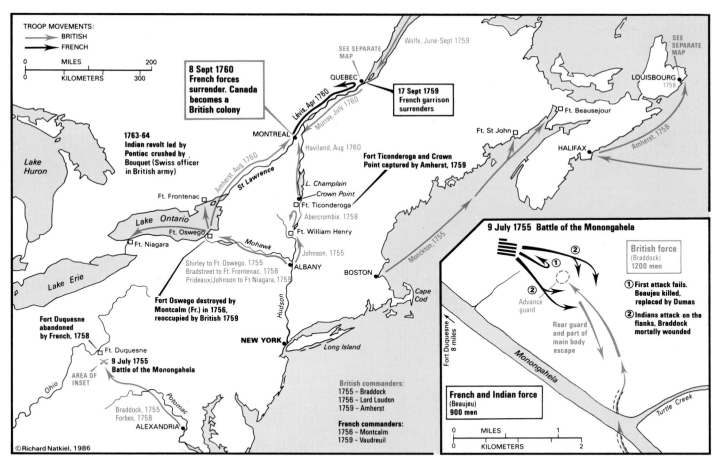

TROOP MOVEMENTS:

BRITISH
FRENCH

MILES 200
KILOMETERS 300

8 Sept 1760
French forces
surrender. Canada
becomes a
British colony

Wolfe, June-Sept 1759

SEE SEPARATE
MAP

QUEBEC

17 Sept 1759
French garrison
surrenders

LOUISBOURG
1758

SEE
SEPARATE
MAP

Lévis, Apr 1760

Murray, July 1760

Ft. Beausejour

Ft. St John

1763-64
Indian revolt led by
Pontiac crushed by
Bouquet (Swiss officer
in British army)

Amherst, Aug 1760

Haviland, Aug 1760

HALIFAX

Amherst, 1758

*Lake
Huron*

MONTREAL

St Lawrence

L. Champlain

Crown Point

Fort Ticonderoga and Crown
Point captured by Amherst, 1759

Ft. Frontenac

Ft. Ticonderoga

Abercrombie, 1758

Lake Ontario

Ft. Oswego

Ft. Niagara

Ft. William Henry

Mohawk

Johnson, 1755

Monckton, 1755

Shirley to Ft. Oswego, 1755
Bradstreet to Ft. Frontenac, 1758
Prideaux/Johnson to Ft Niagara, 1759

Lake Erie

ALBANY

BOSTON

Cape
Cod

Fort Oswego destroyed by
Montcalm (Fr.) in 1756,
reoccupied by British 1759

Hudson

9 July 1755 Battle of the Monongahela

British force
(Braddock)
1200 men

Advance
guard

Fort Duquesne
abandoned
by French, 1758

Ft. Duquesne

9 July 1755
Battle of the Monongahela

AREA OF
INSET

Ohio

NEW YORK

Long Island

Rear guard
and part of
main body
escape

① First attack fails.
Beaujeu killed,
replaced by Dumas

② Indians attack on the
flanks, Braddock
mortally wounded

Braddock, 1755
Forbes, 1758

Potomac

ALEXANDRIA

British commanders:
1755 – Braddock
1756 – Lord Loudon
1759 – Amherst

French commanders:
1756 – Montcalm
1759 – Vaudreuil

Fort Duquesne
8 miles

Monongahela

Turtle Creek

French and Indian force
(Beaujeu)
900 men

MILES 1
KILOMETERS 2

The French and Indian Wars

The next year, 1756, England and France officially declared war, a conflict that would be known in Europe as The Seven Years War, and in America as the French and Indian War of 1756–1763. In America the widely scattered fighting was at first indecisive, the French scoring some minor successes against British forward bases in New York and foiling an intended amphibious attack on the key port of Louisbourg on Ile Royale, guardian of the St Lawrence estuary. In 1758, however, the British began to make substantial gains. Fort Duquesne was finally taken, as was Fort Frontenac on Lake Ontario. Most important, Louisbourg was at last captured. For the assault on Louisbourg the British assembled a formidable 12,000-man force under the overall command of General Jeffrey Amherst. This was dispatched to Ile Royale in a fleet of 120 transport vessels, supported by a naval squadron of 22 battleships and 15 frigates, under the command of

Admiral Edward Boscawen. To defend Louisbourg the French had only the town's 3000-man garrison, commanded by le chevalier de Drocour, and five warships. The British landed on Ile Royale on 8 June 1758. By mid-July they had completely invested Louisbourg and had captured its outlying fortifications. On 25 July the last of the defending French warships was taken, and two days later Drocour surrendered. The British now controlled the mouth of the St Lawrence, and the way was open for an attack on Quebec, 350 miles upriver.

This attack was mounted the following year, Major General James Wolfe commanding the 8500-man land force, and Admiral Sir Charles Saunders the supporting naval squadron. The expedition arrived in the vicinity of Quebec in late June 1759 but could make no headway against the heavily-fortified city, which occupied a nearly impregnable position atop the high cliffs that line the river's north bank. During the summer Wolfe succeeded in setting up a battery on the south shore, opposite Quebec, and in landing some of his troops on the north shore, considerably to the west of the

city. But the French had no difficulty either in withstanding the battery's fire or in containing the landing force, although to do the latter the French commander, Louis Joseph, le marquis de Montcalm, was obliged to detach a portion of his 16,000-man garrison. The deadlock was finally broken in September when Wolfe's scouts discovered a narrow track up the steep cliffs just to the west of the city. During the night of 12 September some 3500 British regulars scaled these cliffs and deployed on the Plains of Abraham, the mile-wide plateau immediately behind Quebec. The French attacked them the next morning. The battle that ensued was a classic eighteenth-century linear confrontation. Much blood was shed – both Wolfe and Montcalm were killed – but superior British musketry prevailed, and thus, in the words of historian Francis Parkman, "the capital of New France passed into the hands of its hereditary foes."

Although the fall of Quebec did not end the war, it probably ensured the ultimate British victory. During the following year, 1760, the British captured most of the remaining key French forts and, finally, Montreal. The extent of these military successes was acknowledged three years later in the Treaty of Paris, by which France ceded all of Canada to Great Britain.

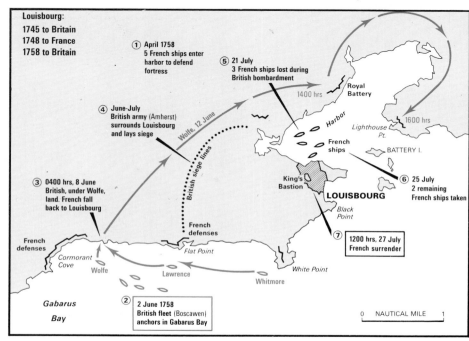

Louisbourg:
1745 to Britain
1748 to France
1758 to Britain

① April 1758
5 French ships enter harbor to defend fortress

④ June-July
British army (Amherst) surrounds Louisbourg and lays siege

⑤ 21 July
3 French ships lost during British bombardment

③ 0400 hrs, 8 June
British, under Wolfe, land. French fall back to Louisbourg

Wolfe, 12 June

British siege lines

French defenses

Royal Battery

1400 hrs

Harbor

Lighthouse Pt.

1600 hrs

BATTERY I.

French ships

King's Bastion

LOUISBOURG

⑥ 25 July
2 remaining French ships taken

Black Point

⑦ 1200 hrs, 27 July
French surrender

French defenses

Cormorant Cove

Wolfe

Flat Point

Lawrence

White Point

Whitmore

Gabarus Bay

② 2 June 1758
British fleet (Boscawen) anchors in Gabarus Bay

0   NAUTICAL MILE   1

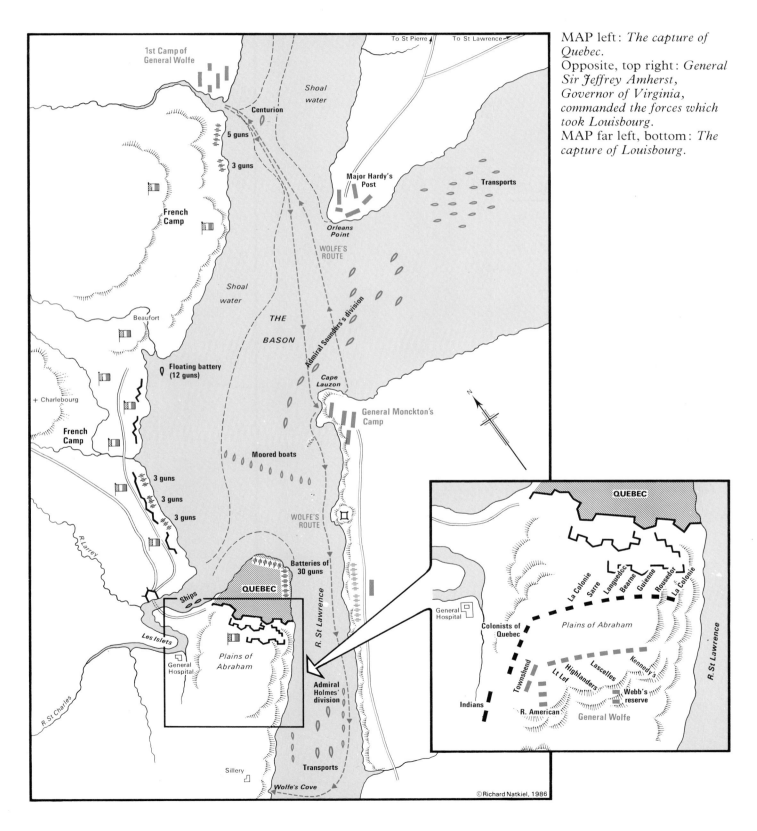

1st Camp of
General Wolfe

To St Pierre   To St Lawrence

Shoal
water

Centurion

5 guns

3 guns

Major Hardy's
Post

Transports

French
Camp

Orleans
Point

WOLFE'S
ROUTE

Beaufort

Shoal
water

THE

BASON

Floating battery
(12 guns)

+ Charlebourg

Cape
Lauzon

General Monckton's
Camp

French
Camp

N

3 guns

3 guns

3 guns

Moored boats

WOLFE'S
ROUTE

R. Larrey

Batteries of
30 guns

QUEBEC

General
Hospital

Ships

R. St Lawrence

Les Islets

General
Hospital

Plains of
Abraham

R. St Charles

Admiral
Holmes'
division

Sillery

Transports

Wolfe's Cove

©Richard Natkiel, 1986

QUEBEC

La Colonie   Sarre   Languedoc   Bearne   Guienne   Rousedor   La Colonie

General
Hospital

Colonists of
Quebec

Plains of Abraham

R. St Lawrence

Townshend   Lt Lef   Highlanders   Lascelles   Kennedy's

Webb's
reserve

Indians

R. American

General Wolfe

MAP left: *The capture of
Quebec.*
Opposite, top right: *General
Sir Jeffrey Amherst,
Governor of Virginia,
commanded the forces which
took Louisbourg.*
MAP far left, bottom: *The
capture of Louisbourg.*

THE REVOLUTIONARY WAR

The Revolution Begins

Even before the end of the French and Indian War relations between the English colonies in America and the mother country had begun to erode. Within a decade of the signing of the Treaty of Paris in 1763 American resentment over British policies towards local self-rule, taxation, trade, territorial expansion and a host of other issues had so fulminated that the colonies were on the brink of rebellion. Hostilities began in earnest on 18 April 1775 when a band of Massa-

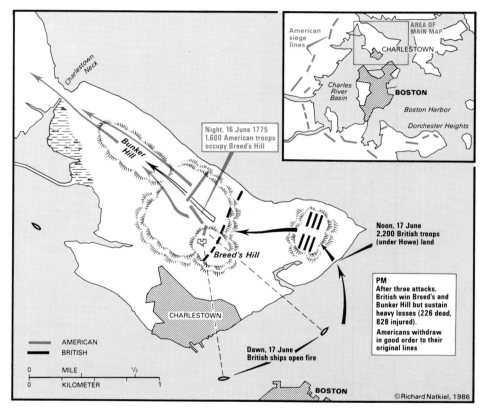

Night, 16 June 1775
1,600 American troops occupy Breed's Hill

Noon, 17 June
2,200 British troops (under Howe) land

PM
After three attacks, British win Breed's and Bunker Hill but sustain heavy losses (226 dead, 828 injured).
Americans withdraw in good order to their original lines

Dawn, 17 June
British ships open fire

AMERICAN
BRITISH

©Richard Natkiel, 1986

chusetts militiamen clashed with British regulars at Lexington, 20 miles outside Boston. In the ensuing 48-hour skirmish 95 militiamen and nearly 275 British soldiers were killed. Thereafter the spread of fighting could not be contained. While a large force of Colonial militiamen surrounded Boston, placing the British garrison there under loose siege, other militias seized British forts at Ticonderoga, Crown Point and St Johns. On 15 June the American Second Continental Congress created a Continental Army and named General George Washington as its commander.

Two days later, on the outskirts of Boston, a force of 2200 British regulars, under the command of Major General William Howe, assailed an American fortified position atop Breed's Hill on the Charleston peninsula. Only after two sanguinary failures did the British close-order frontal assault finally succeed in overrunning the hill, and then perhaps only because the militiamen had run short of ammunition. In this so-called Battle of Bunker Hill (named for a neighboring hill), the British had accomplished virtually nothing, at a cost of 1150 casualties. Most of the defenders had

MAP right: *The New York campaign.*
Below: *George Washington at the*
Battle of Trenton.
Bottom: *General Howe, as seen in a*
contemporary etching.

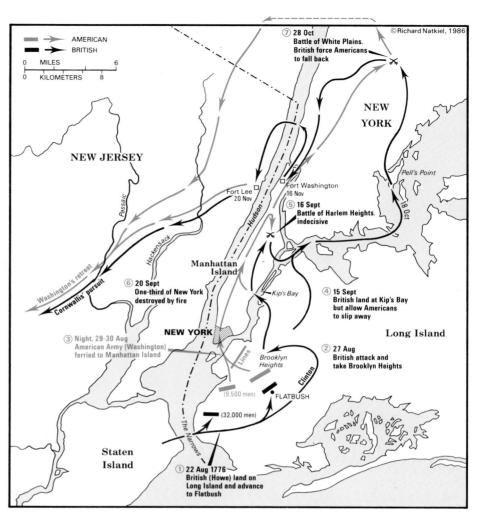

AMERICAN
BRITISH

0 MILES 6
0 KILOMETERS 8

©Richard Natkiel, 1986

⑦ 28 Oct
Battle of White Plains.
British force Americans
to fall back

NEW
YORK

NEW JERSEY

Pell's Point

Fort Lee
20 Nov

Fort Washington
16 Nov

⑤ 16 Sept
Battle of Harlem Heights,
indecisive

18 Oct

Hudson

Manhattan
Island

Kip's Bay

④ 15 Sept
British land at Kip's Bay
but allow Americans
to slip away

⑥ 20 Sept
One-third of New York
destroyed by fire

Washington's retreat

Cornwallis pursuit

Hackensack

Passaic

Long Island

③ Night, 29-30 Aug
American Army (Washington)
ferried to Manhattan Island

NEW YORK

Lines

Brooklyn
Heights

Clinton

② 27 Aug
British attack and
take Brooklyn Heights

(9,500 men)

FLATBUSH

(32,000 men)

Staten
Island

The Narrows

① 22 Aug 1776
British (Howe) land on
Long Island and advance
to Flatbush

escaped, simply to take up new positions nearby, and the siege of Boston
remained unbroken. It continued into
the spring of the following year, the
size and firepower of the investing
forces, now under Washington's personal direction, growing the while. At
last, on 13 April 1776, the British
garrison began its evacuation of the
city.

MAP above left: *The Battle of*
Bunker Hill.
MAP left: *Major battles of the*
Revolutionary War.

The New York
Campaign and the
Battle of Trenton

Washington, correctly anticipating
that the next British move would be a
thrust at New York City, quickly
moved south with about 19,000 men –
a nucleus of Continentals and a large
preponderance of militia. The bulk of
this force he positioned on Brooklyn
Heights on Long Island, hoping thereby to dominate the southern tip of
Manhattan. Sir William Howe's seaborne British invasion force, 32,000
strong, duly arrived at New York on 4
July 1776. On 22 August Howe landed
troops behind Washington's Brooklyn
Heights position, forcing the outflanked Americans to retire across the
East River to Manhattan. Howe pursued them, inexorably driving them
north up the narrow island. When the
Americans attempted to make a stand

at Harlem Heights, Howe again outflanked them (on 18 October) by landing four brigades at Pell's Point,
behind the American lines. Once
again Washington narrowly escaped
encirclement, but he was now obliged
to split his retreating army, sending
half his troops to the comparative
safety of New Jersey while the remainder fought on to try to slow the
momentum of Howe's northward advance. In the event, Howe concluded
that this remnant was not worth
pursuing beyond White Plains, 20
miles north of Manhattan.

While Howe's main force retired to
winter quarters in New York City, a
large detachment, under General
Charles, Lord Cornwallis, was dispatched southwest into New Jersey to
mop up what was left of the American
army there. Though Washington now
had barely 3000 effective Continentals
and militiamen left under his command, he was not content to leave the
initiative to the British. Under cover
of darkness on 25 December he ferried

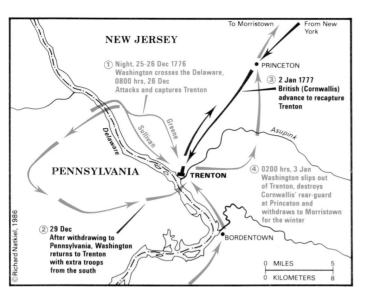

his ragged troops across the Delaware River, marched down the east bank and at dawn on the 26th made a surprise attack on the three Hessian regiments stationed at Trenton. This was a brilliant success, netting over 900 prisoners at the cost of only eight American casualties. Cornwallis at once concentrated a powerful force of 8000 regulars on Trenton, but Washington eluded them, wheeling his small army northeast towards Princeton. There, on 3 January 1777, he encountered three British regiments, not yet joined to Cornwallis' main body, and defeated them in a brief, savage battle of encounter. This ended the campaigning in New Jersey for the remainder of the winter: the British, unable to bring Washington to bay and worried about the safety of their supply lines, retired east to defensive positions around Brunswick, while Washington led his army north to winter quarters near Morristown.

MAP above: *The Battle of Trenton.*
Right: *General Burgoyne surrenders at Saratoga, as seen in the painting by John Trumbull.*

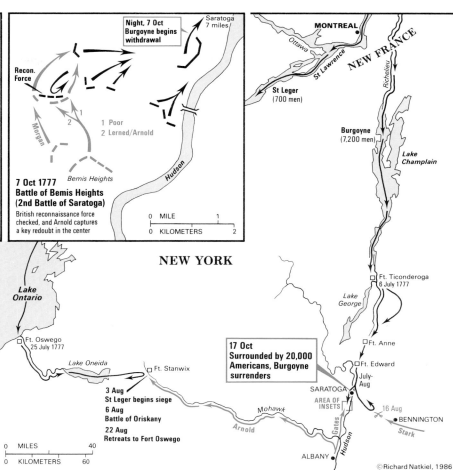

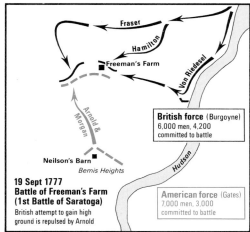

MAP right & above: *The Saratoga campaign and the Battles of Freeman's Farm and Bemis Heights.*
Left: *Washington's forces cross the partially frozen Delaware River in the approach to the Battle of Trenton.*

Map annotations (left inset):

Fraser
Hamilton
Von Riedesel
Freeman's Farm
Arnold & Morgan
Neilson's Barn
Bemis Heights
Hudson

British force (Burgoyne)
6,000 men, 4,200 committed to battle

19 Sept 1777
Battle of Freeman's Farm
(1st Battle of Saratoga)
British attempt to gain high ground is repulsed by Arnold

American force (Gates)
7,000 men, 3,000 committed to battle

Map annotations (center inset):

Night, 7 Oct
Burgoyne begins withdrawal

Saratoga 7 miles

Recon. Force
Morgan
1 Poor
2 Lerned/Arnold
Bemis Heights
Hudson

7 Oct 1777
Battle of Bemis Heights
(2nd Battle of Saratoga)
British reconnaissance force checked, and Arnold captures a key redoubt in the center

0 MILE 1
0 KILOMETERS 2

Map annotations (right map):

MONTREAL
Ottawa
St Lawrence
NEW FRANCE
Richelieu
St Leger (700 men)
Burgoyne (7,200 men)
Lake Champlain
Ft. Ticonderoga 6 July 1777
Lake George
Ft. Anne
Ft. Edward
July-Aug
NEW YORK
Lake Ontario
Ft. Oswego 25 July 1777
Lake Oneida
Ft. Stanwix
3 Aug St Leger begins siege
6 Aug Battle of Oriskany
22 Aug Retreats to Fort Oswego
Mohawk
Arnold
SARATOGA
AREA OF INSETS
Gates
Hudson
16 Aug
BENNINGTON
Stark

17 Oct
Surrounded by 20,000 Americans, Burgoyne surrenders

ALBANY

0 MILES 40
0 KILOMETERS 60

©Richard Natkiel, 1986

The Philadelphia and Saratoga Campaigns

When active campaigning resumed in the spring of 1777 the British mounted two independent large-scale offensives. One, directed by Howe, was aimed at taking the American capital of Philadelphia. The second, under the overall command of General Sir John Burgoyne, was intended as an ambitious pincer movement that would originate from the vicinity of Montreal and would ultimately close its jaws on the key New York city of Albany. With Albany secured, it was planned that Howe would move north from New York to join forces with Burgoyne, thus establishing a line that would effectively cut off all of New England from the other colonies.

Howe's somewhat ponderous seaborne campaign against Philadelphia was successful, but of secondary strategic importance. Washington failed to halt Howe's advance on the city when the Americans were defeated at Brandywine Creek in September, and Washington's subsequent efforts to dislodge Howe from Philadelphia were equally unsuccessful. By December, the American general was obliged to withdraw his battered army to winter quarters at Valley Forge. Yet, contrary to Howe's hopes, the fall of the capital did not in itself significantly blunt the American war effort.

Burgoyne's much more dangerous campaign began in June 1777, his main force moving due south along Lake Champlain, while a smaller right wing, under Lieutenant Colonel Barry St Leger, swung southwest down the St Lawrence to Lake Ontario, thence to re-curve southeast through the Mohawk Valley towards the common objective of Albany. By early July Burgoyne had taken Fort Ticonderoga, roughly halfway to Albany, but St Leger's advance in the Mohawk Valley had been decisively stopped by American militia at the Battle of Oriskany, fought near Fort Stanwix. Burgoyne nevertheless pressed on against stiffening American resistance. On 19 September American troops

Above: *General Charles Cornwallis.*
Below: *Francis Marion, the 'Swamp Fox' led a guerrilla campaign in the south. He is seen here with a captured British officer.*

under General Daniel Morgan (the principal lieutenant of the American theater commander, General Horatio Gates) checked Burgoyne's southward advance at the savage battle of Freeman's Farm. For the next 18 days, while American local forces swelled to an unprecedented 22,000, the two armies skirmished in place. Then, on 7 October, Burgoyne tried to break the impasse with an assault on the American positions on Bemis Heights. In this battle Gates and Morgan so routed the attackers that the British were forced to beat a hasty retreat eight miles north to Saratoga. There, on 17 October 1777, Burgoyne formally surrendered his remaining 5700 men to Gates. This victory was in some ways the most decisive of the war, for in addition to lifting American morale at a critical time and proving that major British forces could be defeated in open battle, it at last persuaded hesitating France to enter the war on the American side.

The Invasion of the South

In the following year, 1778, British strategy took a completely new turn. General Sir Henry Clinton, Howe's successor, evacuated Philadelphia and concentrated his troops in New York, thereafter fighting only small holding actions against Washington's forces in the north. Meantime, the British launched a major land/sea campaign against the southern colonies. In December Savannah was captured, and by the following spring Augusta and most of the rest of Georgia was under British control. By April 1780 the British had captured the port of Charleston, South Carolina, and were preparing to subdue that colony, as well. Washington attempted to prevent this by sending 4000 men under Gates into South Carolina, but on 16 August this force was roundly defeated

Above: *Baron von Steuben, the most influential of a number of foreign officers who helped train the Continental Army.*
Below: *Recruiting poster for the 'Tory' or Loyalist forces.*

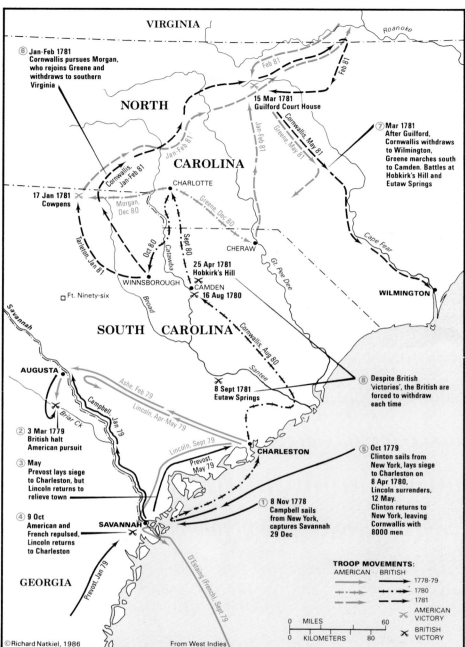

MAP above: *The campaign in the South.*

at Camden by General Cornwallis' disciplined regulars, and it now seemed that both of the Carolinas and Virginia must shortly share the fate of Georgia.

That this did not happen was due to the skillful resistance put up both by local independent militias and by the two small Continental armies (one under Daniel Morgan and another under General Nathaniel Greene) still operating in the Carolinas. Though by the spring of 1781 Cornwallis had advanced as far north as Virginia, virtually none of the areas through which he had passed since leaving Charleston had been truly pacified, and now he faced two fresh Continental armies, led respectively by General Friedrich Wilhelm, Baron von Steuben, and by General Marie-Joseph du Motier, le marquis de Lafayette. Rather than try to deal with these armies (which he could still probably have defeated in open battle) Cornwallis withdrew to the Virginia port of Yorktown.

Yorktown

Quick to seize the opportunity presented by Cornwallis' withdrawal to Yorktown, Washington rushed reinforcements to the Yorktown area – his own forces from New York and those of General Jean-Baptiste de Vimeur, le comte de Rochambeau, from Rhode Island. In short order, Cornwallis was well and truly besieged in Yorktown, and the timely intercession of the British fleet had become for him not a convenience but a necessity. Now the full value of the Franco-American alliance became fully manifest. When, on 5 September, Admiral Thomas Graves' relieving fleet approached the entrance to Chesapeake Bay, it found its way blocked by a slightly larger

MAP right: *Battle of Chesapeake Bay*.
Below: *An attack at Yorktown*.

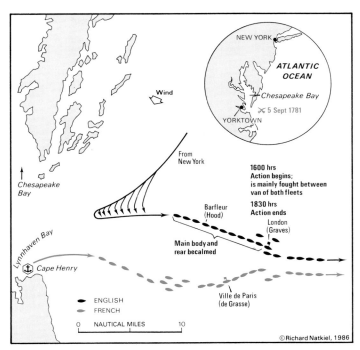

ATLANTIC OCEAN

NEW YORK

Chesapeake Bay

5 Sept 1781

YORKTOWN

Wind

Chesapeake Bay

From New York

1600 hrs
Action begins;
is mainly fought between
van of both fleets

1830 hrs
Action ends

Barfleur
(Hood)

London
(Graves)

Main body and
rear becalmed

Lynnhaven Bay

Cape Henry

Ville de Paris
(de Grasse)

ENGLISH
FRENCH

0   NAUTICAL MILES   10

©Richard Natkiel, 1986

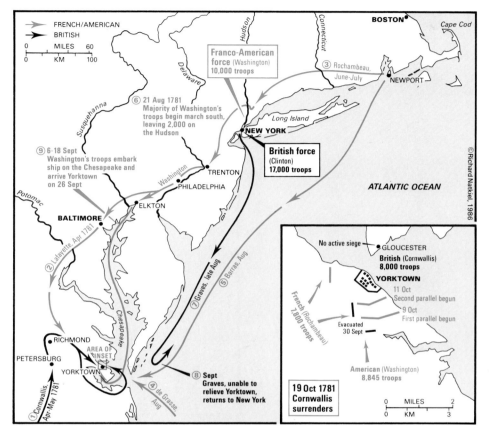

French squadron under the command of Admiral François-Joseph, le comte de Grasse. In strictly naval terms the desultory battle that followed was decisive only in that Graves could not force his way past the French, but that was quite enough to decide the outcome of the war on land. Denied hope either of reinforcement or of evacuation by sea, surrounded by 9000 American and 8000 French troops, Cornwallis had no choice but to surrender.

The American victory at Yorktown marked the end of all serious British military activity in North America. Although a formal state of war persisted for another two years, it was clear that American independence had been won and that only the details of a peace treaty remained to be worked out. A draft of this treaty was negotiated in November 1782; it was ratified by the Continental Congress the following April; and on 3 September 1783, with the formal signing of the Treaty of Paris, the war ended.

MAP left: *The Yorktown campaign.*
Below: *Cornwallis surrenders.*

THE BARBARY WARS

The forty-year 'interbellum' between the end of the American Revolution and the start of the War of 1812 was not, in fact, a period of perfect peace for the new American republic. Between 1798 and 1801 the US Navy fought an undeclared naval war with France (in reaction to the French policy of seizing American merchantmen suspected of trading with Britain). In the course of this quasi-war the Americans captured 85 French vessels, and the US frigate *Constellation* fought and won two duels with French warships of roughly equal force.

More popular, because less fraught with political and sentimental ambiguities, was the military action which the United States took against the Barbary pirates. For years the Arab states of Morocco, Tunis, Algeria and Tripoli had brazenly extorted tribute from various maritime powers in exchange for not attacking their merchant ships in the Mediterranean. The United States had been paying such tribute since 1796, but when the Pasha of Tripoli, Yusuf Karamanli, proposed a much increased level of payment, the United States refused, and Yusuf declared war in May 1801. The American response was to dispatch a small naval squadron to protect US shipping in the Mediterranean, an enterprise that was, at best, only marginally successful. Then, in October 1803, one of the American warships, the 38-gun heavy frigate *Philadelphia*, grounded on a reef off Tripoli and was captured by a fleet of Tripolitanian gunboats, which towed her triumphantly into Tripoli harbor. De-termined not to leave so valuable a prize in enemy hands, the Americans organized a cutting-out expedition. On the dark night of 16 February 1804 US Navy Lieutenant Stephen Decatur and 83 volunteers sailed the ketch *Intrepid* into the harbor, recaptured *Philadelphia* after a brisk fight and, upon finding that the frigate was not in condition to be taken out, burnt her to the waterline. This exemplary action, in which the Americans suffered not a single casualty, was characterized by

Below right: *Commodore Richard Dale, one of the US commanders in the Barbary War.*
Below far right: *Lieutenant Stephen Decatur, hero of the Barbary War.*
Below: *The* USS Constellation *vs the French* Insurgente.

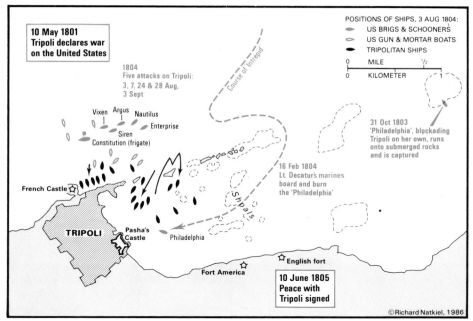

10 May 1801
Tripoli declares war on the United States

1804
Five attacks on Tripoli:
3, 7, 24 & 28 Aug,
3 Sept

POSITIONS OF SHIPS, 3 AUG 1804:
US BRIGS & SCHOONERS
US GUN & MORTAR BOATS
TRIPOLITAN SHIPS

0 MILE ½
0 KILOMETER 1

Course of Intrepid

Vixen Argus Nautilus
Enterprise
Siren
Constitution (frigate)

31 Oct 1803
'Philadelphia', blockading
Tripoli on her own, runs
onto submerged rocks
and is captured

16 Feb 1804
Lt. Decatur's marines
board and burn
the 'Philadelphia'

French Castle

Shoals

TRIPOLI Pasha's Castle

Philadelphia

Fort America English fort

10 June 1805
Peace with Tripoli signed

©Richard Natkiel, 1986

MAP left: *The burning of the Philadelphia and attacks on Tripoli.*
MAP below: *The capture of Derna.*

Britain's Admiral Horatio, Viscount Nelson, as "the most bold and daring act of the age."

The following year American soldier-diplomat William Eaton and US Marine Lieutenant Presley O'Bannon persuaded Ahmet Bey, Yusuf's deposed elder brother, then living in exile in Egypt, to finance an overland expedition to strike at Yusuf's fortress city of Derna. On 6 March Eaton, O'Bannon and Ahmet, having assembled a 400-man force of mercenaries and US Marines, set out from the outskirts of Alexandria on a grueling 600-

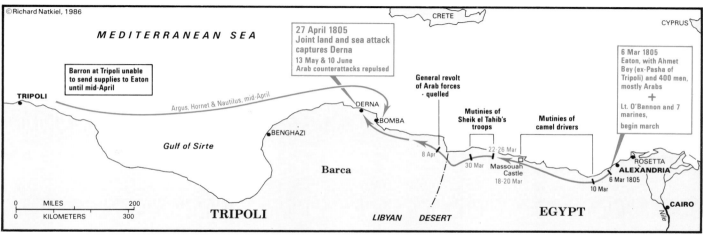

©Richard Natkiel, 1986

MEDITERRANEAN SEA

CRETE

CYPRUS

27 April 1805
Joint land and sea attack captures Derna
13 May & 10 June
Arab counterattacks repulsed

6 Mar 1805
Eaton, with Ahmet Bey (ex-Pasha of Tripoli) and 400 men, mostly Arabs
Lt. O'Bannon and 7 marines, begin march

Barron at Tripoli unable to send supplies to Eaton until mid-April

General revolt of Arab forces - quelled

Mutinies of Sheik el Tahib's troops

Mutinies of camel drivers

TRIPOLI

Argus, Hornet & Nautilus, mid-April

DERNA
BOMBA

BENGHAZI

8 Apr

22-26 Mar
30 Mar Massouah Castle
18-20 Mar

ROSETTA
ALEXANDRIA
6 Mar 1805
10 Mar

Gulf of Sirte

Barca

CAIRO
Nile

0 MILES 200
0 KILOMETERS 300

TRIPOLI LIBYAN DESERT EGYPT

mile trek across the Libyan Desert. They did not arrive at Derna until 27 April 1805, but once there, supported by off-shore fire from three American ships, they took Derna the same day. For the next month and a half they successfully repelled every attempt to dislodge them. This surprising victory, coupled with a steadily escalating US naval bombardment of Tripoli itself, persuaded Yusuf to sign a peace treaty, which he did on 4 June. The Barbary war, thus ended, had been minor in scale and only partially satisfactory in result, since the pirates' annual tribute, though diminished, continued to be exacted. But perhaps its real significance lay in the fact that it was the first of many historic occasions in which the United States would undertake to project her military power far beyond her own borders.

THE WAR OF 1812

The War Begins

The reasons that prompted the United States to go to war with Great Britain in 1812 were less substantive than emotional. The British policy of interdicting all neutral maritime trade with France had occasioned the seizure of numerous American merchant ships, causing some genuine financial distress to American shipowners and tempting many other Americans to blame – not always accurately – various domestic economic difficulties on the loss of foreign markets. Even more offensive to American pride was the Royal Navy's practice of routinely impressing into British naval service American merchant crewmen who could not prove they were not British subjects. When the British tried to extend their insatiable hunt for 'deserters' to the crews of American warships a succession of inflammatory naval incidents inevitably followed. Diplomatic efforts to defuse this dangerous situation came too late. Amidst rumours that the British were fomenting Indian attacks on American frontier settlements the US Congress at last succumbed to the national war fever and declared war on 18 June 1812.

The small, ill-prepared US Army immediately took the offensive in an ambitious three-pronged attack on Canada. By mid-August the westernmost of these attacks had been utterly defeated, with the losses of Fort Mackinac, Fort Dearborn and Detroit leaving most of the Northwest Territory under British control. The central attack, across the Niagara Frontier, foundered in October, when nearly 1000 American troops were surrounded and forced to surrender at Queenston, Canada. The easternmost attack, on Montreal, petered out by the end of November.

MAP right: *The campaigns of the War of 1812.*

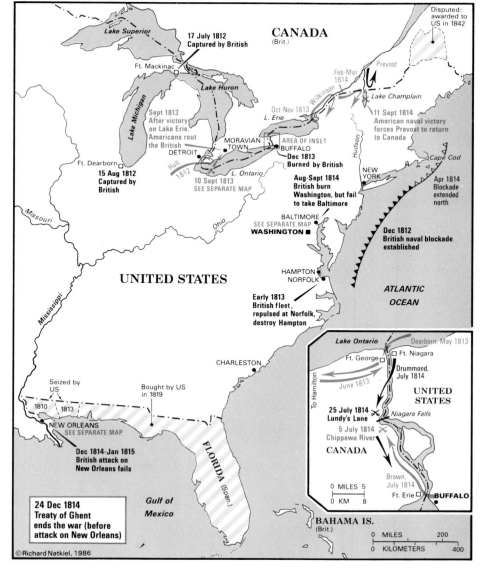

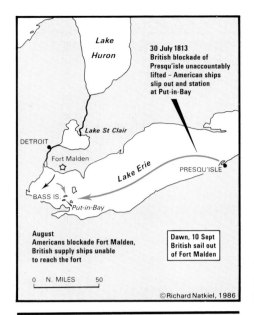

Lake Huron

30 July 1813
British blockade of Presqu'isle unaccountably lifted – American ships slip out and station at Put-in-Bay

Lake St Clair

DETROIT

Fort Malden

Lake Erie

PRESQU'ISLE

BASS IS.

Put-in-Bay

August
Americans blockade Fort Malden, British supply ships unable to reach the fort

Dawn, 10 Sept
British sail out of Fort Malden

0   N. MILES   50

© Richard Natkiel, 1986

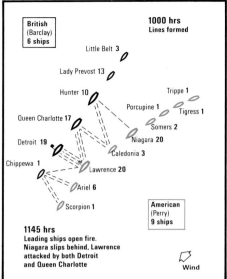

British (Barclay) 6 ships

1000 hrs
Lines formed

Little Belt 3

Lady Prevost 13

Hunter 10

Trippe 1

Porcupine 1

Tigress 1

Queen Charlotte 17

Somers 2

Detroit 19

Niagara 20

Caledonia 3

Chippewa 1

Lawrence 20

Ariel 6

Scorpion 1

American (Perry) 9 ships

1145 hrs
Leading ships open fire. Niagara slips behind, Lawrence attacked by both Detroit and Queen Charlotte

Wind

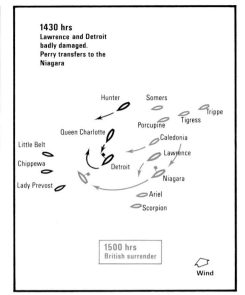

1430 hrs
Lawrence and Detroit badly damaged. Perry transfers to the Niagara

Hunter

Somers

Trippe

Queen Charlotte

Porcupine

Tigress

Little Belt

Caledonia

Chippewa

Detroit

Lawrence

Lady Prevost

Niagara

Ariel

Scorpion

1500 hrs
British surrender

Wind

The Naval War

For the Americans the effects of these initial disasters on land were somewhat mitigated by the simultaneous successes of the little US Navy. On 19 August the frigate USS *Constitution*, 44, Captain Isaac Hull, destroyed HMS *Guerrière*, 38, off Nova Scotia. In short order thereafter USS *Essex*, 32, took HMS *Alert*, 20; and in October *Constitution*'s sister ship, USS *United States*, Captain Stephen Decatur, took HMS *Macedonian*, 38. The climax of this dazzling season came in December, when *Constitution*, now under Captain Thomas Bainbridge, took HMS *Java*, 38, off the coast of Brazil. Though these single-ship actions amounted to the greatest humiliation the Royal Navy had endured for a generation, they were not of great strategic importance. By early 1813 the overwhelmingly powerful British fleet held America's Atlantic seaboard under such tight blockade that American warships had the greatest difficulty in making sorties from their ports.

On land, throughout 1813 the Americans continued to try to press their attacks on Canada. From the Niagara Frontier east, these efforts again came to nothing. (Indeed, so sharp were the British ripostes that the town of Buffalo was burned and the key American base at Sackett's Harbor

MAPS top: *The Battle of Lake Erie.* Right: *William Henry Harrison, general of the War of 1812. Harrison later became 9th President of the USA.*

23

was nearly lost to siege.) But to the west, on Lake Erie and in the Michigan peninsula, progress was made. On Lake Erie Commander Oliver Hazard Perry, USN, had assembled a small squadron of two gun brigs and seven schooners. On 10 September this flotilla decisively defeated a British squadron of two ships, two brigs and two schooners, commanded by Commodore R H Barclay. Perry's victory made the key British positions on the western end of the lake – Detroit and Fort Malden – suddenly vulnerable. Under pressure from advancing American troops, led by Brigadier General William Henry Harrison, the British abandoned both these bases and fell back into the interior of Upper

Canada. On 5 October Harrison caught up with and destroyed this retreating British army on the Thames River. As a result, most of the Northwest Territory, including Lake Erie and the proximate part of Upper Canada, passed under American control.

The British naval blockade had effectively drawn the fangs of America's 16-ship seagoing Navy, and in May 1813 the British broke the string of American frigate victories when HMS *Shannon*, 38, Captain Philip Broke, defeated USS *Chesapeake*, 38, Captain James Lawrence, off Boston. But of far greater consequence was the fulmination of American privateering. By early 1813 some 600 American privateers were scourging British com-

Above: *Commodore Perry transfers his flag from the shattered* Lawrence *to the* Niagara *ready to turn the tables in the Battle of Lake Erie.*
Bottom right: *British attack on Fort Oswego, Lake Ontario, May 1814.*

merce in the North and South Atlantic, the Caribbean, the North Sea and even the English Channel. By the war's end they had taken over 1300 British merchantmen (and some naval vessels), had driven maritime insurance rates to ruinous heights and had prompted merchant's associations in such cities as Bristol, Glasgow and Liverpool to petition the government to end the war before England's merchant marine was destroyed.

Campaigns of 1814

In 1814 the Americans renewed their attack on the Niagara Frontier. A well-trained 3500-man American force, under Brigadier Generals Jacob Brown and Winfield Scott, began well enough by capturing Fort Erie, at the mouth of the Niagara River, and then, on 5 July, by besting the regular troops of Sir Gordon Drummond and General Phineas Riall at the Battle of the Chippewa River. But on 25 July the two armies clashed again at Lundy's Lane, a bloody encounter which, though indecisive in itself, so weakened the Americans that they could not continue. In the following months the British were reinforced and the Americans were not, and by November the Americans had been forced out of the Niagara Peninsula entirely.

To the east, along the Montreal-Lake Champlain-Albany axis, the situation was reversed, for here the British launched an invasion of their own. A 12,000-man army, under the command of General Sir George Prevost, and a naval squadron of one frigate, one brig, two sloops and 12

Below: *The Battle of Lundy's Lane on 25 July 1814 was one of the hardest fought of the War of 1812.*

Below: 'Macdonough Pointing the
Gun,' a famous incident during the
Battle of Lake Champlain when
Macdonough personally directed the
fire of his ship.
Bottom: General Winfield Scott, US
commander at Lundy's Lane.

Macdonough sank or captured every one of the British vessels. Deprived of naval support, Prevost concluded that his invasion could not succeed and returned to Canada.

In the meantime, far to the south, a British amphibious raiding force had sailed into Chesapeake Bay, marched on virtually undefended Washington and burnt the Capitol, the White House and several other government buildings. This force then reembarked and sailed on to Baltimore. Here, on 13 September, they were met with a spirited defense. Their land attack, led by Major General Robert Ross, failed to get past the earthwork redoubts that Major General Samuel Smith's Maryland militia had set up east of the city; and Vice-Admiral Alexander Cochrane's powerful naval squadron could not force its way past Fort McHenry, guardian of the entrance to Baltimore's harbor. Frustrated at Baltimore, the British force returned to the West Indies, there to plan another operation: an attack on New Orleans.

galley-gunboats, under the command of Commodore George Downie, moved rapidly down Lake Champlain to Plattsburg. At this point Downie's squadron was intercepted by Commodore Thomas Macdonough's US Navy lake squadron, composed of a corvette, a brig, a schooner, a sloop and 10 galley-gunboats. Although outnumbered and considerably outgunned,

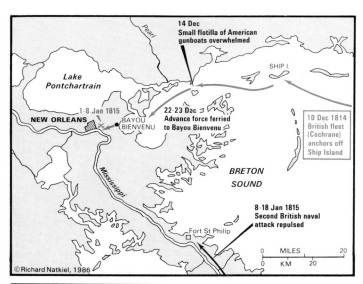

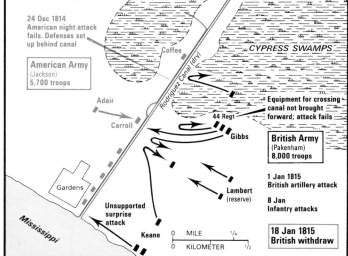

The Battle of New Orleans

For the New Orleans assault the British assembled 8000 veteran troops, under the command of Major General Sir Edward Pakenham, and some 50 supporting warships and transports. Defending the city were 5000 troops, mostly irregular, under the command of Major General Andrew Jackson. The British came on shore at Bayou Bienvenu on 23 December and made their way west towards the city. Their approach route left little room for maneuver, since the Mississippi River lay on their left, and a nearly impenetrable cypress swamp lay on their right. Between these obstacles the Americans had erected a high earthwork fortification, well defended by artillery and supported by additional artillery sited on the Mississippi's opposite bank. When the British attempted a frontal assault, on 8 January 1815, the inevitable result was carnage – 2000 British dead, among them Pakenham. The shattered British expeditionary force then withdrew to the

MAPS top: *The Battle of New Orleans.*
Right: *The death of General Sir Edward Pakenham.*

Below: *The Battle of New Orleans as painted by Jean Hyacinthe de Laclotte in 1815. Although crude in style, the painting gives a good impression of the ground on which the battle was fought.*
Bottom: *Jackson encourages the American defenders during the battle.*

coast, made a half-hearted attack on Fort Bowyer, at the entrance to Mobile harbor and finally, upon learning that peace negotiations had been concluded in Ghent two weeks before the Battle of New Orleans had been fought, sailed back to the West Indies.

The news that the war was over took even longer to reach ships at sea. Thus the famous *Constitution*, now under the command of Captain Charles Stewart, fought her last, and in some ways most brilliant fight on 20 February 1815, when she took HMS *Cyane*, 32, and HMS *Levant*, 20, in a single engagement. The fact that this victory occurred nearly two months after the formal cessation of hostilities was of a piece with the confused manner in which this largely pointless war had been fought from the outset.

THE FIGHT FOR TEXAN INDEPENDENCE

The Alamo and San Jacinto

Between 1820 and 1830 about 20,000 Americans had settled in the northern Mexican province of Texas. At first the Mexican government encouraged this immigration, thinking the settlers would help to cultivate the barren land and to subdue the local Indians, but the newcomers soon proved to be troublesome. They ignored both the government's injunctions that they convert to Catholicism and its proscriptions against slave-owning. Worse, they set up an insistent clamor for ever more extensive rights of self-government. In 1830 Mexico forbade further immigration into Texas; and in 1835 the government, now under the control of strongman General Antonio López de Santa Ana, attempted to bring the Texans to heel by garrisoning the province with Federal troops. Several violent clashes occurred between settlers and these troops, and the Texans now threatened secession. Determined to quash this, Santa Ana led a punitive expedition of 6000 regulars into the fractious province.

His first target was the Alamo in San Antonio, an abandoned mission that the Texans had fortified. The Alamo garrison, under the command of Lieutenant Colonel William Travis, consisted of only 183 men – among them the famous frontiersmen Davy Crockett and Jim Bowie – too few to man effectively the quarter-mile of perimeter wall that enclosed the mission compound. Yet the Texans managed to withstand Santa Ana's siege for 10 days, until, on 6 March 1836, they were overwhelmed by a massive 3000-man assault. In all, the Mexicans lost 1500 men at the Alamo: the few Texans who survived the fight were summarily executed. Three weeks later 300 Texans who had surrendered to Santa Ana's lieutenant, General José Urrea, at Goliad were similarly executed. "Remember the Alamo;

Below: *The defeated General Santa Ana surrenders to the injured Sam Houston at San Jacinto.*

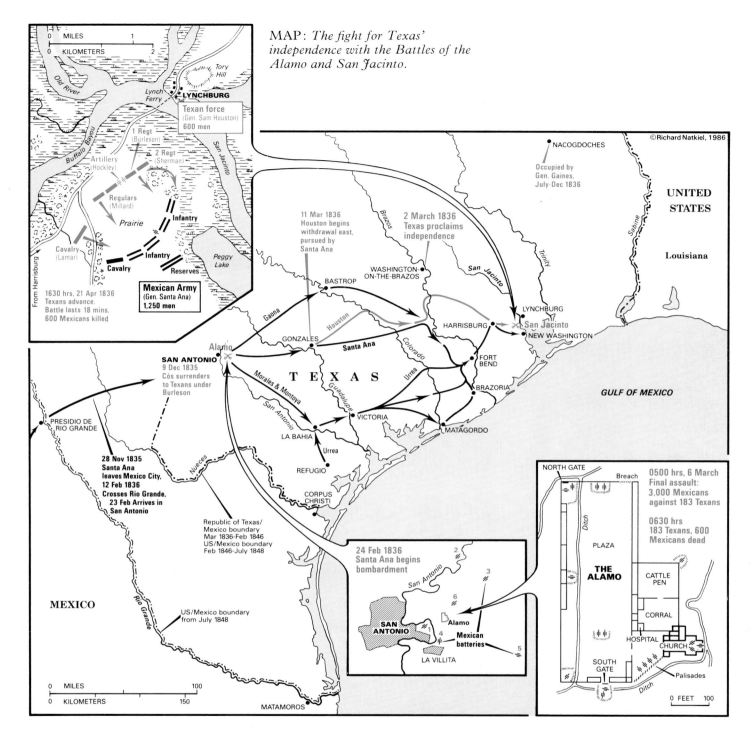

MAP: *The fight for Texas'*
independence with the Battles of the
Alamo and San Jacinto.

©Richard Natkiel, 1986

Inset — San Jacinto battle (top left):

Tory Hill

Old River

Lynch Ferry
LYNCHBURG

Buffalo Bayou

San Jacinto

Texan force
(Gen. Sam Houston)
600 men

1 Regt
(Burleson)

2 Regt
(Sherman)

Artillery
(Hockley)

Regulars
(Millard)

Prairie

Infantry

Infantry

Cavalry

Cavalry
(Lamar)

Reserves

Peggy Lake

From Harrisburg

1630 hrs, 21 Apr 1836
Texans advance.
Battle lasts 18 mins,
600 Mexicans killed

Mexican Army
(Gen. Santa Ana)
1,250 men

Main map:

UNITED STATES

Louisiana

Sabine

NACOGDOCHES

Occupied by
Gen. Gaines,
July-Dec 1836

11 Mar 1836
Houston begins
withdrawal east,
pursued by
Santa Ana

2 March 1836
Texas proclaims
independence

Brazos

WASHINGTON-
ON-THE-BRAZOS

San Jacinto

Trinity

BASTROP

Houston

GONZALES

Santa Ana

Colorado

LYNCHBURG

San Jacinto

HARRISBURG

NEW WASHINGTON

Alamo

SAN ANTONIO
9 Dec 1835
Cós surrenders
to Texans under
Burleson

T E X A S

Guadalupe

Urrea

FORT BEND

BRAZORIA

GULF OF MEXICO

Morales & Montoya

San Antonio

VICTORIA

MATAGORDO

PRESIDIO DE
RIO GRANDE

LA BAHIA

Urrea

**28 Nov 1835
Santa Ana
leaves Mexico City,
12 Feb 1836
Crosses Rio Grande,
23 Feb Arrives in
San Antonio**

Nueces

REFUGIO

CORPUS CHRISTI

Republic of Texas/
Mexico boundary
Mar 1836-Feb 1846
US/Mexico boundary
Feb 1846-July 1848

MEXICO

Rio Grande

US/Mexico boundary
from July 1848

0 MILES 100

0 KILOMETERS 150

MATAMOROS

Inset — San Antonio (bottom center):

24 Feb 1836
Santa Ana begins
bombardment

San Antonio

2

3

6

SAN ANTONIO

1

Alamo

4

Mexican
batteries

5

LA VILLITA

Inset — The Alamo (bottom right):

NORTH GATE

Breach

Ditch

PLAZA

THE ALAMO

CATTLE PEN

CORRAL

HOSPITAL

CHURCH

SOUTH GATE

Palisades

Ditch

0500 hrs, 6 March
Final assault:
3,000 Mexicans
against 183 Texans

0630 hrs
183 Texans, 600
Mexicans dead

0 FEET 100

remember Goliad" became the rally-ing cry of the Texas revolt, now in full spate.

The only significant Texan force left in the field consisted of about 600 men led by Sam Houston, who had been chosen to command the army of Texas after the province declared its independence on 2 March. Santa Ana relentlessly pursued this small force westward, but in the process he per-mitted his army to become divided. Thus when he caught up with Houston in April his effective local command numbered only about 1250. Sensing an opportunity, Houston quickly turn-ed and attacked, catching Santa Ana by surprise. The engagement, which took place on a grassy plain between San Jacinto Creek and Buffalo Bayou on 21 April, was a fairly straightfor-ward linear confrontation, a cavalry duel occupying the western flank, while Texan infantry assailed the center and attempted to turn the Mexican right on the east. In the center and on both flanks the Texans prevailed. The Mexicans lost about 600 men, against only 9 Texans, and Santa Ana was taken prisoner.

The victory at the Battle of San Jacinto confirmed Texas' de facto independence. But because Mexico continued to lay claim to the territory and because the Texans were now actively petitioning to become one of the United States, the seeds of a new international conflict were rapidly being sown.

THE MEXICAN WAR

The US Invades

The self-proclaimed Republic of Texas began asking to be admitted into the United States almost immediately after Sam Houston's victory over the Mexicans at San Jacinto in 1836. But American domestic political considerations (would Texas be admitted as a slave or a free state?) and fear of offending Mexico, which still claimed Texas, prevented the United States from acting on the Texans' request for nearly ten years. In March 1845, however, an expansion-minded president and Congress were finally able to set aside such inhibitions and invited Texas to join the Union. Mexico at once broke off diplomatic relations. Anticipating war, newly-elected President James Polk ordered Brevet Brigadier General Zachary Taylor to move US troops into the Texas territory.

By the time Mexico formally declared war, on 25 April 1846, Taylor had assembled about 4000 men in southeastern Texas. On 7 May an approximately equal Mexican force set upon Taylor at Palo Alto, a little north of the mouth of the Rio Grande, and was bloodily defeated, mainly by superior American artillery. Taylor pursued the retreating Mexicans westward, inflicting further casualties on them at Resaca de la Palma, but lost touch with them when they fled south across the Rio Grande. After being reinforced Taylor also crossed the river, taking Monterrey on 24 September and Saltillo on 16 November. Subsequently, and much to Taylor's disgust, Polk ordered him to detach the bulk of his army and send it off to reinforce another army that Major General

Winfield Scott was assembling at Tampico in preparation for an attack on Vera Cruz. Thus Taylor had less than 5000 men left in his command when, on 23 February 1847, 15,000 Mexican regulars, under the command of General Antonio López de Santa Ana, attacked him near the hacienda Buena Vista, south of Saltillo. Although the issue of the Battle of Buena Vista was several times in doubt, Taylor's accurate artillery fire and the success of his dragoons in breaking up Mexican infantry charges finally tilted the decision in the Americans' favor. This victory, combined with another won by a force of Missouri volunteers farther north, at Chihuahua, effectively put northern Mexico in American hands. Even before that time US Army, Navy and militia forces had succeeded in removing all Mexican military presence from New Mexico and California. Thus the Americans' sole remaining objective was the conquest of central Mexico.

General Scott's 13,000-man army at Tampico mounted an amphibious attack on Vera Cruz in March and, after a two-week siege, took the city on the 27th. Scott then made his way slowly west towards Mexico City, defeating Santa Ana's 12,000-man opposing army at Cerro Gordo on 18 April and finally arriving in the vicinity of the capital in August. For more than a month Scott was obliged to fight a succession of fierce (and, on his part, brilliantly conducted) battles around the city's periphery – at El Pedregal, Contraras, Churubusco, El Molino de Rey, Chapultepec and several other points – and it was not until 14 September that Santa Ana at last surrendered the city itself. On 2

Above: *General Winfield Scott at Vera Cruz.*
MAP above right: *The Mexican War.*
Right: *Contemporary impression of the Battle of Buena Vista.*

February 1848 the war was formally ended and the present southern boundary of the United States was fixed by the signing of the Treaty of Guadelupe Hidalgo.

In strict military terms, American prosecution of the war had been exemplary, for the opposing Mexican armies were usually more numerous and were at all times well equipped and led. Whether America's motives for fighting the war in the first place were equally praiseworthy is less clear.

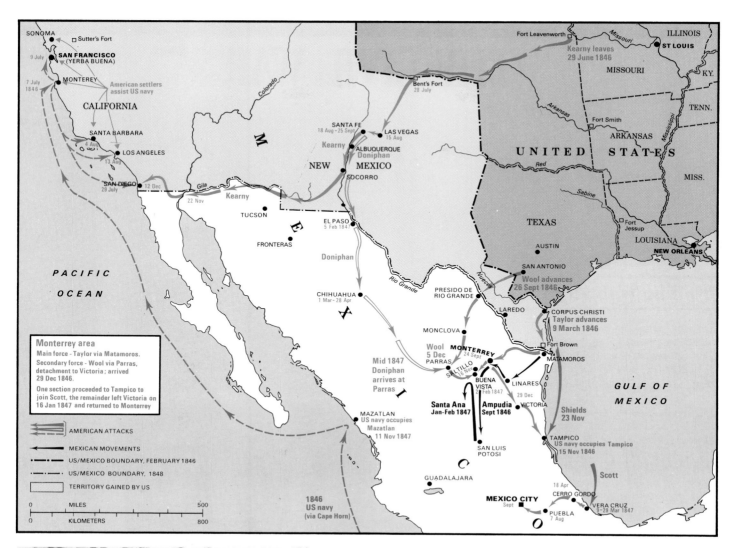

Monterrey area

Main force - Taylor via Matamoros.
Secondary force - Wool via Parras, detachment to Victoria; arrived 29 Dec 1846.

One section proceeded to Tampico to join Scott, the remainder left Victoria on 16 Jan 1847 and returned to Monterrey

AMERICAN ATTACKS
MEXICAN MOVEMENTS
US/MEXICO BOUNDARY, FEBRUARY 1846
US/MEXICO BOUNDARY, 1848
TERRITORY GAINED BY US

| 0 | MILES | 500 |
| 0 | KILOMETERS | 800 |

SONOMA
Sutter's Fort
9 July
SAN FRANCISCO (YERBA BUENA)
7 July 1846
MONTEREY
American settlers assist US navy
CALIFORNIA
SANTA BARBARA
4 Aug
LOS ANGELES
13 Aug
SAN DIEGO 12 Dec
29 July
22 Nov
Kearny
Gila
TUCSON
FRONTERAS
PACIFIC OCEAN
Colorado
SANTA FE 18 Aug - 25 Sept
LAS VEGAS 15 Aug
Kearny
Doniphan
ALBUQUERQUE
NEW MEXICO
SOCORRO
EL PASO 5 Feb 1847
Doniphan
Rio Grande
CHIHUAHUA 1 Mar - 28 Apr
Fort Leavenworth
Kearny leaves 29 June 1846
Missouri
ST LOUIS
ILLINOIS
MISSOURI
KY.
Bent's Fort 28 July
Arkansas
Fort Smith
ARKANSAS
TENN.
Mississippi
UNITED STATES
Red
TEXAS
AUSTIN
SAN ANTONIO
Wool advances 26 Sept 1846
Nueces
Sabine
MISS.
Fort Jessup
LOUISIANA
NEW ORLEANS
PRESIDO DE RIO GRANDE
LAREDO
MONCLOVA
CORPUS CHRISTI Taylor advances 9 March 1846
Fort Brown
MATAMOROS
Wool 5 Dec
PARRAS
MONTERREY 24 Sept
SALTILLO 16 Nov
BUENA VISTA 22 Feb 1847
LINARES
GULF OF MEXICO
Mid 1847 Doniphan arrives at Parras
Santa Ana Jan-Feb 1847
Ampudia Sept 1846
VICTORIA 29 Dec
Shields 23 Nov
MAZATLAN US navy occupies Mazatlan 11 Nov 1847
SAN LUIS POTOSI
TAMPICO US navy occupies Tampico 15 Nov 1846
Scott
1846 US navy (via Cape Horn)
GUADALAJARA
MEXICO CITY Sept
PUEBLA 7 Aug
CERRO GORDO 18 Apr
VERA CRUZ 9-28 Mar 1847

THE CIVIL WAR

The War Begins

Disputes over a variety of moral and economic issues related to the institution of slavery – and especially to the question of whether it should be allowed to spread into new states and the western Territories – had progressively envenomed relations between the Northern and Southern United States since the early years of the nineteenth century. By the mid-1850s the government's capacity to paper over these irreconcilable sectional differences with legislative compromise was exhausted. When, in 1860, Abraham Lincoln, candidate of the anti-slavery Republican party, was elected president, many in the Deep South concluded that they could no longer go on working within the Constitutional framework of the Union. By the time of Lincoln's inauguration on 4 March 1861 seven Southern states had seceded, formed a Confederate States of America and elected Jefferson Davis as its president. Lincoln's efforts to undo this crisis through conciliation collapsed when, on 12 April, South Carolinian troops attacked the Federal garrison at Fort Sumter, in Charleston harbor. Three days later Lincoln declared the secessionist states to be in rebellion. With war now plainly inevitable, and as four more border states hastened to join the CSA, both sides began to assemble their armies.

The war about to be fought was the bloodiest in American history. War-related deaths would total nearly 500,000, about 90,000 more than the total for World War II. (In relation to contemporary populations, the Civil

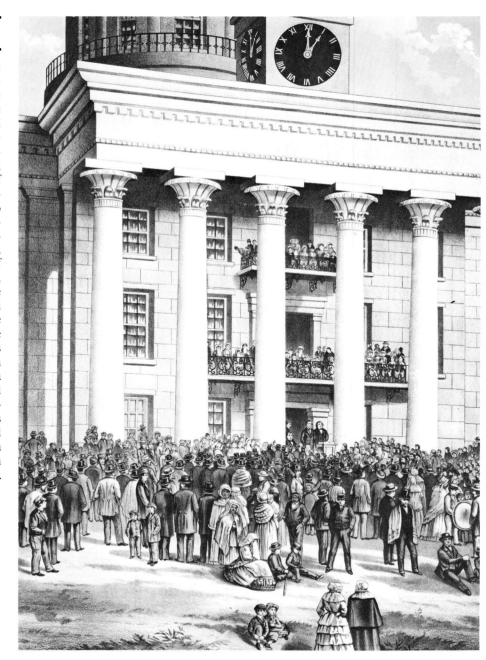

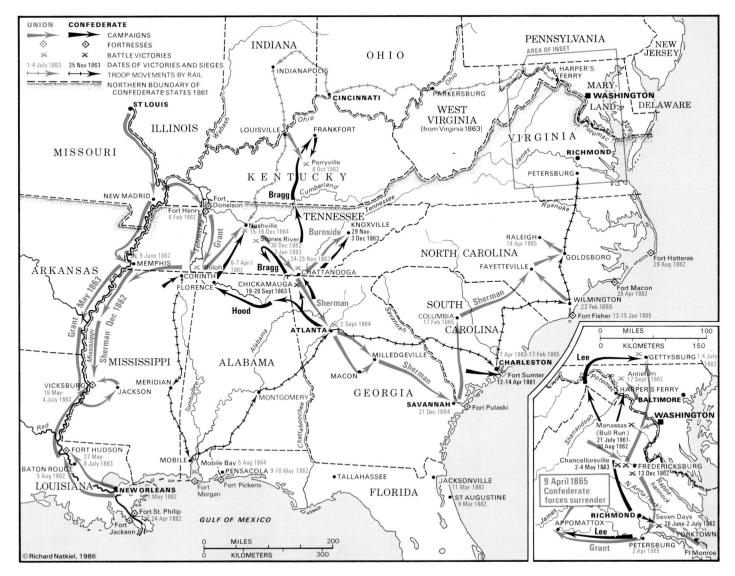

War death rate was more than five times that of World War II.) Technological innovations that vastly increased battlefield firepower made this slaughter possible and, in the process, profoundly affected the tactics – and even the fundamental character – of war. In time these new technologies would also help the more industrialized North to win, but at the outset the preponderance of Northern strength was by no means so great as to give it a decisive advantage. This was perhaps even more true since the burden of the offensive lay entirely with the North.

MAP above: *The campaigns of the Civil War.*
Left: *The inauguration of Jefferson Davis as President of the Confederacy.*
Right: *Inside Fort Sumter during the bombardment, April 1861.*

The First Battle of Bull Run

The North quickly settled on a three-part strategy: a primary offensive intended to drive south from the vicinity of Washington and capture the Confederate capital of Richmond, Virginia; a second offensive designed to secure the entire length of the Mississippi River; and a total naval blockade of the Confederate coast.

The attack on Richmond began on 16 July 1861. An army of 35,000 Federal troops, under the command of Brigadier General Irwin McDowell, set out from Washington to engage a Confederate army of 20,000, commanded by Brigadier General P G T Beauregard, that had taken up station at Manassas Junction, just 30 miles away. McDowell arrived at Manassas on the 18th, to find Beauregard well positioned for defence behind Bull Run Creek. But the Union commander did not launch his attack until three days had passed, long enough for Beauregard to be reinforced by 9000 additional men brought to him by Brigadier General Joseph E Johnston.

When McDowell did attack, on the 21st, his effort to break the Confederate left flank failed. When he attempted to disengage his troops became disorganized, and the retreat turned into a rout that swept the Federals all the way back to the outskirts of Washington. Here the Union army remained for the rest of the year.

MAP far right: *The approach to the Battle of Shiloh.*
MAPS right: *The First Battle of Bull Run.*
Below: *Engraving of the action during the First Battle of Bull Run.*

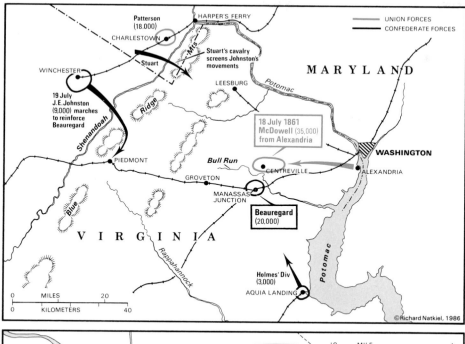

UNION FORCES
CONFEDERATE FORCES

HARPER'S FERRY

Patterson (18,000)
CHARLESTOWN

Stuart's cavalry screens Johnston's movements

Stuart

M A R Y L A N D

WINCHESTER

LEESBURG

Potomac

19 July J.E.Johnston (9,000) marches to reinforce Beauregard

Ridge

18 July 1861 McDowell (35,000) from Alexandria

WASHINGTON

PIEDMONT

Bull Run

GROVETON

CENTREVILLE

ALEXANDRIA

Shenandoah

MANASSAS JUNCTION

Beauregard (20,000)

Blue

V I R G I N I A

Rappahannock

Holmes' Div (3,000)

Potomac

AQUIA LANDING

0   MILES   20
0   KILOMETERS   40

©Richard Natkiel, 1986

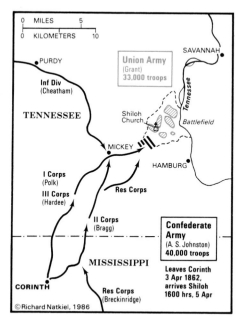

0   MILES   5
0   KILOMETERS   10

PURDY

SAVANNAH

Inf Div (Cheatham)

Union Army (Grant) 33,000 troops

TENNESSEE

Shiloh Church

Battlefield

Tennessee

MICKEY

HAMBURG

I Corps (Polk)

III Corps (Hardee)

Res Corps

II Corps (Bragg)

MISSISSIPPI

CORINTH

Res Corps (Breckinridge)

Confederate Army (A. S. Johnston) 40,000 troops

Leaves Corinth 3 Apr 1862, arrives Shiloh 1600 hrs, 5 Apr

©Richard Natkiel, 1986

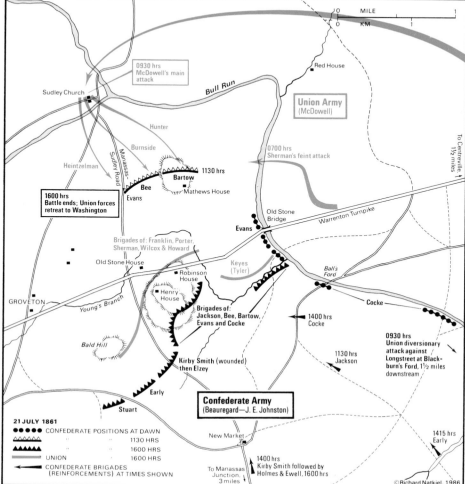

0   MILE   1
0   KM   1

Red House

0930 hrs McDowell's main attack

Sudley Church

Bull Run

Hunter

Union Army (McDowell)

Burnside

0700 hrs Sherman's feint attack

Heintzelman

Sudley Road

Manassas

1130 hrs

Bartow

Bee

Mathews House

Evans

1600 hrs Battle ends; Union forces retreat to Washington

Old Stone Bridge

Evans

Warrenton Turnpike

To Centreville, 1½ miles

Brigades of: Franklin, Porter, Sherman, Wilcox & Howard

Old Stone House

Keyes (Tyler)

Ball's Ford

Robinson House

Henry House

Young's Branch

Brigades of: Jackson, Bee, Bartow, Evans and Cocke

Cocke

GROVETON

1400 hrs Cocke

Bald Hill

0930 hrs Union diversionary attack against Longstreet at Black-burn's Ford, 1½ miles downstream

1130 hrs Jackson

Kirby Smith (wounded) then Elzey

Early

Confederate Army (Beauregard—J. E. Johnston)

Stuart

21 JULY 1861
●●●●● CONFEDERATE POSITIONS AT DAWN
▲▲▲▲▲ 1130 HRS
▬▬▬ 1600 HRS
UNION 1600 HRS
➤ CONFEDERATE BRIGADES (REINFORCEMENTS) AT TIMES SHOWN

New Market

1415 hrs Early

1400 hrs Kirby Smith followed by Holmes & Ewell, 1600 hrs

To Manassas Junction, 3 miles

©Richard Natkiel, 1986

The Battle of Shiloh

The campaign of 1862 began in the West. In February Brigadier General Ulysses S Grant's Union army moved from Kentucky into northwestern Tennessee, capturing Forts Henry and Donelson and some 15,000 Confederate prisoners. Major General Henry W Halleck, the Western Theater commander, then ordered Grant to proceed south to Shiloh, in southern Tennessee, there to join forces with another Union army that Major General Don Carlos Buell would bring down from Nashville. The opposing Confederate generals, Beauregard and Albert Sidney Johnston, made haste to strike before this juncture could take place. On 6 April they caught Grant completely by surprise at Shiloh when they attacked his men with a slightly larger force of 40,000. Their initial assault nearly carried the day, but Brigadier General William T Sherman's highly spirited defense of Grant's flank frustrated the Confederates' attempt to roll up the Union army from right to left and gave the Union commander time to consolidate his decimated forces for a last-ditch

stand on the bank of the Tennessee
River. Buell's reinforcements, which
arrived only just in time to prevent a
Union disaster, permitted Grant to
make a successful counterattack the
next day, but the Federal troops were
by then too exhausted to pursue the
withdrawing Confederates. The final
butcher's bill for this inconclusive
battle, about 24,000 dead or wounded,
shocked both sides. Worse was to
come.

Right: *Confederate forces repel a
Union charge during the Battle of
Shiloh.*
MAPS below: *The fighting at Shiloh.*

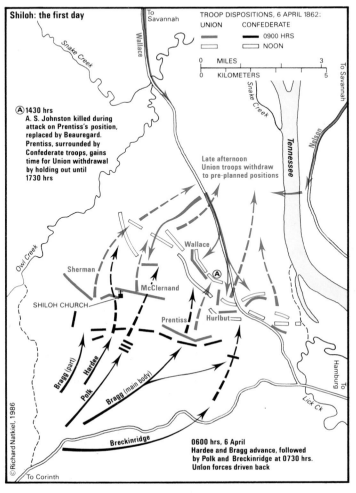

Shiloh: the first day

To Savannah

TROOP DISPOSITIONS, 6 APRIL 1862:
UNION   CONFEDERATE
              0900 HRS
              NOON

0   MILES   3
0   KILOMETERS   5

Snake Creek

Wallace

Ⓐ 1430 hrs
A. S. Johnston killed during
attack on Prentiss's position,
replaced by Beauregard.
Prentiss, surrounded by
Confederate troops, gains
time for Union withdrawal
by holding out until
1730 hrs

Snake Creek

Tennessee

Nelson

Late afternoon
Union troops withdraw
to pre-planned positions

Owl Creek

Wallace

Ⓐ

Sherman

McClernand

SHILOH CHURCH

Prentiss

Hurlbut

Bragg (part)

Hardee

Polk

Bragg (main body)

Breckinridge

To Hamburg

Lick Ck

0600 hrs, 6 April
Hardee and Bragg advance, followed
by Polk and Breckinridge at 0730 hrs.
Union forces driven back

© Richard Natkiel, 1986

To Corinth

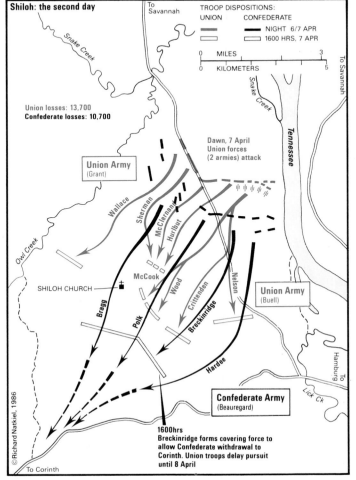

Shiloh: the second day

To Savannah

TROOP DISPOSITIONS:
UNION   CONFEDERATE
              NIGHT 6/7 APR
              1600 HRS, 7 APR

0   MILES   3
0   KILOMETERS   5

Snake Creek

Snake Creek

Tennessee

To Savannah

Union losses: 13,700
Confederate losses: 10,700

Dawn, 7 April
Union forces
(2 armies) attack

Union Army
(Grant)

Wallace

Sherman

McClernand

Hurlbut

Owl Creek

McCook

SHILOH CHURCH

Bragg

Polk

Wood

Crittenden

Nelson

Breckinridge

Union Army
(Buell)

Hardee

To Hamburg

Lick Ck

Confederate Army
(Beauregard)

1600hrs
Breckinridge forms covering force to
allow Confederate withdrawal to
Corinth. Union troops delay pursuit
until 8 April

© Richard Natkiel, 1986

To Corinth

MAP below right: *The Battle of New Orleans; Farragut's fleet forces its way up the Mississippi toward the city.*
Below: *David Farragut, hero of New Orleans and Mobile Bay.*
Bottom right: *The* Hartford, *Farragut's flagship in his victories.*

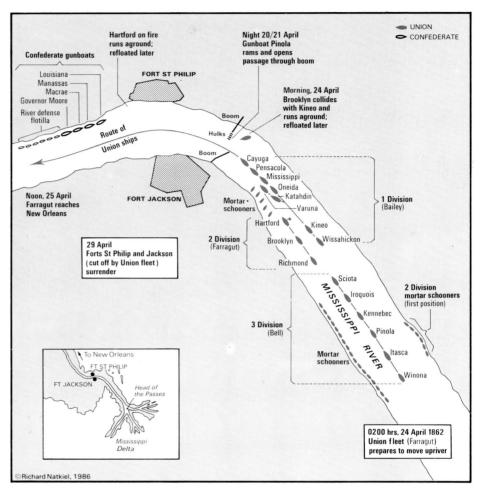

The Battle of New Orleans

While Grant had been moving through Tennessee towards Shiloh, combined Army and Navy forces had been methodically extending Union control over the central Mississippi River, and by 6 June they had secured the river as far south as Memphis. At about the same time the Navy was scoring even more spectacular successes on the lower Mississippi. On 24 April Commodore David G Farragut's 46-vessel naval squadron fought its way past the forts guarding the southern approaches to New Orleans and the next day captured the city. As Farragut continued to force his way upriver, Federal troops followed in his wake, eventually pushing as far north as Baton Rouge. Confederate control of the riverbank had now been compressed to the section between Port Hudson, Louisiana, and Vicksburg, in central Mississippi. Inland, a limited Confederate autumn counteroffensive into central Kentucky produced some alarm and a good deal of fierce fighting, but failed to undo the effects of the steady gains the Union had made in the West throughout the year.

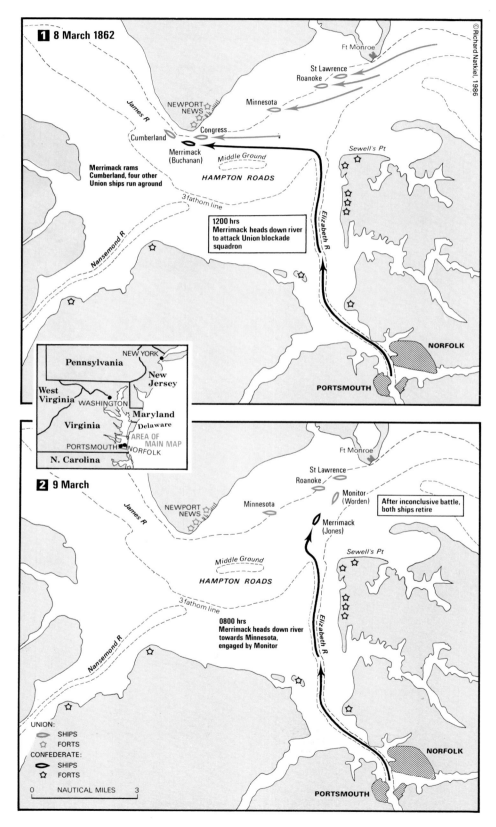

1 8 March 1862

Ft Monroe

St Lawrence
Roanoke
Minnesota

James R

NEWPORT
NEWS

Congress
Cumberland

Merrimack
(Buchanan)

Middle Ground

Sewell's Pt

Merrimack rams Cumberland, four other Union ships run aground

HAMPTON ROADS

3 fathom line

Nansemond R

1200 hrs Merrimack heads down river to attack Union blockade squadron

Elizabeth R

NORFOLK

PORTSMOUTH

©Richard Natkiel, 1986

Inset map:

NEW YORK

Pennsylvania

New Jersey

West Virginia

WASHINGTON

Maryland

Delaware

Virginia

AREA OF MAIN MAP

PORTSMOUTH NORFOLK

N. Carolina

2 9 March

Ft Monroe

St Lawrence
Roanoke

Monitor
(Worden)

After inconclusive battle, both ships retire

Merrimack
(Jones)

James R

NEWPORT
NEWS

Minnesota

Sewell's Pt

Middle Ground

HAMPTON ROADS

3 fathom line

Nansemond R

0800 hrs Merrimack heads down river towards Minnesota, engaged by Monitor

Elizabeth R

NORFOLK

PORTSMOUTH

UNION:
◯ SHIPS
☆ FORTS
CONFEDERATE:
⬭ SHIPS
★ FORTS

0   NAUTICAL MILES   3

The Battle of Hampton Roads

In the East, 1862 produced no more clear-cut strategic decision than had 1861, though the scale and violence of the fighting vastly increased. The year's first major battle in the East was a historic naval engagement. Searching for a weapon to counter the Union blockade the Confederates had built a massive steam-driven ironclad, CSS *Virginia* (ex-*Merrimack*), armed with powerful 8 inch, 7 inch and 6 inch guns. On 8 March 1862 this monster sortied from Norfolk, Virginia, and set upon a five-ship blockading squadron in Hampton Roads. In short order *Virginia* sank the sloop-of-war USS *Cumberland*, 24, and then battered the frigate USS *Congress*, 50, into surrender. The next day, when *Virginia* headed for the frigate USS *Minnesota*, 50, which had grounded while trying to come to the aid of *Congress*, she found herself confronted by another self-propelled ironclad, USS *Monitor*, which mounted two 11 inch guns in a revolving turret. Though in four hours of fighting neither ship managed to sink the other, *Virginia* had the worst of the exchange and retired to Norfolk, never to sortie again. History remembers this famous duel as marking a symbolic end to the age of fighting sail. Its more immediate significance was that it dashed Southern hopes of gaining a technological advantage with which to break the blockade.

MAPS left: *The Battle of Hampton Roads.*
MAP above right: *Jackson's Valley Campaign.*
Right: *The* Monitor *and the* Virginia *exchange fire during their stalemated battle.*

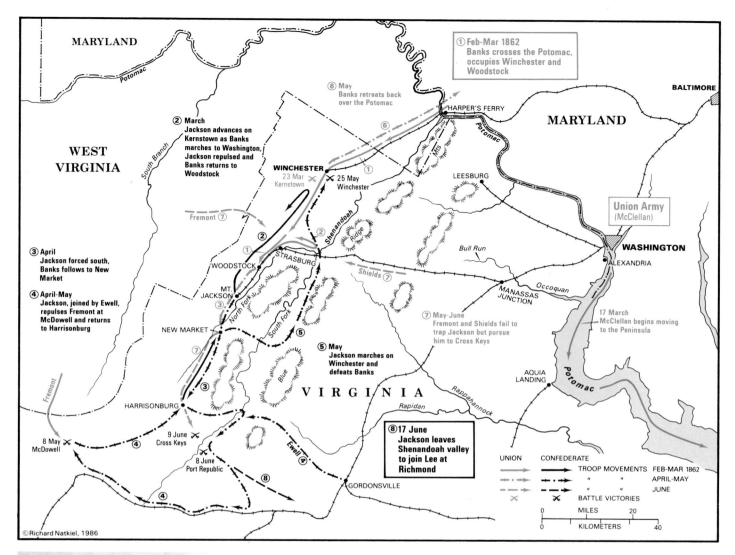

① Feb-Mar 1862
Banks crosses the Potomac, occupies Winchester and Woodstock

⑥ May Banks retreats back over the Potomac

MARYLAND

BALTIMORE

② March
Jackson advances on Kernstown as Banks marches to Washington, Jackson repulsed and Banks returns to Woodstock

WEST VIRGINIA

Fremont ⑦

③ April
Jackson forced south, Banks follows to New Market

④ April-May
Jackson, joined by Ewell, repulses Fremont at McDowell and returns to Harrisonburg

WINCHESTER
23 Mar Kernstown
✗ 25 May Winchester

LEESBURG

Union Army (McClellan)

WOODSTOCK
STRASBURG
MT. JACKSON

Shields ⑦

Bull Run

WASHINGTON
ALEXANDRIA

17 March McClellan begins moving to the Peninsula

NEW MARKET

⑦ May-June
Fremont and Shields fail to trap Jackson but pursue him to Cross Keys

MANASSAS JUNCTION

Occoquan

⑦

⑤ May
Jackson marches on Winchester and defeats Banks

V I R G I N I A

AQUIA LANDING

Rappahannock

Fremont

HARRISONBURG

Rapidan

Blue Ridge

8 May ✗ McDowell

9 June ✗ Cross Keys

Ewell ④

⑧ 17 June
Jackson leaves Shenandoah valley to join Lee at Richmond

8 June Port Republic

④

⑧

GORDONSVILLE

UNION	CONFEDERATE		
→	►	TROOP MOVEMENTS	FEB-MAR 1862
→	►	" " "	APRIL-MAY
→	►	" " "	JUNE
✗	✗	BATTLE VICTORIES	

MILES 0 — 20
KILOMETERS 0 — 40

©Richard Natkiel, 1986

Jackson's Valley Campaign

The land war in the East also resumed in March, with a two-pronged Union offensive designed to capture Richmond. The major attack was to be delivered by a 100,000-man army, under Major General George B McClellan, which was to be landed on the tip of the Virginia Peninsula, thence to march on the Confederate capital, only 75 miles away. A secondary attack, to be launched overland, was to clear the Shenandoah Valley of Confederate forces and then converge on Richmond from the northwest. In the event it was the Valley campaign that was the more decisive, for here the brilliant defensive tactics of Confederate General Thomas J 'Stonewall' Jackson not only frustrated the Union advance but pinned down

41

troops badly needed by McClellan to reinforce his army on the Peninsula. Throughout March and April Jackson had fought a skillful delaying action against the southward advance of Major General Nathaniel Banks, and when, in May, Banks attempted to trap Jackson between his own forces and those of Major General John C Frémont, who had entered the southern end of the valley from West Virginia, Jackson defeated both in succession. In early June Union Generals Frémont and James Shields again attempted to trap Jackson between converging columns, and again he defeated his pursuers individually in the battles of Cross Keys and Port Republic, fought in 24 hours.

Having reduced the Union advance in the Shenandoah to near chaos, Jackson withdrew from the valley in mid June to join with the new commander of the Army of Northern Virginia, General Robert E Lee, in defending Richmond against McClellan's slow-moving advance up the Peninsula.

The Seven Days' Battle

McClellan had reached the Peninsula in early April but had wasted a month besieging Major General John Magruder's forces at Yorktown. The Confederates abandoned the town early in May and withdrew toward Richmond, fighting a delaying action at Williamsburg on the 5th. By the end of the month McClellan's army was closing in on Richmond but had become badly dispersed en route. Confederate General J E Johnston mounted an unsuccessful attempt to take advantage of this and defeat McClellan in detail in the Battle of Fair Oaks on 31 May. Johnston's subordinate commanders let him down and he himself was wounded and replaced in charge by General Lee.

On 25 June Lee began his counteroffensive with a series of relentless attacks (subsequently known as the Seven Days' Battle). In engagements at Mechanicsville (26 June) and Gaines Mill (27 June) he forced McClellan to retreat toward a new base at Harrison's Landing. The Federal rear guard held Lee off at Savage Station and Fraser's Farm and by 1 July the Union army was in a strong position at Malvern Hill. Although Lee's attacks on this position were beaten off the Union forces retired to Harrison's Landing and abandoned the Peninsula campaign. McClellan's army was withdrawn from the Peninsula in early August.

Left: *Stonewall Jackson seen at the First Battle of Bull Run. Jackson was probably the most able of Lee's Lieutenants.*
MAP above right: *The Seven Days' Battle.*
Right: *Typical example of the sort of defensive position constructed by both sides during the Civil War.*

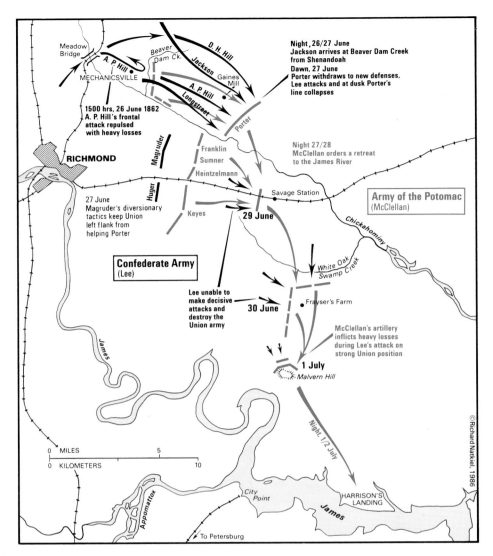

Night, 26/27 June
Jackson arrives at Beaver Dam Creek
from Shenandoah
Dawn, 27 June
Porter withdraws to new defenses,
Lee attacks and at dusk Porter's
line collapses

1500 hrs, 26 June 1862
A. P. Hill's frontal
attack repulsed
with heavy losses

Night 27/28
McClellan orders a retreat
to the James River

27 June
Magruder's diversionary
tactics keep Union
left flank from
helping Porter

Army of the Potomac
(McClellan)

Confederate Army
(Lee)

Lee unable to
make decisive
attacks and
destroy the
Union army

McClellan's artillery
inflicts heavy losses
during Lee's attack on
strong Union position

1 July
Malvern Hill

Night 1/2 July

City
Point

HARRISON'S
LANDING

To Petersburg

©Richard Natkiel, 1986

0 MILES 5
0 KILOMETERS 10

Manassas and Antietam

The North next attempted to recapitulate the strategy of the preceding year with direct overland offensives, originating from Washington and aimed at Richmond. Once again the contending armies clashed at Manassas, this time on 29 August 1862, and once again the Federal troops were routed, retreating in disorder back to Washington. Lee immediately seized the initiative and launched an offensive into Maryland. McClellan, at the head of 90,000 troops, caught up with Lee's 50,000 at Antietam Creek, near Sharpsburg, Maryland, in mid-September, and on the 17th McClellan attacked. None of his efforts to turn Lee's flanks was successful, and for the most part the battle was fought as a murderous confrontational slugging match, with neither side winning a clear decision. The Battle of Antietam was, however, the bloodiest battle of the war so far, producing 12,000 Union and 10,000 Confederate casualties. In the face of

MAP below: *The Second Battle of Bull Run.*
MAP bottom: *Battle of Antietam.*
Below right: *Union forces cross the river and go into the attack at Fredericksburg in December 1862.*

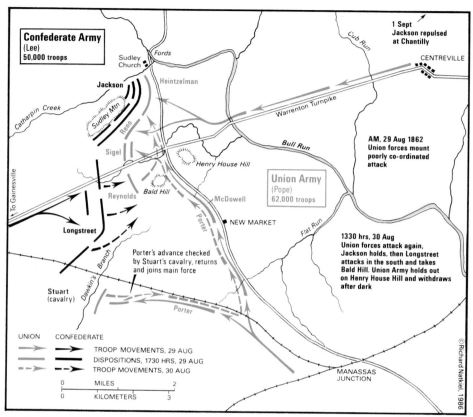

Confederate Army
(Lee)
50,000 troops

1 Sept Jackson repulsed at Chantilly

CENTREVILLE

Cub Run

Sudley Church

Fords

Jackson

Heintzelman

Sudley Mtn

Reno

Warrenton Turnpike

Sigel

Bull Run

AM, 29 Aug 1862 Union forces mount poorly co-ordinated attack

Henry House Hill

To Gainesville

Catharpin Creek

Reynolds

Bald Hill

McDowell

Union Army
(Pope)
62,000 troops

Longstreet

Porter

NEW MARKET

Flat Run

1330 hrs, 30 Aug Union forces attack again, Jackson holds, then Longstreet attacks in the south and takes Bald Hill. Union Army holds out on Henry House Hill and withdraws after dark

Dawkin's Branch

Porter's advance checked by Stuart's cavalry, returns and joins main force

Stuart (cavalry)

Porter

© Richard Natkiel, 1986

UNION   CONFEDERATE

→ → TROOP MOVEMENTS, 29 AUG
━ ━ DISPOSITIONS, 1730 HRS, 29 AUG
--→ --→ TROOP MOVEMENTS, 30 AUG

MANASSAS JUNCTION

0   MILES   2
0   KILOMETERS   3

such devastating losses, Lee felt compelled to abandon his offensive and withdraw across the Potomac River into Virginia on the next day.

At the year's end the North made yet another attempt on Richmond. This offensive, involving about 100,000 troops led by Major General Ambrose E Burnside, was conceived as a relatively straightforward advance south to Fredericksburg, on the Rappahannock River, and thence southeast to the Confederate capital. By the time (13 December) Burnside was ready to cross the Rappahannock and assail Fredericksburg, Lee's 70,000 troops were strongly entrenched in the hills around the town. Though the situation plainly called for some form of enveloping tactics, the unimaginative Burnside chose a frontal assault across the river and up the slopes before the town, always under heavy fire. The inevitable result: 15,000 Union casualties to a much smaller Confederate loss of about 5000, Fredericksburg still in Confederate hands and the Union offensive brought to a standstill.

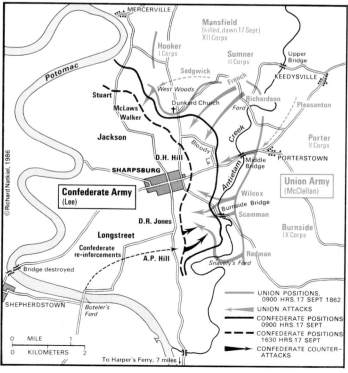

MERCERVILLE

Mansfield (killed, dawn 17 Sept) XII Corps

Hooker I Corps

Sumner II Corps

Upper Bridge

Potomac

Sedgwick

West Woods

French

KEEDYSVILLE

Stuart

McLaws

Walker

Dunkard Church

Richardson

Pleasanton

Jackson

Bloody La.

Porter V Corps

D.H. Hill

Middle Bridge

PORTERSTOWN

SHARPSBURG

Antietam

Confederate Army
(Lee)

Wilcox

Burnside Bridge

Scamman

D.R. Jones

Longstreet

Burnside IX Corps

Confederate re-inforcements

A.P. Hill

Redman

Bridge destroyed

Snavely's Ford

SHEPHERDSTOWN

Boteler's Ford

© Richard Natkiel, 1986

━ UNION POSITIONS, 0900 HRS, 17 SEPT 1862
← UNION ATTACKS
━ CONFEDERATE POSITIONS 0900 HRS. 17 SEPT
-- CONFEDERATE POSITIONS 1630 HRS.17 SEPT
▶ CONFEDERATE COUNTER-ATTACKS

0   MILE   1
0   KILOMETERS   2

To Harper's Ferry, 7 miles ↓

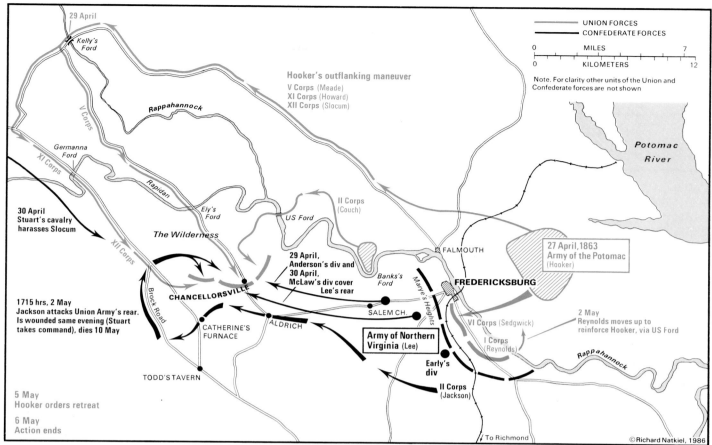

The map shows:

UNION FORCES
CONFEDERATE FORCES

0 MILES 7
0 KILOMETERS 12

Note. For clarity other units of the Union and Confederate forces are not shown

29 April — Kelly's Ford

Rappahannock

V Corps

Germanna Ford

XI Corps

Rapidan

30 April
Stuart's cavalry
harasses Slocum

XII Corps

The Wilderness

Ely's Ford

US Ford

Hooker's outflanking maneuver
V Corps (Meade)
XI Corps (Howard)
XII Corps (Slocum)

Potomac River

29 April, Anderson's div and 30 April, McLaw's div cover Lee's rear

II Corps (Couch)

FALMOUTH

27 April, 1863
Army of the Potomac
(Hooker)

1715 hrs, 2 May
Jackson attacks Union Army's rear.
Is wounded same evening (Stuart takes command), dies 10 May

Brock Road

CHANCELLORSVILLE

CATHERINE'S FURNACE

ALDRICH

Banks's Ford

SALEM CH.

Marye's Heights

FREDERICKSBURG

Army of Northern Virginia (Lee)

VI Corps (Sedgwick)

I Corps (Reynolds)

2 May
Reynolds moves up to reinforce Hooker, via US Ford

Rappahannock

TODD'S TAVERN

Early's div

II Corps (Jackson)

5 May
Hooker orders retreat

6 May
Action ends

To Richmond

©Richard Natkiel, 1986

The Battle of Chancellorsville

The North sought to break the stalemate before Fredericksburg the following spring. Burnside's successor, Major General Joseph Hooker, now attempted a combined frontal assault and northern envelopment. Lee adroitly counterattacked Hooker's enveloping right wing and forced it to assume a defensive position at the town of Chancellorsville. Then Lee rapidly assembled a force of about 60,000 men, 42,000 of which he launched in a direct attack on Chancellorsville, while another 28,000, mostly cavalry, under the command of Lieutenant General Thomas J Jackson, swung around the town on Hooker's right. The ferocity of this attack (begun on 2 May 1863) nearly undid Hooker's 90,000-man army. Though in the end it barely managed to hang together, Hooker ordered it to begin its retreat on 5 May. Again, casualties were enormous: 17,000 Union and 13,000 Confederate (of whom Jackson was one).

While the dismayed Union command was trying to think what to do next, Lee acted with characteristic boldness. Virtually ignoring the Federal forces still before Fredericksburg (he left only a single corps to defend the town), he abruptly hurled 75,000 troops northwest in an invasion of Pennsylvania. As panic spread in the North Hooker could only turn his army around and follow as best he might.

MAP above: *The Battle of Chancellorsville.*
Below: *Hooker's headquarters.*

MAP right: *The capture of Vicksburg.*
MAPS below right: *The Battle of Chickamauga.*
MAP below left: *The Battle of Gettysburg.*

The Battle of Gettysburg

For the better part of the month of June 1863 Lee's forces fanned out over southern Pennsylvania, spreading chaos and destruction and capturing much-needed supplies. Only by the month's end had the fragmented elements of the Union army, now commanded by Hooker's replacement, Major General George G Meade, begun to coalesce sufficiently to prompt Lee to concentrate his own forces. He did so before the small crossroads town of Gettysburg, where Union troops were desperately trying to set up defensive positions. On 1 July 1863 the Confederates attacked Gettysburg from the northwest and drove the defenders south from the town into a chain of low hills. All through the following day of savage fighting Lee's lieutenants tried in vain to dislodge the Union defenders from this high ground: Cemetery Hill and Culp's Hill on the north, Cemetery Ridge in the center, and Round Top and Little Round Top on the south. On 3 July the Confederates made a last all-out assault – 15,000 men led by Major General George Pickett – on Cemetery Ridge. It was bloodily repulsed, costing the attackers an appalling 60 percent in casualties. Lee, who had thus far lost nearly 30,000 men in his Pennsylvania offensive, realized he could do no more and on 4 July ordered his army back to Virginia. This decisive Union victory broke forever the South's capacity to mount major offensive operations in the Eastern theater.

Vicksburg and the Western Campaign: 1863

Meantime, equally dramatic developments had been unfolding in the West. At the beginning of 1863 the South had only one remaining important foothold on the Mississippi River, the fortress city of Vicksburg. But Grant was finding this 'Gibraltar of the West' a tough nut to crack. Natural and man-made defences made the city almost impregnable on its north, west and south sides, while the eastern approaches were guarded both by the city's strong garrison and by Joseph E Johnston's potentially formidable Confederate army headquartered just 40 miles due east in Jackson. None of the several attempts that Grant made on Vicksburg during the first quarter of the year met with any success. Then, in April, he moved a 45,000-man force down the west bank of the Mississippi, crossed the river at a point about 50 miles below the city and marched rapidly northeast towards Jackson. He took that city on 14 May, driving Johnston's troops off to the north, then wheeled west and struck at Vicksburg. The city gallantly withstood his grim siege for six weeks, surrendering only on 4 July, the same day Lee began his withdrawal from Gettysburg.

With the capture of Vicksburg the Union had achieved the preliminary goal of its Western strategy: the Greater South was now bisected along a north-south axis. The next goal would be to split the Old South along an east-west axis, and the necessary first step in this enterprise would be the capture of Chattanooga, a key Confederate stronghold on Tennessee's southern border with Georgia. Defending Chattanooga was Major General Braxton Bragg, with an army of about 62,000. Marching all too slowly to the attack was Major General William S Rosecrans, with an army of about 65,000. By the time the dilatory Rosecrans arrived on the scene in

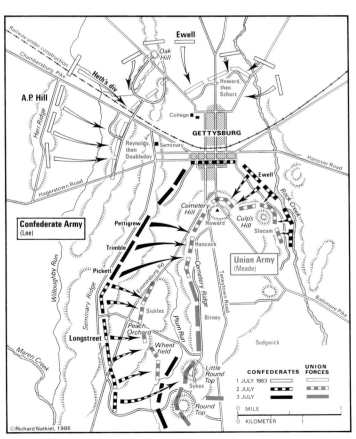

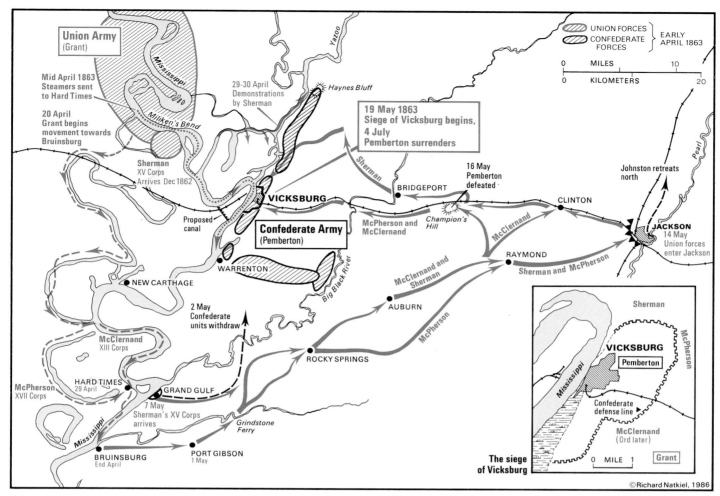

Union Army
(Grant)

Mid April 1863
Steamers sent
to Hard Times

20 April
Grant begins
movement towards
Bruinsburg

Mississippi

Milliken's Bend

Yazoo

29-30 April
Demonstrations
by Sherman

Haynes Bluff

Sherman
XV Corps
Arrives Dec 1862

Proposed
canal

VICKSBURG

Confederate Army
(Pemberton)

WARRENTON

Big Black River

NEW CARTHAGE

2 May
Confederate
units withdraw

McClernand
XIII Corps

McPherson
XVII Corps

HARD TIMES
29 April

GRAND GULF

7 May Sherman's XV Corps
arrives

Grindstone Ferry

Mississippi

BRUINSBURG
End April

PORT GIBSON
1 May

ROCKY SPRINGS

McClernand and
Sherman

AUBURN

McPherson

19 May 1863
Siege of Vicksburg begins,
4 July
Pemberton surrenders

Sherman

16 May
Pemberton defeated

BRIDGEPORT

Champion's Hill

McPherson and
McClernand

McClernand

RAYMOND

Sherman and McPherson

CLINTON

Johnston retreats
north

Pearl

JACKSON

14 May
Union forces
enter Jackson

14 May
Union forces enter Jackson

UNION FORCES
CONFEDERATE
FORCES

EARLY
APRIL 1863

0   MILES   10
0   KILOMETERS   20

**The siege
of Vicksburg**

Sherman

VICKSBURG

Pemberton

McPherson

Confederate
defense line

McClernand
(Ord later)

Mississippi

0   MILE   1

Grant

©Richard Natkiel, 1986

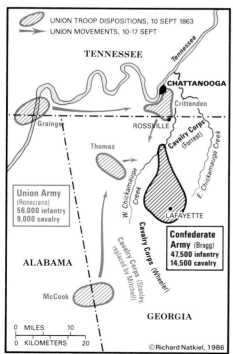

UNION TROOP DISPOSITIONS, 10 SEPT 1863
UNION MOVEMENTS, 10-17 SEPT

TENNESSEE

Tennessee

CHATTANOOGA

Crittenden

Grainger

ROSSVILLE

Thomas

Cavalry Corps
(Forrest)

W. Chickamauga Creek

E. Chickamauga Creek

LAFAYETTE

Union Army
(Rosecrans)
56,000 infantry
9,000 cavalry

Cavalry Corps
(Stanley,
replaced by Mitchell)

Cavalry Corps
(Wheeler)

**Confederate
Army** (Bragg)
47,500 infantry
14,500 cavalry

ALABAMA

McCook

GEORGIA

0   MILES   10
0   KILOMETERS   20

©Richard Natkiel, 1986

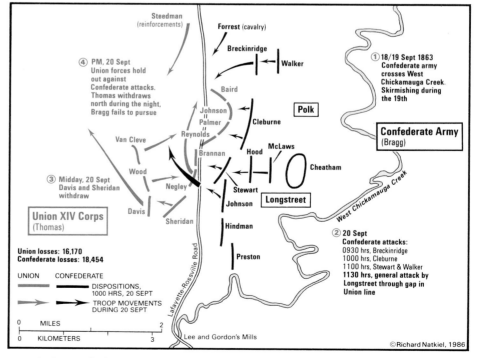

Steedman
(reinforcements)

Forrest (cavalry)

Breckinridge

Walker

④ PM, 20 Sept
Union forces hold
out against
Confederate attacks.
Thomas withdraws
north during the night,
Bragg fails to pursue

Baird

Johnson
Palmer

Reynolds

Van Cleve

Cleburne

Polk

Brannan

Hood

McLaws

Cheatham

Wood

Stewart

Negley

Johnson

Longstreet

③ Midday, 20 Sept
Davis and Sheridan
withdraw

Davis

Sheridan

Hindman

Preston

Union XIV Corps
(Thomas)

Union losses: 16,170
Confederate losses: 18,454

UNION   CONFEDERATE

DISPOSITIONS,
1000 HRS, 20 SEPT

TROOP MOVEMENTS
DURING 20 SEPT

0   MILES   2
0   KILOMETERS   3

Lafayette-Rossville Road

Lee and Gordon's Mills

① 18/19 Sept 1863
Confederate army
crosses West
Chickamauga Creek.
Skirmishing during
the 19th

Confederate Army
(Bragg)

West Chickamauga Creek

② 20 Sept
Confederate attacks:
0930 hrs, Breckinridge
1000 hrs, Cleburne
1100 hrs, Stewart & Walker
1130 hrs, general attack by
Longstreet through gap in
Union line

©Richard Natkiel, 1986

early September Bragg had not only established himself in a superb defensive position south of the city but also was being reinforced by extra men from Lieutenant General James T Longstreet's corps, brought all the way from Virginia. When Bragg realized he had gained numerical superiority, he quickly went over to the attack,

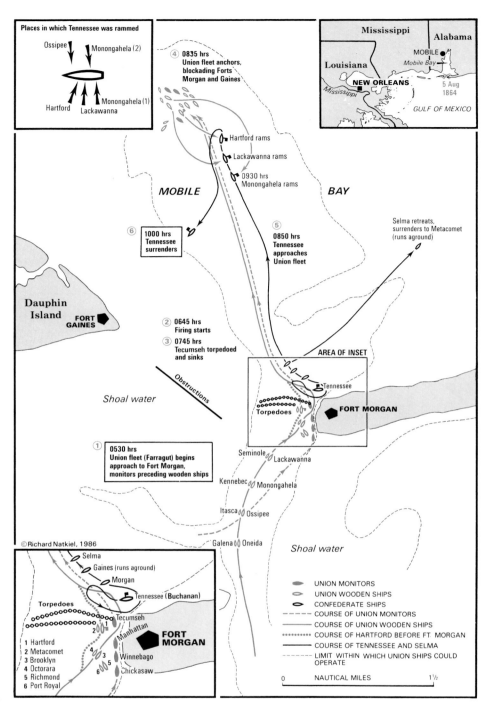

Places in which Tennessee was rammed

Ossipee — Monongahela (2)

Hartford — Lackawanna — Monongahela (1)

④ 0835 hrs
Union fleet anchors, blockading Forts Morgan and Gaines

Hartford rams

Lackawanna rams

0930 hrs
Monongahela rams

MOBILE   BAY

⑥ 1000 hrs
Tennessee surrenders

⑤ 0850 hrs
Tennessee approaches Union fleet

Selma retreats, surrenders to Metacomet (runs aground)

Dauphin Island   FORT GAINES

② 0645 hrs
Firing starts

③ 0745 hrs
Tecumseh torpedoed and sinks

AREA OF INSET

Obstructions

Shoal water

Tennessee

Torpedoes

FORT MORGAN

① 0530 hrs
Union fleet (Farragut) begins approach to Fort Morgan, monitors preceding wooden ships

Seminole

Lackawanna

Kennebec   Monongahela

Itasca   Ossipee

© Richard Natkiel, 1986

Galena   Oneida

Shoal water

Selma

Gaines (runs aground)

Morgan

Tennessee (Buchanan)

Torpedoes

Tecumseh

Manhattan

FORT MORGAN

1 Hartford
2 Metacomet
3 Brooklyn
4 Octorara
5 Richmond
6 Port Royal

Winnebago

Chickasaw

🟢 UNION MONITORS
⬭ UNION WOODEN SHIPS
⬛ CONFEDERATE SHIPS
---- COURSE OF UNION MONITORS
—— COURSE OF UNION WOODEN SHIPS
···· COURSE OF HARTFORD BEFORE FT. MORGAN
—— COURSE OF TENNESSEE AND SELMA
---- LIMIT WITHIN WHICH UNION SHIPS COULD OPERATE

0   NAUTICAL MILES   1½

Mississippi   Alabama

Louisiana

MOBILE
Mobile Bay

NEW ORLEANS

5 Aug 1864

Mississippi

GULF OF MEXICO

MAP left: *The Battle of Mobile Bay.*
MAP right: *Sherman's advance to Atlanta and the capture of the city.*

Chickamauga. But he finally did so, the climax coming on 25 November 1863, when, in the freakish battle of Missionary Ridge, his troops stormed up the side of a small mountain to overwhelm strongly-entrenched Confederate positions at the top (an almost unheard-of feat in this war of intense firepower). This success cracked the entire Confederate line, and the dispirited Bragg was forced to retreat to Dalton, Georgia, some 25 miles away. The Union offensive into the Deep South could now begin.

The North finds a Winning Strategy: 1864

Early in 1864 Lincoln appointed Grant General in Chief of the US Army and brought him back east to help plan what the president expected to be the closing phase of the war. This final Union strategy was again tripartite. First, the great offensive from the West into the Deep South would of course continue: directed by Sherman, it was intended to drive southeast from Chattanooga all the way through Georgia to the coast, capturing Atlanta along the way. Second, in the East, yet another attempt would be made on Richmond: several armies would be employed in this task, but the main thrust was to be made by Meade, now commander of the Army of the Potomac, starting from a point about 35 miles northwest of Fredericksburg. Last, far to the south, Major General Nathaniel Banks was to move east from New Orleans to capture Mobile, Alabama, and then, Montgomery.

It was as well that the third part of this plan was the least important, for Banks failed utterly. Yet thanks to the US Navy Mobile was, if not captured, effectively neutralized as a Confederate port. This occurred in the summer of 1864, well after the major offensives in the West and East had begun. On 5 August now-Admiral David Farragut led an 11-ship squadron, spearheaded

striking at the Union army on 19 September in a wooded area near Chickamauga Creek. The main phase of the battle was fought the following day, with Bragg unsuccessfully concentrating his main attack on Rosecrans' well-defended left. In the midst of the fighting, Longstreet noticed that a gap (the result of a misunderstood order) had opened in the Union center. Longstreet immediately led a charge through the gap, collapsing the Union right flank and threatening to roll up the whole line. Only a dogged delaying

action on the Union left, coupled with Bragg's pig-headed refusal to give Longstreet the support he needed, saved Rosecrans' disintegrating army from annihilation. The price of this victory to the Confederates was very high – 18,000 casualties that the South could ill-afford – but the beaten Union army had been driven back into Chattanooga and had to remain there in a humiliating state of siege until relieved by Grant in October.

It took Grant a full month of campaigning to repair the damage done at

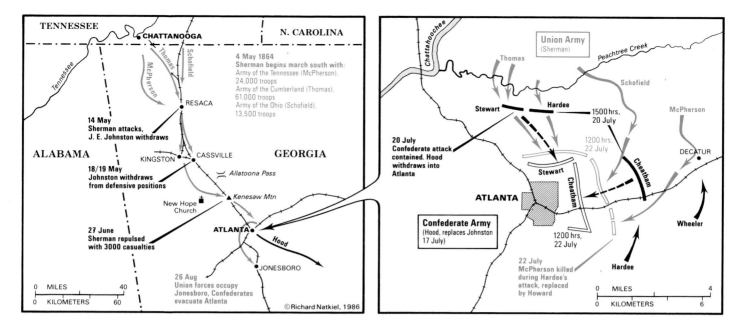

by four ironclad monitors, in an attack on Mobile Bay. The narrow navigation channels leading into the bay, along with strategically placed Confederate minefields and underwater obstructions, forced the attackers to pass close under the guns of Fort Morgan, the most powerful of the forts that guarded the bay's entrance. In addition to suffering a punishing barrage from the forts, Farragut's ships had to endure severe enfilading fire from CSS *Tennessee*, a more heavily armed version of the ironclad *Virginia*, which had taken up station in the channel beyond the forts. Many of the Union ships were roughly handled in this passage, and one, the monitor *Tecumseh*, was sunk by a mine. At last the battered Union flotilla straggled past the forts to confront the formidable, virtually unsinkable *Tennessee*. Neither cannonades nor repeated rammings seemed to harm this armor-plated giant, and it was not until a lucky shot carried away her rudder chain, leaving her dead in the water and unable to bring her guns to bear, that the Union ships were finally able to pound her into surrender. Farragut then returned to the forts and succeeded in capturing them all (Morgan by assault from the land). Now in complete control of the waters of Mobile Bay, Farragut had effectively sealed off the Confederacy's last major Gulf port.

The two big offensives in the West and the East had begun on the same day: 4 May 1864. Sherman, with 100,000 men, had left Chattanooga, slowly making his way towards Atlanta

in the teeth of stiff resistance from Joseph Johnston's 65,000-man Army of Tennessee. The fighting was incessant, several times flaring into major battles. Sherman's losses were staggering, and by July the Union army had advanced only 100 miles. It was not until 9 August (and after Johnston had been relieved, for political reasons, by the less successful General John B Hood) that Sherman reached Atlanta, and it was not until 1 September that he was finally able to force Hood to withdraw to Alabama and fight his way into the city. He would remain there in occupation for two months.

Grant's Advance on Richmond

On the day that Sherman left Chattanooga (4 May 1864) Grant, with Meade's 99,000-man Army of the Potomac, began his long advance southeast towards Richmond. Lee and his 64,000-man Army of Northern Virginia counterattacked immediately. For two days the armies fought a series of savage battles near Chancellorsville in an area known as The Wilderness. By 6 May Grant's forces had suffered 17,000 casualties, and Lee's, 6000; but no decision had been reached, and Grant doggedly resumed his advance. Lee next tried to halt the momentum of the Union offensive by setting up an immense fortified roadblock about ten miles farther southwest at Spotsylvania. Here, and at a flank redoubt at

North Anna Creek, the armies fought another bloody, inconclusive series of battles of attrition between 9 and 18 May. Again Grant disengaged and continued his advance. And again Lee raced south to intercept him, this time at Cold Harbor, where, between 3 and 12 June, the antagonists fought yet a third round of battles as sprawling, sanguinary and indecisive as their predecessors. By now Grant's casualties stood at an awesome 55,000 (to Lee's 32,000), yet still he persisted. For the last time he disengaged and, in a brilliantly executed maneuver, contrived to transfer his whole army across the James River in such secrecy that Lee did not realize he had been outflanked until six days after the operation had begun. By the time Lee caught up with him on the 18th, Grant was already south of Richmond and preparing to lay siege to Petersburg, an important rail junction on one of the capital's major supply routes.

Lee now sought to create a diversion dramatic enough to draw Grant away from Richmond. In early July he sent Major General Jubal A Early's cavalry corps up the Shenandoah Valley to threaten Washington. But Grant refused to be drawn, and Early's alarming attack was eventually beaten off by local forces. Grant then ordered Major General Philip H Sheridan to pursue the overextended Early back down the valley. This Sheridan did, and by the end of the year he had thrice defeated Early and driven him from the Valley, securing it once and for all for the Union.

49

MAP below: *Grant's advance on Richmond.*
Below right: *General Philip Sheridan, one of the most able Union cavalry commanders.*

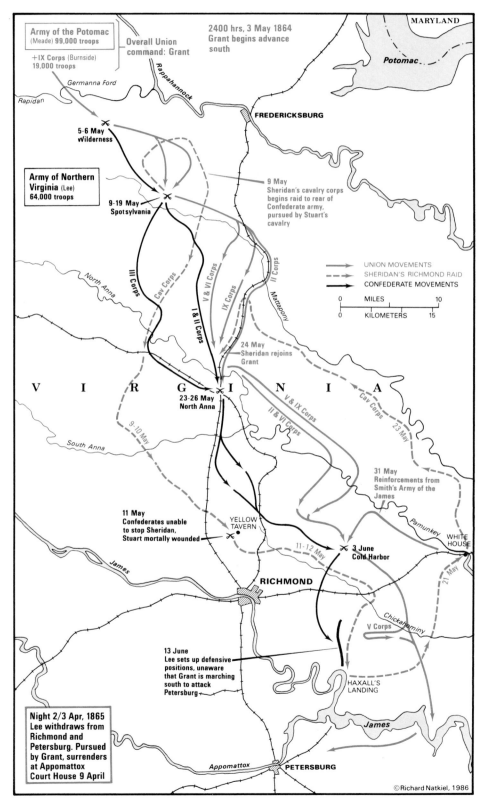

Army of the Potomac
(Meade) 99,000 troops
+IX Corps (Burnside)
19,000 troops

Overall Union
command: Grant

2400 hrs, 3 May 1864
Grant begins advance
south

MARYLAND

Potomac

Rappahannock

Germanna Ford

Rapidan

FREDERICKSBURG

5-6 May
Wilderness

Army of Northern
Virginia (Lee)
64,000 troops

9-19 May
Spotsylvania

9 May
Sheridan's cavalry corps
begins raid to rear of
Confederate army,
pursued by Stuart's
cavalry

North Anna

III Corps

Cav Corps

V & VI Corps

IX Corps

I & II Corps

II Corps

Mattapony

UNION MOVEMENTS
SHERIDAN'S RICHMOND RAID
CONFEDERATE MOVEMENTS

0   MILES   10
0   KILOMETERS   15

24 May
Sheridan rejoins
Grant

V I R G I N I A

23-26 May
North Anna

V & IX Corps

II & VI Corps

Cav Corps

23 May

South Anna

9-10 May

31 May
Reinforcements from
Smith's Army of the
James

Pamunkey

WHITE
HOUSE

11 May
Confederates unable
to stop Sheridan,
Stuart mortally wounded

YELLOW
TAVERN

11-12 May

3 June
Cold Harbor

21 May

James

RICHMOND

Chickahominy

V Corps

13 June
Lee sets up defensive
positions, unaware
that Grant is marching
south to attack
Petersburg

HAXALL'S
LANDING

James

Night 2/3 Apr, 1865
Lee withdraws from
Richmond and
Petersburg. Pursued
by Grant, surrenders
at Appomattox
Court House 9 April

Appomattox   PETERSBURG

©Richard Natkiel, 1986

Meantime, Grant's forces had settled in for a long siege of Petersburg. The Confederates had set up an arc of formidable earthwork fortifications before the town, and major Union efforts to breach these defenses in June and July (the second involving a spectacular – though ultimately unsuccessful – use of mines) had been bloodily repulsed. For the remainder of the year the two armies remained stalemated on the Petersburg front.

Victory for the Union

In Atlanta, however, Sherman was now preparing to launch the final phase of his great offensive from the West. After sending 30,000 men north to reinforce Major General George H Thomas in Nashville, Tennessee (Sherman rightly guessed that Hood might make an attempt on that key Union base), Sherman burned Atlanta and, on 15 November, set out with 62,000 men on his famous march through Georgia to the sea. Virtually unopposed, he left a trail of deliberate and highly demoralizing devastation in his wake. By 21 December he had reached the coast, had captured Savannah and was ready to wheel north and join forces with Grant. Simultaneously, Thomas had repelled Hood's anticipated attack on Nashville and by 16 December, while Sherman was investing Savannah, had counterattacked

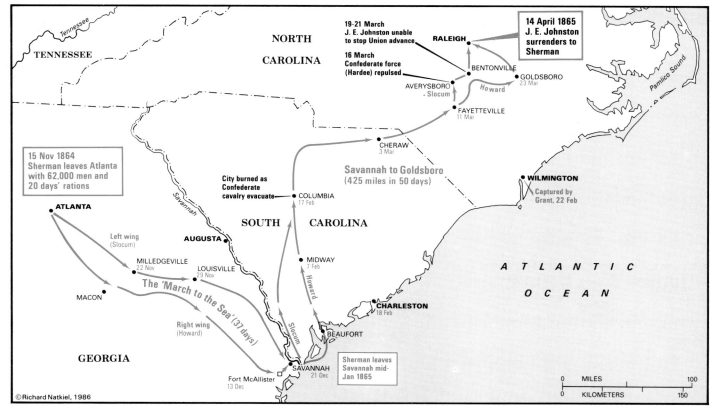

19-21 March
J. E. Johnston unable
to stop Union advance

16 March
Confederate force
(Hardee) repulsed

**NORTH
CAROLINA**

**14 April 1865
J. E. Johnston
surrenders to
Sherman**

RALEIGH

BENTONVILLE

GOLDSBORO
23 Mar

AVERYSBORO
. Slocum

Howard

FAYETTEVILLE
11 Mar

TENNESSEE

CHERAW
3 Mar

Savannah to Goldsboro
(425 miles in 50 days)

**15 Nov 1864
Sherman leaves Atlanta
with 62,000 men and
20 days' rations**

City burned as
Confederate
cavalry evacuate

COLUMBIA
17 Feb

WILMINGTON
Captured by
Grant, 22 Feb

ATLANTA

Savannah

**SOUTH
CAROLINA**

Left wing
(Slocum)

AUGUSTA

MILLEDGEVILLE
22 Nov

LOUISVILLE
29 Nov

MIDWAY
7 Feb

Howard

A T L A N T I C

O C E A N

MACON

The 'March to the Sea' (37 days)

Right wing
(Howard)

Slocum

CHARLESTON
18 Feb

BEAUFORT

GEORGIA

SAVANNAH
21 Dec

Fort McAllister
13 Dec

Sherman leaves
Savannah mid-
Jan 1865

Pamlico Sound

© Richard Natkiel, 1986

MILES 0 — 100
KILOMETERS 0 — 150

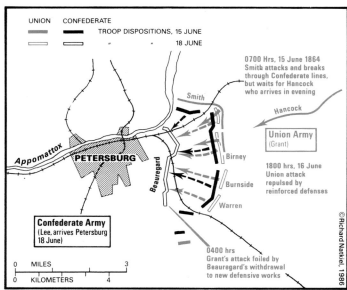

UNION   CONFEDERATE

TROOP DISPOSITIONS, 15 JUNE

" " 18 JUNE

0700 Hrs, 15 June 1864
Smith attacks and breaks
through Confederate lines,
but waits for Hancock
who arrives in evening

Smith

Hancock

Union Army
(Grant)

1800 hrs, 16 June
Union attack
repulsed by
reinforced defenses

Appomattox

PETERSBURG

Birney

Beauregard

Burnside

Warren

Confederate Army
(Lee, arrives Petersburg
18 June)

0400 hrs
Grant's attack foiled by
Beauregard's withdrawal
to new defensive works

MILES 0 — 3
KILOMETERS 0 — 4

© Richard Natkiel, 1986

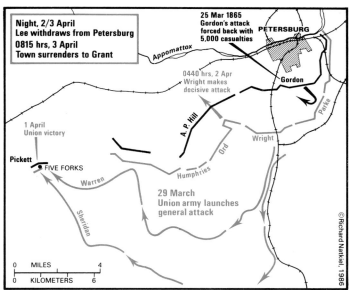

**Night, 2/3 April
Lee withdraws from Petersburg
0815 hrs, 3 April
Town surrenders to Grant**

25 Mar 1865
Gordon's attack
forced back with
5,000 casualties

PETERSBURG

Appomattox

Gordon

0440 hrs, 2 Apr
Wright makes
decisive attack

A. P. Hill

Parke

1 April
Union victory

Pickett

Ord

Wright

FIVE FORKS

Warren

Humphries

29 March
Union army launches
general attack

Sheridan

MILES 0 — 4
KILOMETERS 0 — 6

© Richard Natkiel, 1986

so successfully as to destroy Hood's army.

Lee's army at Petersburg was now the only major military organization left to the Confederacy, and by early 1865 its position there was becoming untenable: Sheridan had completed his conquest of the Shenandoah Valley and was already beginning to rejoin Grant, while Sherman was rapidly approaching from the south. On 25 March Lee made a final, unsuccessful attempt to break out of the trap by trying to open a corridor through Grant's line at Fort Stedman. Four days later Grant sent Sheridan off to the southwest to try to turn Lee's right flank, and on 1 April, at the Battle of Five Forks, Sheridan succeeded in doing so. The next day Grant mounted a frontal assault on the disintegrating Confederate line, and within another twenty-four hours he was at long last in Richmond. On 9 April Lee formally surrendered at Appomattox Court House, Virginia.

MAP top: *Sherman's march through Georgia.*
MAP above left: *The siege of Petersburg.*
MAP above: *Battle of Five Forks.*

With Lee's capitulation Southern resistance collapsed. The remaining Southern military forces were still in the process of laying down their arms when, on 14 April, at Ford's Theater in Washington, Abraham Lincoln was assassinated.

THE INDIAN WARS

Indian Wars Before 1860

Within twelve hours of first setting foot on the shores of the New World the Jamestown settlers in Virginia were skirmishing with the local Algonquin Indians. Within sixteen years of their arrival at Plymouth the New England colonists were engaged in a war with the Pequots. These were but the opening rounds of a bitter territorial struggle between Europeans and Indians that would persist for the next two and a half centuries, until the newcomers at last succeeded in swallowing up all the valuable land between the two oceans.

Because the English came to the New World primarily as settlers, and the French primarily as traders, the French were able to enlist many

Zachary Taylor leads his men, aided by bloodhounds, in an attack on the Seminoles during the bitter seven-year-long war in Florida.
LIBRARY OF CONGRESS

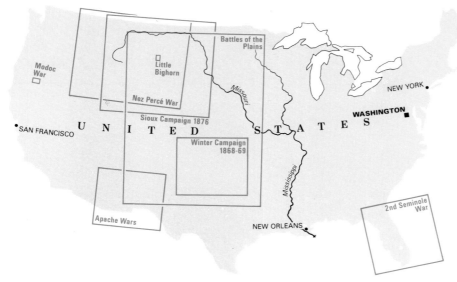

Above: *Colonel Zachary Taylor leads his men against the Seminole Indians.*
MAP left: *Guide to the overall position of the maps in this chapter.*

Indians as allies in the long course of the French and Indian Wars (1689–1763); but since the Indians' essential interests had little to do with European colonial rivalries, their armed resistance to the spread of English settlement continued unabated after the final French defeat. This resistance, though incessant, was largely formless, in that it occurred sporadically at various points along the perimeter of the settled areas and involved many different tribes. It did, however, often rise to considerable levels of menace and violence, especially during the

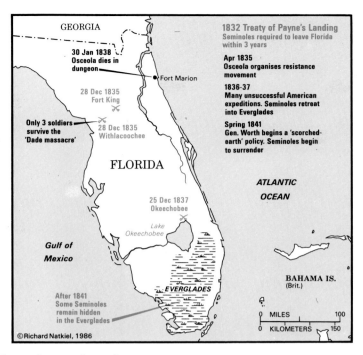

MAP above: *Battles and campaigns of the Second Seminole War*.

Revolution and the War of 1812, and by the end of the 1820s finding a solution to the 'Indian Problem' stood high on the young United States' list of priorities.

The draconian solution finally adopted (under the Indian Removal Act of 1830) was simply to round up Indians living in the East and deport them to reservations that had been set up west of the Mississippi: Indians who resisted would be moved forcibly by the US Army. Typical of the violent reaction this policy produced was the so-called Second Seminole War (1835–42), which began on 28 December 1835 when a 108-man Seminole war party set upon a marching column of 112 Army regulars in central Florida and killed all but three. A few days later the Seminoles, now commanded by their great war leader Osceola, defeated a force of 300 regulars and 500 Florida militiamen on the banks of the Withlacoochee River. The Seminoles thereafter fought a hit-and-run campaign, avoiding pitched battle so successfully that for two years they frustrated utterly a series of punitive expeditions sent against them by both the Federal and Florida

governments. Even after Colonel Zachary Taylor caught up with and defeated them at the Battle of Lake Okeechobee (25 December 1837) the Seminoles fought on, and only after a protracted and massive scorched earth campaign had brought them to the edge of starvation did they finally capitulate in 1842. In all, the effort to remove just this one relatively minor tribe had obliged the United States to commit most of its small Army, had caused the death of nearly 2000 soldiers and had cost an estimated $40 million.

To the extent that it succeeded, the Removal Policy did not so much solve the Indian problem as defer it. When, about mid-century, significant numbers of white settlers and gold-seekers began crossing the Mississippi to challenge the Indians for control of territory in the West, the Indian Wars entered a new and more ferocious phase. In the decade before the Civil War the frequency, intensity and geographic distribution of violent confrontations in the West increased apace. Between 1851 and 1858 the Army was obliged to conduct no less than three campaigns in the far Northwest to subdue the fractious Coeur d'Alenes and Yakimas. And this was only a pale foreshadowing of the trouble it would soon be having with the Cheyennes and Siouan tribes of the Great Plains and with the Kiowas, Comanches, Apaches and Navajos in the Southwest.

Indian Wars of the Southwest

So fluid and wide-ranging were the Indian Wars in the West that it is easier to describe them discretely, in terms of geographic regions and specific tribal groupings, than as a single unfolding chronology of events. Thus in the Southwest the principal militant Indian groups were 1) the Kiowas and Comanches, who operated in Oklahoma and Texas, 2) the Navajos of Arizona and New Mexico, 3) the Apaches, also of Arizona and New Mexico and 4) the Arapahos and Southern Cheyenne, who sometimes drifted as far south as Oklahoma and Northern Texas.

Settlers and local militias, as well as regular and (during the Civil War) Volunteer Army troops, had all been involved in intermittent skirmishing with Kiowas and Comanches since the 1850s. When these warlike tribes at last agreed, under the terms of the Medicine Lodge Treaty of 1867, to settle on a large reservation in Oklahoma, it was widely hoped that a measure of peace might be restored to the Texas-Oklahoma region. But though the Indians were content to make their homes on the reservation, certain bands, such as that led by the Kiowa chief Satanta, continued to make raids outside its borders. In June 1874 Satanta and other Kiowas, Arapahos and Southern Cheyenne joined the Kwahadi Comanche chief Quanah Parker in a large-scale attack on a white buffalo-hunters' settlement, Adobe Walls, in the Texas Panhandle. This (unsuccessful) attack touched off a state of general warfare, the so-called Red River War, that reached as far north as central Kansas, eventually involved some 1200 Indian braves and 3000 Federal troops and did not end until February 1875, when the Indians were surrounded in Palo Duro Canyon in Texas, starved into surrender and forcibly returned to their reservation.

After this defeat, the Kiowas and Comanches gave little more trouble.

Ten years earlier the Navajos had been subdued in somewhat similar fashion. In July 1863 they had rejected an ultimatum delivered by James Carleton (a general in the militia-like Volunteer Army that replaced regular troops in the West during the Civil War) to move onto a reservation in northern Arizona/New Mexico. Carleton then sent the famous Indian fighter Colonel Christopher 'Kit' Carson and a force of 736 to bring the Navajos to heel. In a shrewdly conducted campaign Carson gradually forced the Indians back to their stronghold at Canyon de Chelly in Arizona and besieged them. By the end of 1864 he had forced some 8000 of them to surrender, and by 1866 all the remaining Navajos had been settled on the reservation, where they remained peacefully.

Even before this campaign Carleton and Carson had been involved in the beginning of what would be one of the longest and bitterest struggles on the Frontier: the Apache Wars, which lasted from 1861 to 1886. Prior to 1860 the ferocious Apaches had done most of their raiding in Mexico, but in 1861 the Chiricahua Apache chief Cochise, abetted by his father-in-law, chief Mangas Coloradas of the Warm Springs Apaches, initiated a series of raids north of the border that spread terror in Arizona and New Mexico. After the death of Mangas in 1863 (he was murdered while in captivity) the level of the guerrilla attacks slackened somewhat, but it flared again in 1871 after some Arizona vigilantes made an unprovoked attack on a peaceful Aravaipa Apache settlement near Camp Grant. It took the US Army's General George Crook two years of constant diplomacy and hard fighting (which culminated in a major Indian defeat at Turret Peak in March 1873) to restore temporary peace to the Arizona Territory. This peace collapsed four years later as the result of premature government efforts to move the truculent Indians onto

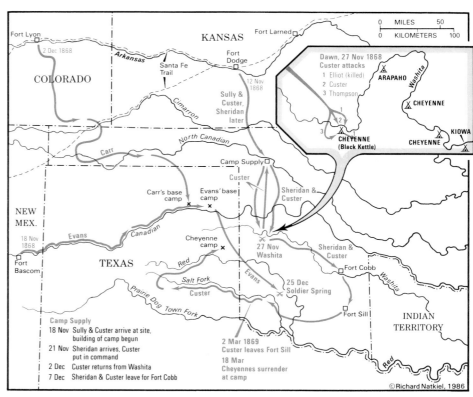

MAP below left: *Battles of the Apache Wars.*

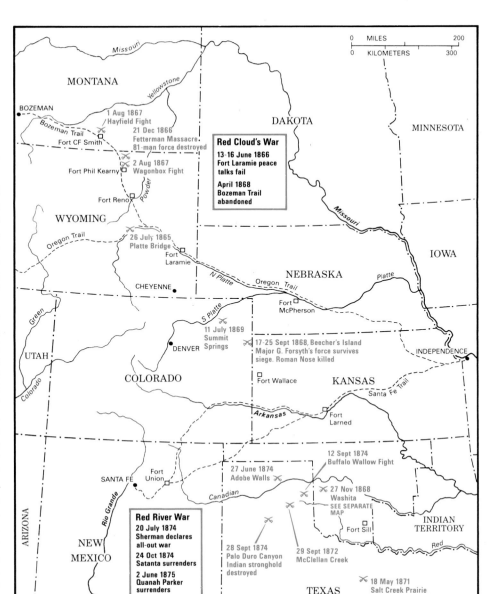

reservations, from which chief Victorio soon led a defiant mass exodus of Chiricahua and Warm Springs Apaches in 1877. The fighting which ensued briefly subsided after Victorio's death in battle in October 1880, but it was soon revived by his successor, the relentless Chiricahua war leader Geronimo, who was not finally induced to surrender until September 1886, thus at last bringing to an end a quarter century of often atrocious fighting.

The Cheyenne were essentially peoples of the Great Plains, but it was in the Southwest, in Oklahoma, that one of their bands was involved in one of the most famous and portentous incidents of the Indian Wars. In 1868 General Philip Sheridan, commander of the Department of the Missouri (which included most of the US between the Mississippi River and the Nevada Territory) decided on a policy of lightning surprise offensives to try to subdue the troublesome Plains Indians. Unfortunately, he chose as his first target a body of Southern Cheyenne led by the generally pacific and conciliatory chief Black Kettle. Sheridan's most promising young protégé, Colonel George Armstrong Custer, without warning attacked Black Kettle's camp on the banks of the Washita River on the morning of 27 November 1868. Whether the mêlée that followed is better called a battle or a massacre is moot: 20 troopers and 103 Indians (including Black Kettle and many women and children) were killed. Custer then skillfully extricated himself from the Washita Valley before Indians from neighboring camps could retaliate. This raid made Custer's reputation in the Indian-fighting Army and, in a very different sense, made it as well among the Cheyenne and all the other Plains tribes.

MAP left: *The winter campaign of 1868–69 and the Battle of the Washita.*
MAP above right: *Battles of the Plains.*

Indian Wars of the Great Plains

The Indians of the Great Plains – notably the congeries of Siouan tribes and the Cheyenne – were, if only because of their great numbers, potentially the most formidable opponents of the westward-moving white settlers, miners and hunters. They proved to be so in fact.

The first big eruption of violence on the Plains occurred in Minnesota during the Civil War. In August 1862 the normally peaceful Santee Sioux, annoyed both by the economic pressure created by settlers thronging into the state and by the neglect and dishonesty of the Federal Indian Agents, rose up in bloody revolt, attacking settlements and, for a time, besieging Fort Ridgely. It took the Volunteer Army and local militias over a month to put down this uprising, by which time some 700 whites had been killed. Many Santee fled to the Dakota Territory. Of those who surrendered or were captured, 38 were condemned to death.

Of the many incidents illustrative of the hatred that burgeoned between whites and the Plains Indians during the Civil War, one of the best remembered is the infamous Sand Creek Massacre, in which, on 29 November 1864, Colonel John Chivington led 700 Colorado Volunteers in a surprise attack on Chief Black Kettle's encampment of Southern Cheyenne on Sand Creek, a tributary of the Arkansas

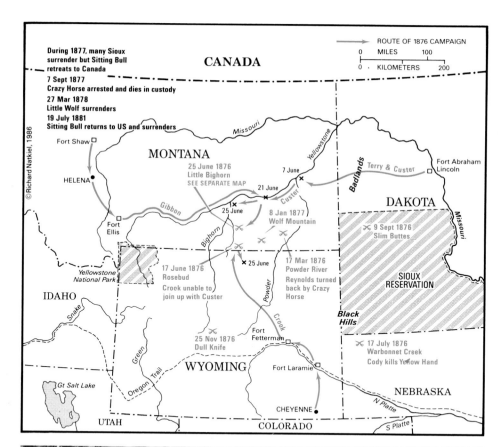

MAP left: *The Sioux campaign of 1876.*

During 1877, many Sioux surrender but Sitting Bull retreats to Canada
7 Sept 1877
Crazy Horse arrested and dies in custody
27 Mar 1878
Little Wolf surrenders
19 July 1881
Sitting Bull returns to US and surrenders

ROUTE OF 1876 CAMPAIGN
0 MILES 100
0 KILOMETERS 200

CANADA

MONTANA

Missouri

Fort Shaw
HELENA

Yellowstone
7 June
Badlands
Terry & Custer
Fort Abraham Lincoln

25 June 1876
Little Bighorn
SEE SEPARATE MAP
21 June
Custer

Gibbon
25 June
8 Jan 1877
Wolf Mountain

DAKOTA

Fort Ellis

Bighorn

9 Sept 1876
Slim Buttes

Missouri

Yellowstone
National Park

17 June 1876
Rosebud
Crook unable to join up with Custer

25 June

Powder

17 Mar 1876
Powder River
Reynolds turned back by Crazy Horse

SIOUX
RESERVATION

IDAHO

Snake

Crook

Black
Hills

Fort Fetterman

25 Nov 1876
Dull Knife

17 July 1876
Warbonnet Creek
Cody kills Yellow Hand

Green

Gt Salt Lake

WYOMING

Oregon Trail

Fort Laramie

NEBRASKA

N Platte

UTAH

CHEYENNE

COLORADO

S Platte

Above: *The Hunkpapa Sioux chief Sitting Bull seen here in 1885.*
Left: *Major General Custer (left) during the Civil War. In the smaller postwar army Custer and many other officers had to accept reduced rank.*
MAP right: *The Battle of the Little Bighorn.*

River. Ignoring the Indians' truce flags, Chivington's raiders slaughtered over 200 Indians. Chivington was subsequently condemned for this brutality by a Congressional Investigating Committee, but in essence it would be repeated four years later (again against Black Kettle's Cheyenne) by the regular Army's Colonel George Custer at the Battle of the Washita (qv).

Hardly had the regular Army returned to the West after the end of the Civil War before it was engaged in a major campaign in the Wyoming and southern Montana Territories against Sioux, Cheyenne and Arapaho tribesmen who opposed the building of a chain of new Army forts along the Bozeman Trail. This so-called Red Cloud's War, which lasted the better part of a year, began with the ambush and annihilation of an 81-man Army detachment led by Captain William Fetterman (the Fetterman Massacre,

21 December 1866), included a siege of the Army's Fort Phil Kearny and several famous small battles (such as the Hayfield Fight and the Wagon-box Fight, both in August 1867) and only subsided in the autumn of 1867 after the signing of the Medicine Lodge Treaty.

In 1868 the Army's campaigns against the Plains Indians shifted south. Custer's Battle of the Washita in Oklahoma has been described else-where. That same autumn Major George Forsyth was fighting the Cheyenne in Colorado in a campaign that culminated in the desperate Battle of Beecher's Island (17–25 September), in which the Cheyenne war leader Roman Nose was killed.

The Army was temporarily diverted from the Plains wars in the early 1870s by the Modoc War in California (qv), but by the middle of the decade a major new confrontation developed in the Dakota Territory as the result of a white gold rush into the Black Hills, an area sacred to many Sioux and Cheyenne and reserved to them by treaty. By 1876 some 50,000 Indians were in rebellion, and the Army's General George Crook had been sent to put it down. Crook's strategy was to converge three columns on the Indians' main camp in the Valley of the Little Bighorn River in the Montana Territory: He would approach from the south, Colonel John Gibbon from the west and General Alfred Terry from the east. But the great Sioux war leader Crazy Horse succeeded in halting Crook's advance at the Battle of the Rosebud on 17 June. Terry and Gibbon joined forces on 21 June and, afraid that the Indians might elude them before Crook's arrival, ordered Colonel George Custer's 7th Cavalry Regiment to go on ahead and try to bottle up the Indians in the Valley. Unknown to them was the enormous size of the Indian encampment, which included over 3000 braves under the overall command of the Sioux leader Sitting Bull. Upon discovering the Indians, Custer not only rashly decided to attack but weakened his force by dividing it into three groups. In the ensuing Battle of the Little Bighorn, fought on 25 June 1876, Custer's group (five troops) was surrounded and annihilated, and the other two were forced to retreat with heavy losses. It took the Army another year and a half of vigorous campaigning to restore peace to the Western Plains.

This peace was broken for the last time in 1890. The Army became alarmed by what it considered the militant fervor induced in the tribes by a new religious movement, the Ghost Dance cult, and sent an expedition into the Dakotas to restore order. This inept effort produced, on 29 December, the last battle of the Indian Wars, that of Wounded Knee, in which 150 Sioux were killed in something very like the massacres at Sand Creek and the Washita – perhaps a fitting end to a sorry chapter of American history.

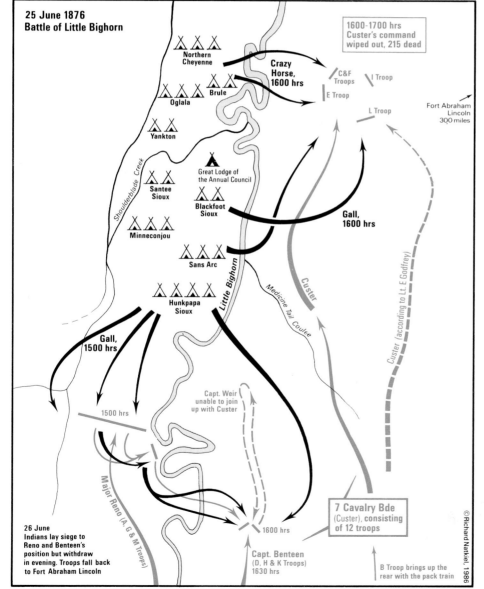

25 June 1876
Battle of Little Bighorn

Northern Cheyenne

Crazy Horse, 1600 hrs

1600-1700 hrs Custer's command wiped out, 215 dead

C&F Troops   I Troop

E Troop

L Troop

Fort Abraham Lincoln 300 miles

Brule

Oglala

Yankton

Shoulderblade Creek

Great Lodge of the Annual Council

Santee Sioux

Blackfoot Sioux

Gall, 1600 hrs

Minneconjou

Sans Arc

Little Bighorn

Medicine Tail Coulee

Custer

Custer (according to Lt. E Godfrey)

Hunkpapa Sioux

Gall, 1500 hrs

Capt. Weir unable to join up with Custer

1500 hrs

Major Reno (A, G & M Troops)

1600 hrs

7 Cavalry Bde (Custer), consisting of 12 troops

26 June
Indians lay siege to Reno and Benteen's position but withdraw in evening. Troops fall back to Fort Abraham Lincoln

Capt. Benteen (D, H & K Troops) 1630 hrs

B Troop brings up the rear with the pack train

© Richard Natkiel, 1986

Indian Wars of the Northwest

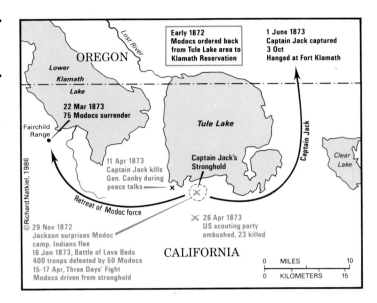

The Northwest – northern California, Oregon, Washington and Idaho – was no more exempt from the scourge of warfare between whites and Indians in the second half of the 19th century than any other trans-Mississippi region. In the Washington and Oregon Territories friction between local Indians and the rising tide of white gold-seekers and settlers had produced a pattern of increasingly violent confrontation since the early 1850s. In Washington it reached such proportions that in 1856 the US Army was forced to intercede in a mercifully bloodless campaign (the Yakima War) to restore order to the Columbia Basin. In the same year the Army had also to intervene in fierce fighting between settlers and Rogue River Indians in the Siskiyou Trail area of southern Oregon. Here, however, pacification was not achieved until the Rogues were broken in the Battle of Big Meadow, fought on 27 May. Then, within two years of the end of the Rogue River War, violence again reached such levels in Washington that the Army had to return to fight what is now called the Coeur d'Alene (or Second Yakima) War, which lasted between May and September 1858 and involved three good-sized battles, the Army's ultimate victory being won at the Battle of Spokane Plain on 5 September.

During the Civil War only one major (Volunteer) Army campaign was fought in the Northwest area, against the Shoshones of Idaho. Both the causes and result of this war followed the now-familiar pattern, though the Army victory that ended the fighting (the Battle of Bear River, 27 January 1863) was particularly bloody, perhaps as many as 400 Indians being killed.

The first major post-Civil War campaign that the regular Army fought in the Northwest was one of the oddest in all the history of the Indian Wars. Under pressure from land-hungry settlers, the Federal government had moved the small Modoc tribe of northern California onto the Klamath Reservation in Oregon. The Modocs were unhappy there, and in 1870 a small band of them, under the leadership of an Indian known to the whites as Captain Jack, left the reservation and eventually, to escape capture, headed into the 'Land of the Burnt Out Fires,' a desolate area of lava beds south of Tule Lake in California. Although Jack's effectives only numbered between 50 and 75, they were able to take expert advantage of the natural defenses this bizarre landscape provided and repelled all attempts made by civilian posses to extirpate them. When, in January 1873, the US Army attempted to do what the posses had not, they too were bloodily repulsed. Colonel Frank Wheaton, leader of this failed expedition, subsequently estimated that it would require 1000 men, supported by mortars and howitzers, to storm the positions held by Jack's 50-odd Modocs. In April the Army tried diplomacy, but during the course of the parlays a fight broke out, during which Jack fatally shot the chief Army negotiator, General E R S Canby. Now the Army had no choice: the 1000 men and artillery were

assembled and a full-scale offensive was mounted. It raged through the lava beds for a full month, from mid-April to mid-May, and even after Modoc power had obviously been broken (at the Battle of Dry Lake, 14 May), nearly another month passed before Jack finally surrendered. He and three other Modocs were hanged at Fort Klamath on 3 October 1873.

The Army's final campaign in the Northwest, the Nez Percé War, was, in its very different way, even more extraordinary than the Modoc War. Since 1863 the Government had been trying to move the Nez Percés, who lived on Idaho's Salmon River and in the Wallowa Valley of Oregon, to a reservation in northwest Idaho. The Indians adamantly refused, and in 1876 the Army finally moved into the Wallowa Valley to remove them by force. After some fighting, the Nez Percé chief Joseph withdrew his people eastward to join with the Salmon River Nez Percés. A US Army force under the command of General O O Howard defeated the combined Nez

MAP top: *The Modoc War of 1873.*
MAP top right: *The pursuit of the Nez Percés.*
Right: *The Nez Percé leader Chief Joseph and one of his adversaries General O O Howard.*

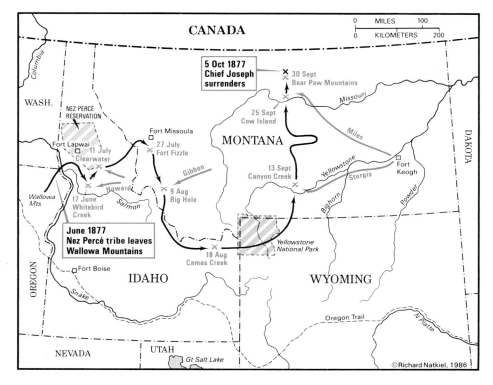

Percé tribes at the Battle of the Clearwater on 11 July but failed to halt their flight eastward along Lewis and Clark's old Lolo Trail. Coming from the east, another US infantry column under Colonel John Gibbon again failed to deflect the Indians at the Battle of Big Hole, fought in western Montana on 9 August. And again, on 13 September at the Battle of Canyon Creek, still another Army force commanded by Colonel Samuel Sturgis failed to deter the Nez Percés as they made their way into the Yellowstone country of central Montana. Finally, at the end of September, a fourth force under Colonel Nelson Miles intercepted them at Bear Paw Mountain, just short of the Canadian border, and after a 5-day siege forced their surrender. During their three-month 1700-mile retreat the 800 Nez Percés had lost 120 tribesmen and had killed about 180 whites. Although frustrated in their purpose, they had won the admiration of the entire country.

THE SPANISH-AMERICAN WAR

The Philippines Campaign

Throughout the 19th century a succession of Latin American nations had won their independence from Spanish imperial rule, and by 1895 the only New World colonies left to Spain were Cuba and Puerto Rico. In that year the Cubans, as they had several times before, rebelled in an effort to throw off the Spanish yoke. The measures taken by the Spanish to put down the insurrection, harsh enough in fact, were wildly sensationalized in the American 'yellow' press and in the propaganda issued by the Cuban lobby. Popular sentiment for intervention in Cuba was already high in the US when, on 15 February 1898, the battleship USS *Maine* blew up in Havana harbor, an incident that most Americans immediately attributed (though without compelling evidence) to Spanish sabotage. By 20 April an enraged Congress had authorized the president to use military force to secure Cuban independence and shortly thereafter Spain declared war. But since the small US Army was not immediately capable of fighting a foreign war, and a mobilization plan had yet to be drawn up, the initial burden of offensive operations perforce fell to the Navy – in the form of a largely ineffective blockade of Cuba and an unexpectedly effective attack on the Spanish-held Philippines.

In the early morning hours of 1 May 1896 Commodore George Dewey of the Navy's Asiatic Squadron led the cruisers *Olympia*, *Baltimore*, *Boston* and *Raleigh*, accompanied by two gunboats and a revenue cutter, into Manila Bay. Anchored at the southern end of the bay, off Cavite, was Admiral Patricio Montojo's Spanish squadron, consisting of the modern cruiser *Reina Cristina* and ten other elderly light cruisers and gunboats. Braving fire from both the Spanish shore and naval batteries Dewey approached to the limit of his guns' range and opened fire at 0548. The ensuing gunnery duel was interrupted at 0735 when, acting on mistaken information about a shortage of ammunition, Dewey withdrew to count casualties. There were none, so the Americans had a leisurely breakfast and then returned to the fray at 1116. By this time the dense smoke of battle had cleared sufficiently to reveal that the Spanish line was in a bad way, with the *Cristina* and the wooden-hulled *Castilla* sunk and most of the other ships heavily damaged. In a little over an hour all the remaining ships had been put out of action. The only US casualties had been eight men injured when *Baltimore* was hit by a shell fired from the Cavite arsenal. It was nearly three months before the Army could take advantage of this decisive naval victory. In late July General Wesley Merritt's 15,000-man VIII Corps landed in the Manila area, to find the Spanish garrison on Luzon eager to negotiate surrender terms. They were duly accepted on 13 August, two days after Spain and the US signed an armistice to end the fighting in all theaters.

Under the terms of the final peace treaty, ratified by Congress on 6 February 1899, Spain ceded the Philip-

CHINA
Formosa
© Richard Natkiel, 1986
HONG KONG
PACIFIC OCEAN
Hainan I.
25 April 1898
Dewey sails
30 April
Insurgent
leaders
put ashore
Luzon
1 May
MANILA
PHILIPPINE
ISLANDS
South China Sea
MINDORO
SAMAR
PANAY
LEYTE
CEBU
PALAWAN
NEGROS
Mindanao
NAUTICAL
MILES
0   200
Borneo

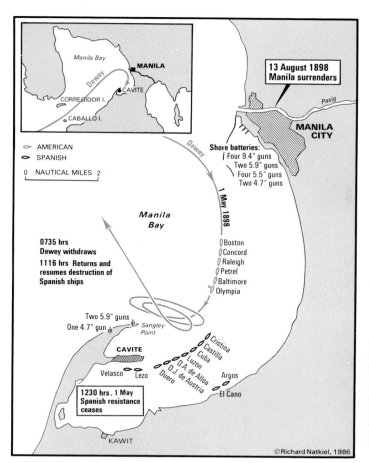

MAP above: *Battle of Manila Bay.*
MAP below left: *Dewey's approach to the Philippines before the battle.*
Above right: *Commodore Dewey (seated) aboard his flagship.*
MAP below right: *Naval preliminaries of the Cuban campaign.*

pines to the US, but while the Americans were still debating what to do with this unlooked-for acquisition, Emilio Aguinaldo's militant Filipino nationalists, impatient with the US military occupation, resorted to armed insurrection. By mid-summer some 35,000 US troops and 40,000 Filipino insurgents were embroiled in a comparatively formless, but nonetheless savage, guerrilla war. Though the US re-established control over Luzon in the autumn of 1899, fighting in other parts of the archipelago did not finally end until 1902, by which time 4000 Americans and perhaps 200,000 Filipinos had been killed. The pointlessness of all this was underscored by the fact that within little more than a decade the US would grant the Philippines virtual domestic autonomy, and, after thirty more years of harmonious relations, complete sovereignty.

The Cuban Campaign

When war broke out between America and Spain in late April 1898 the US Army was subjected to intense public and political pressure to invade Cuba immediately. But the regular Army numbered only 26,000, mobilization of volunteers was just beginning, training facilities and equipment were lacking and the Army's high command had no strategic plan suitable for the occasion. That the Army should have been able to send an expedition to Cuba as early as mid-June is remarkable; that this expedition was relatively small and ill-coordinated is less so.

The first American plan was to land troops somewhere on the northwest shore of Cuba, in the vicinity of Havana, as soon as possible after the US Navy had neutralized Spanish

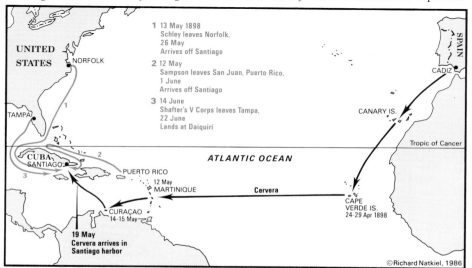

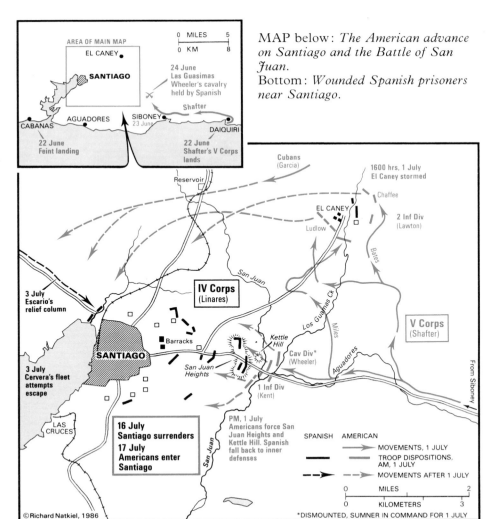

MAP below: *The American advance on Santiago and the Battle of San Juan.*
Bottom: *Wounded Spanish prisoners near Santiago.*

Admiral Pascual Cervera's Caribbean squadron. But Cervera avoided battle and by late May had brought his ships under the protection of the batteries dominating Santiago Bay, at the southeastern end of the island. Thus a new plan was hatched, whereby the Army would first send an expedition against the forts around Santiago Bay and expose Cervera to naval attack. Accordingly, beginning on 22 June 17,000 troops of General William R Shafter's V Corps landed at Siboney and Daiquiri, east of Santiago.

Although the landings were unopposed, Spanish General Arsenio Linares attempted to block the American advance on Santiago at Las Guasimas on 24 June. When he was worsted in this small battle he withdrew to his main defensive position on the San Juan heights, which guarded Santiago from the east. Shafter's plan for the attack on these heights, scheduled for 1 July, included a frontal assault by General Joseph Wheeler's dismounted cavalry and a

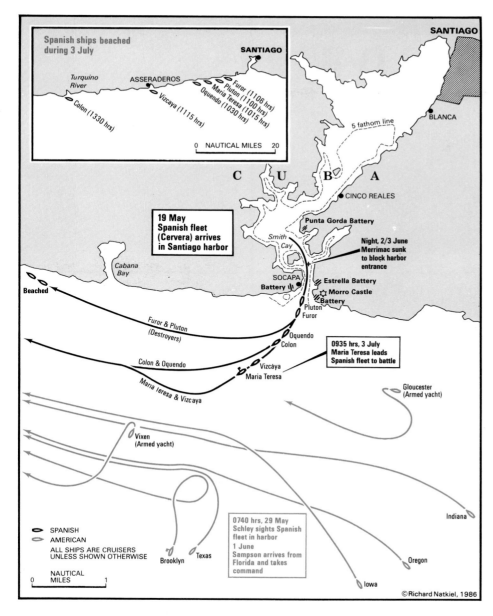

Spanish ships beached during 3 July

Turquino River — ASSERADEROS — *Vizcaya (1115 hrs)* — *Colon (1330 hrs)* — *Maria Teresa (1100 hrs)* — *Pluton (1106 hrs)* — *Oquendo (1030 hrs)* — SANTIAGO

0 NAUTICAL MILES 20

SANTIAGO

C U B A

5 fathom line

BLANCA

CINCO REALES

Punta Gorda Battery

19 May Spanish fleet (Cervera) arrives in Santiago harbor

Smith Cay

Night, 2/3 June Merrimac sunk to block harbor entrance

Cabana Bay

Beached

SOCAPA Battery

Estrella Battery
Morro Castle Battery

Pluton Furor

Furor & Pluton (Destroyers)

Oquendo
Colon

0935 hrs, 3 July Maria Teresa leads Spanish fleet to battle

Colon & Oquendo

Vizcaya
Maria Teresa

Maria Teresa & Vizcaya

Gloucester (Armed yacht)

Vixen (Armed yacht)

Indiana

SPANISH
AMERICAN
ALL SHIPS ARE CRUISERS UNLESS SHOWN OTHERWISE

**0740 hrs, 29 May Schley sights Spanish fleet in harbor
1 June Sampson arrives from Florida and takes command**

Oregon

NAUTICAL MILES
0   1

Brooklyn   Texas

Iowa

© Richard Natkiel, 1986

MAP left: *The crushing American victory in the naval Battle of Santiago.* Bottom: *Colonel Theodore Roosevelt in Cuba in 1898. The reputation Roosevelt gained in the fighting later helped him attain the presidency.*

the 13-inch guns of USS *Oregon* she too was forced ashore. In this decisive action, which lasted three hours and forty minutes, only one US sailor was killed.

The 23,000 Spanish troops in the Santiago area now felt themselves to be in a hopeless position, and on 16 July they surrendered. On 25 July General Nelson Miles, with 3000 men, invaded Puerto Rico and encountered so little resistance that by 16 August he had secured the whole island. By this time Spain had already agreed to an armistice and preparations for peace negotiations were under way.

In all, the Cuban campaign had cost the US only 379 battle deaths, but the real cost was very much higher, since over 5000 troops succumbed to tropical diseases. In return for this, Cuban independence had been won and the US had inadvertently become an imperial power.

simultaneous assault on the left by General Jacob Kent's infantry division. In a coordinated operation General Henry Lawton's infantry was to seize the town of El Caney, two miles to the north, and then return to support Wheeler's right wing. In the event, Lawton encountered stiffer resistance at El Caney than expected and returned too late to participate in the main battle. Neither Wheeler nor Kent received adequate artillery support and for a time were pinned down by withering rifle fire from the Spanish trenches atop the hills. But eventually Black Troopers of the 10th and 19th Cavalry, assisted by Colonel Theodore Roosevelt's volunteer Rough Riders, succeeded in storming Kettle Hill, and a little later, after a Gatling gun bat-tery had driven some of the defenders from their trenches, Kent's infantry took the main Spanish position on San Juan Hill.

While the Army and the War Department were debating what to do next, Cervera, on 3 July, attempted to extricate his four cruisers and two destroyers from Santiago Bay. Even before they made their offing they were intercepted by an American squadron of five cruisers (four of them of near battleship strength) and two armed yachts under the temporary command of Commodore Winfield Scott Schley. In short order five of the Spanish ships had been disabled and driven aground. The sixth, the fast cruiser *Cristobal Colon*, almost escap-ed, but when bracketed by fire from

63

WORLD WAR I

America Enters the War

When World War I erupted in Europe in the summer of 1914 the US, though sympathetic to the Allied cause, was determined not to be drawn into the conflict. Yet in the next three years American hostility to the Central Powers, and particularly to Germany, grew to such a level that on 6 April 1917 the US declared war. Doubtless many factors – Allied propaganda, the pressure of pro-Ally economic interests, the arrogant clumsiness of German diplomacy towards the US – played a part in this decision, but of overwhelming importance was the German military policy of unrestricted submarine warfare against all neutral shipping engaged in commerce with the Allies. This policy had so enraged the Americans that in 1915 the Germans had agreed to modify it; when, in February 1917, they unilaterally resumed it in full force, the Americans took it as an unforgivable affront.

As was so often the case in American history, the US was ill-prepared to go to war. The Army, including National Guardsmen in Federal service, numbered only about 200,000, whereas John J Pershing, the general designated to command the US Expeditionary Force, correctly stated that 3,000,000 would not be too few to ensure victory. While a massive mobilization plan (Selective Service) was slowly being set in motion and US industry was gearing up for wartime production, Pershing began sending his first token forces overseas in June. By October five divisions (around 100,000 men) were in France, but Pershing, over some Allied protest,

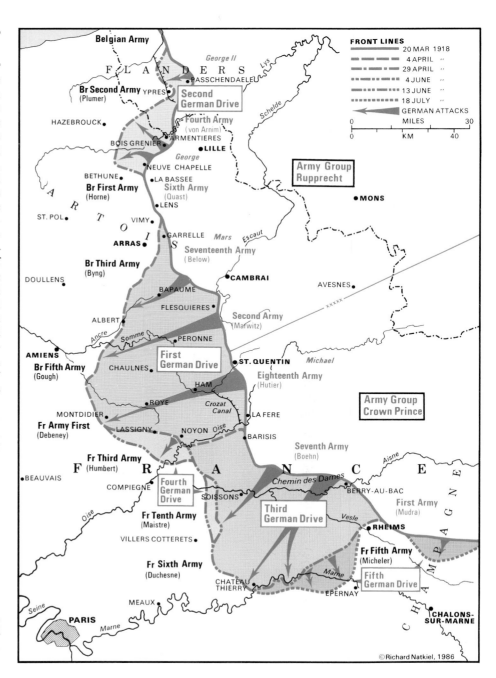

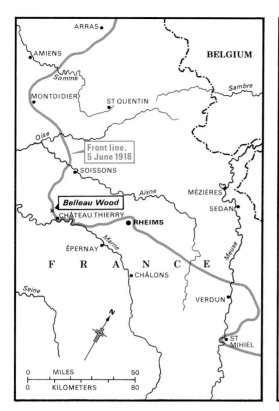

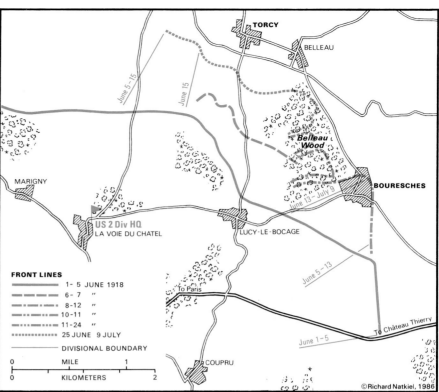

MAP above: *The Battle of Belleau Wood.*
MAP left: *The German offensives in the early months of 1918.*
Left: *Generals Pershing (right) and Foch at a conference in June 1918.*

steadfastly refused to allow them to be sent to the front until their training could be completed. When, in mid-April 1918, he finally did begin to commit some of his forces to the Allied line, it was to the relatively peaceful southern sector, near Château Thierry, that they were sent.

As it happened, this sector was not destined to be peaceful for long. On 20 April a German attack virtually anni-hilated two US companies assigned to hold the village of Sicheprey, a minor victory of which German propagand-ists made much. On 27 May the Allies retaliated when elements of the US 1st Division, well supported by French tanks and artillery, attacked and took the German-held village of Cantigny. But all this was mere prelude, for on that same day the Germans launched a major offensive in the southern sector, starting from their main positions along the Chemin des Dames Ridge and aimed at taking Château Thierry, crossing the Marne and per-haps thereafter driving on to Paris, only 50 miles away.

65

Now all US forces in the area, notably the Army's 2nd and 3rd Divisions and two regiments of Marines, had to be committed unstintingly to assist the French in repelling the German drive. The main locus American action would prove to be Belleau Wood and the nearby town of Bouresches, a little to the north of Château Thierry (which the Germans occupied on 3 June). On 6 June the US Marine 5th and 6th Regiments counterattacked the Germans in the woods and village. Three days of bloody fighting followed, with no very clear result. On the 9th the battered Marines retired to regroup and then resumed the attack on the 12th. Three days later units of the 3rd Division began to reinforce them and by 25 June both the woods and the village were at last in American hands.

The German offensive in the southern sector had been effectively contained by the end of June, but on 14 July the German VII Army made a final effort to break out and resume the drive on Paris. By this time four US divisions (the 26th 'Yankee,' the 3rd, the 28th and the 42nd 'Rainbow') had joined the French units defending the arc that ran southeast from Belleau Wood along the Marne. Again the fighting was fierce, and many of the American units were roughly handled, but after some minor gains this German offensive, too, was blocked, and by the 18th the front had been restabilized.

In this essentially defensive phase of operations the Americans had performed much better than either their allies or the Germans had predicted. How effective they would be on the offense would soon be revealed.

MAP right: *The Aisne-Marne Offensive showing the sectors retaken by the participating American divisions.*

The Aisne-Marne Offensive

The German offensives that both the Americans and French in the southern sector of the Western Front had been engaged in trying to repel between 20 April and 18 July were merely phases of a much larger German strategy. At the beginning of 1918 the German High Command had concluded that it might now be possible to break the three-and-a-half-year-old stalemate in France and force an end to the war on terms acceptable to Germany. What prompted this hope was the Russian Revolution, which had collapsed Russian resistance on the Eastern Front by the autumn of 1917 and had thereby released some 70 German divisions for service in the West. With these large reinforcements the Germans felt they might be able to mount a series of offensives that would either break the

Western allies completely or push their lines so far back into France that they would be compelled to sue for peace. It was imperative, however, that these offensives be initiated before any significant numbers of American troops could arrive in Europe to reinforce the Allies.

The first of these offensives was begun on 21 March in the central sector, and, although it produced some territorial gains, it had been effectively contained by 5 April. A second offensive against the British in the north was similarly halted by the end of April. And, as we have seen, a third major offensive against the French and Americans in the south had been effectively stemmed by mid-July. By this time the exhausted Germans were constrained to face the fact that their strategy had failed.

Although the Allies were not quite yet in a position to mount an all-out counteroffensive, General Ferdinand Foch, the Supreme Allied Command-

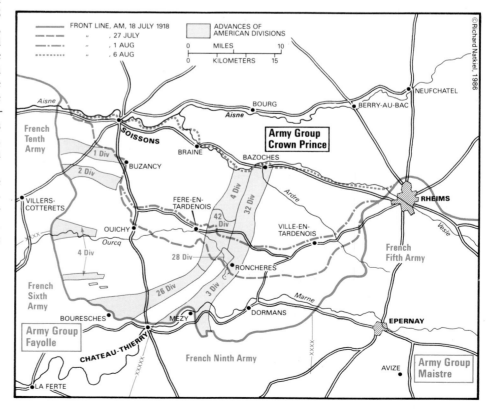

Above: *Members of Battery D, 105th Field Artillery celebrate the Armistice, 11 November 1918.*
Below: *Men of the 132nd Infantry, 32nd Division man a trench during training. The soldier nearest the camera is preparing to fire a rifle grenade.*

er, was nevertheless determined to lose no time in seizing the initiative by mounting a series of limited attacks all along the German line. One of the most important of these, an attack on the Château Thierry salient that was intended to advance the Allied line from the Marne to the Aisne, fell largely to the Americans.

On 18 July, while the US 1st and 2nd Divisions, the 5th Marine Regiment and a French division attacked the western side of the salient, the 4th Division (reinforced by French regiments), the 26th and the 3rd attacked it from the south. After the first day progress was slow and losses mounted alarmingly. By the end of 20 July the 4th and 26th Divisions had suffered 2000 casualties each, and the 1st Division 7000. By 25 July both the 26th and 28th Divisions were too exhausted to continue and had to be replaced by the 42nd 'Rainbow' Division (among whose officers was Colonel Douglas MacArthur). Within 24 hours the 42nd was engaged in violent fighting in the Forêt de Fere, which it only

finally secured on the 27th, and by 1 August it, too, was so decimated that it had to be replaced. Indeed, by this time, casualties everywhere in the sector were so heavy that divisions had constantly to be rotated to and from the front; yet the painful advance continued. By 28 July the Allies had gained a toehold on the Vesle River, east of Rheims, and in the next nine days they succeeded in pushing their whole line up to that river and, into the bargain, retaking Soissons.

By 9 August the Château Thierry salient had been completely eliminated and the weary Allies called a halt to prepare for the expected German counterattack. When it failed to develop, the advance was resumed on the 19th, its focus shifting northwest along the Aisne. The Germans finally made their riposte on the 27th. It was extremely strong, but it recovered very little ground and eventually petered out. It was clear with this victory that the Allies still held the initiative and that more offensives could be expected in a short time.

The St Mihiel Offensive

The desperate need to repel the German offensives of the spring and summer of 1918 had necessarily diluted Pershing's control over the American Expeditionary Force. At Foch's command US divisions had been deployed along the Western Front in somewhat random fashion (one, the 33rd, as far north as Amiens), and as the Aisne-Marne offensive began to wind down Pershing turned his thoughts increasingly to the problem of reconsolidating the American military effort in France. His solution was to propose a new limited offensive that would be American-run and mostly American-conducted. His target would be the southernmost (and perhaps least threatening) of the salients protruding from the German line, that at St Mihiel, southwest of Metz. His plan included both the elimination of this salient and, if a breakthrough could be achieved, the recapture of Metz itself. When Foch hotly protested that such an

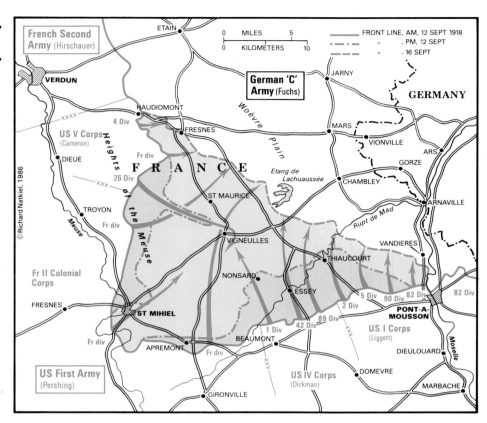

Below: *King George V of Britain decorating Private Harry Shelly with the Medal of Honor for gallantry in action on 4 July 1918.*

attack would merely interfere with preparations for the major offensive he was now planning, Pershing threatened to withdraw all US troops from the Front. In the end a compromise was reached: the attack on the St Mihiel salient would be made, with some French support, but in no circumstance would it be followed by a drive on Metz, and Pershing's forces had to be ready to participate in Foch's main offensive scheduled to begin on 26 September.

Pershing, whose command had now been designated First Army Europe, quickly deployed his troops about the salient. On its south flank he deployed two corps: on the right, US I Corps (the 2nd, 5th, 82nd and 90th Divisions), and on the left, US IV Corps (the 1st, 42nd and 89th Divisions). The French II Colonial Corps was positioned at the salient's apex, and on its north flank was the US V Corps (the US 26th and French 15th Divisions). More than 3000 artillery pieces and 270 tanks (the latter under the overall command of Lieutenant Colonel George S Patton, Jr) were distributed among these forces. A novel addition to the Allied arsenal were some 1500 aircraft, under the overall command of Colonel William J 'Billy' Mitchell, which were to be primarily employed in ground attack missions, the first large-scale close-support operation ever attempted.

Faced with such a daunting assembly of matériel and men, outnumbered by approximately three to one, General Fuchs, commander of the German forces in the salient, had already begun to pull back when the Allies struck at 0100 hours on 12 September 1918. This withdrawal to some extent frustrated Pershing's plans, for it had been intended that the 26th Division and elements of IV Corps would rapidly converge on the village of Vigneulles, thus trapping many Germans between themselves and the advancing French Colonials. In the event, the encirclement, completed by dawn on the 13th, netted fewer enemy troops than had been hoped – about 15,000 –

but this disappointment was to some extent mitigated by the capture of 440 heavy weapons that the Germans had not had time to remove. In the next three days the American and French forces advanced rapidly, and by the 16th the entire salient was in Allied hands. Foch now called a halt to the operation and ordered Pershing to redeploy in preparation for the big offensive on the 26th.

In retrospect it is still difficult to draw up an accurate balance sheet for the St Mihiel offensive. Doubtless Foch had some cause to call it a needless, and possibly risky, sideshow. But in addition to accomplishing Pershing's objective of re-establishing the integrity of American command, its quick and inexpensive success (casual-

ties were less than three percent) certainly boosted Allied – and correspondingly lowered German – morale. In addition, it provided excellent combat training for several more fresh US divisions whose services would be needed in Foch's impending offensive. Finally, it suggested some interesting lessons about the changing nature of war. On the 12th, for example, US horse-mounted cavalry had quickly to be withdrawn in the face of enemy machine-gun fire, a clear indication that a long chapter in military history was fast coming to a close. On the other hand, the surprising effectiveness of Mitchell's air strikes demonstrated, for those who cared to see, that an impressive new chapter was in the process of being written.

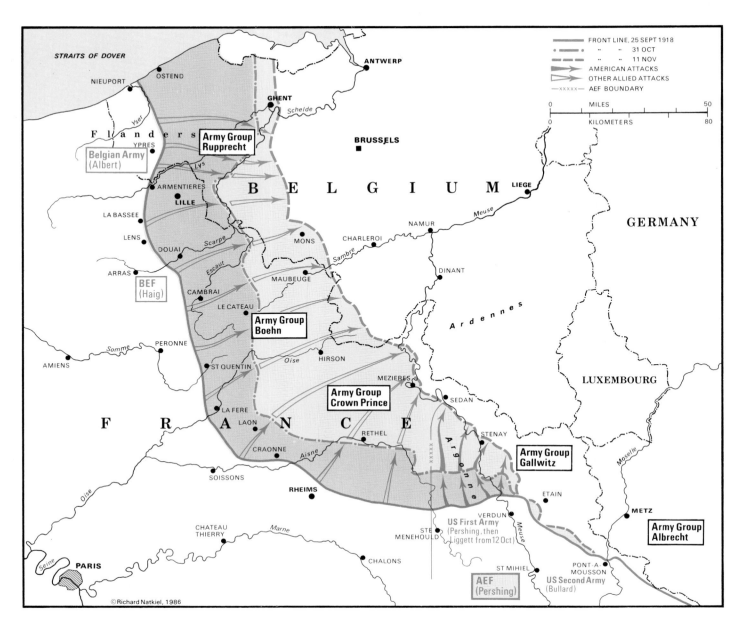

Front line, 25 Sept 1918, 31 Oct, 11 Nov; American attacks; Other Allied attacks; AEF boundary.

© Richard Natkiel, 1986

The Meuse-Argonne Offensive

Foch's plan for the great Allied offensive to be launched in the autumn of 1918 consisted of a rapid succession of blows against every important part of the German line. The Americans and the French Fourth Army would lead off on 26 September with an attack on that segment of the line that stretched between Rheims and the Meuse. The next day the British would attack in the Lens sector. Then British, French and Belgian forces in the far north would assail the part of the front that lay between Armentieres and the sea. And finally the French and British would strike at the center, east of Amiens.

The initial Franco-American assault on the 26th was aimed at driving the Germans back through Sedan to the 'barrier' of the Ardennes Forest, incorrectly thought by the Allied High Command to be impassable and therefore a likely place for a three-sided envelopment. The American half of this sector was to be on the right, from the western side of the Argonne Forest to the Meuse. Although Pershing, ably assisted by some talented staff officers such as Colonel George C Marshall, had performed wonders in bringing the whole US First Army north from the St Mihiel salient in just 10 days, his dispositions on the eve of the attack were less than ideal. On the

American left, opposite the formidable Argonne Forest, was I Corps, composed of the veteran 28th and two green divisions. All three divisions that made up V Corps in the center were green; and of the divisions of III Corps on the right, only the 4th had had any real battle experience. Other veteran US divisions, such as the 1st, 2nd and 42nd, were resting in the rear, waiting to be introduced later.

Preceded by a heavy artillery barrage, the American troops began their advance at 0230 hours on the 26th. Once the Germans had recovered from the shelling they put up fierce resistance, especially (and predictably) under the dense cover of the Argonne. By 28 September, the day on which Pershing had wanted the Argonne cleared, it was clear that the Americans were in for a long hard fight. I Corps' green 35th Division had already sustained 8000 casualties and had to be replaced by the veteran 1st, and in the center two other green divisions had also to be replaced. Many more such rotations would follow.

The Argonne had still not been taken by early October when Pershing halted his exhausted troops for rest and reconsolidation. During this period, which lasted until the end of the month, Pershing relinquished personal command of the First Army to the aggressive General Hunter Liggett and created a new command, Second Army, under General Robert Bullard, responsible for guarding Liggett's rear, southeast of the Meuse.

Liggett resumed the advance on 1 November with a broad attack along a 15-mile front. By 3 November his center had progressed some 12 miles, to the vicinity of Beaumont, but, as usual, his left lagged behind, still entangled in the Argonne. At last, on 4 November, the First Army's left flank, now composed of the 77th and 78th Divisions, fought their way clear of the obstructive forest, and the whole American line was free to pivot northeast and pin the Germans against the Meuse.

But by this time the Allies had achieved major breakthroughs elsewhere on the Western Front and the war was obviously about to end. In a symbolic gesture Liggett now halted his advance and gave to the French Fourth Army the honor of liberating Sedan.

The armistice that ended World War I went into effect at 1100 hours on 11 November 1918. America's participation in the war had come late, and her losses had been trivial in comparison to those suffered by other belligerents (less than four percent of those suffered by France, for example). Yet her contribution to victory had been disproportionately great, and the conduct of American troops in battle had given the country reason for considerable satisfaction.

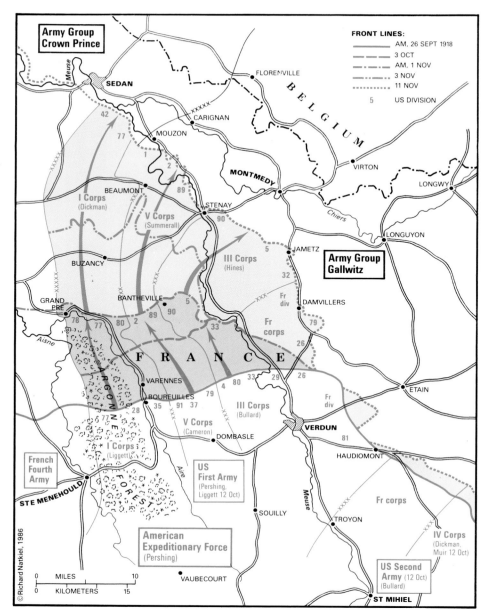

WORLD WAR II

Pearl Harbor

US-Japanese relations, cool since the mid-1930s, began to disintegrate after September 1940 when Japan signed the pointedly anti-US Tripartite Pact with Germany and Italy. By the following August Japanese incursions into French Indochina had provoked the US into joining the British and East Indies Dutch both in pledging mutual military assistance in case of Japanese attack and in imposing an oil embargo. Since Japan was wholly dependent on imports for her petroleum, this embargo, which cut her sources of supply by 90 percent, severely threatened her economy. Now the Japanese had either to compose their differences with the Americans, Dutch and British

or to seize sources of petroleum and other vital raw materials in the Far East by aggression, a course that would certainly bring all concerned into general war. Throughout the autumn of 1941, as successive diplomatic efforts to allay the crisis foundered, official Japanese thinking fixed ever more firmly on the course of war.

Japanese war plans gave priority to neutralizing the US Pacific Fleet, the greatest immediate threat to Japan's freedom of action. The same logic that dictated that this task must be accomplished early in the war soon led to a decision that it should become the *casus belli* itself, and elaborate preparations were undertaken for the Imperial Japanese Navy to deliver a massive surprise air strike on the Pacific Fleet's base at Pearl Harbor.

The order actually to mount this attack was sent to the IJN on 2 December. In the next five days Admiral Chuichi Nagumo sailed a large task force formed around all six of Japan's fleet carriers to within 250 miles of the Hawaiian Islands. On the morning of 7 December a first wave of 189 Kate bombers/torpedo bombers, Val dive bombers and Zero fighters struck Pearl Harbor and nearby airfields. A second wave of 171 aircraft followed about an hour later.

The Americans were caught totally by surprise, and 3681 of them paid for their unpreparedness with their lives. All eight of the US battleships in port were put out of commission (two permanently), as were 10 other warships and auxiliaries and 80 percent of all the military aircraft on Oahu. The

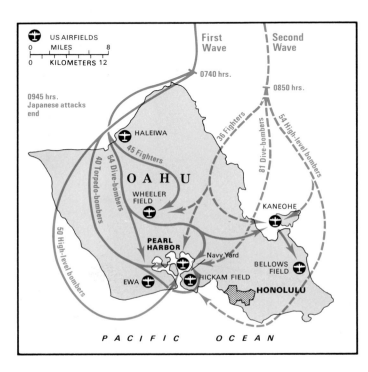

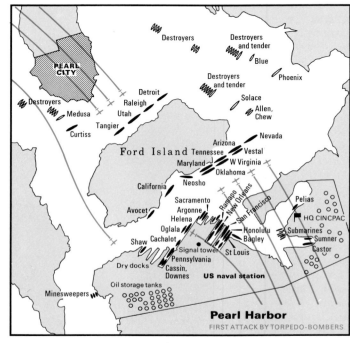

Japanese lost just 29 planes.

Yet this great victory was less overwhelming than it at first seemed. The Pacific Fleet's battleship strength had, to be sure, been reduced from nine to one, but experience was soon to show that battleships were very much less important in the naval balance than carriers, and no American carriers were in port at the time of the raid. Nor was Pearl Harbor, as a naval facility, critically damaged. Perhaps most important, the Japanese seriously underestimated the psychological effect the attack would have on its victims. Many Japanese planners had predicted that the Americans would be demoralized in proportion to the raid's success and might, if hit hard enough, even be receptive to peace negotiations. The unalloyed fury with which the American people and government reacted dissipated such fantasies, and with them any hopes of the short war on which so much of Japanese strategic planning had been predicated.

MAPS left: *Pearl Harbor showing how the airfields and the fleet anchorage were struck. Note the oil storage tanks which were not attacked.*

Above: *Ships of the Pacific Fleet in harbor five weeks before the attack.* Below: *Fire fighting operations around the battleship* Nevada.

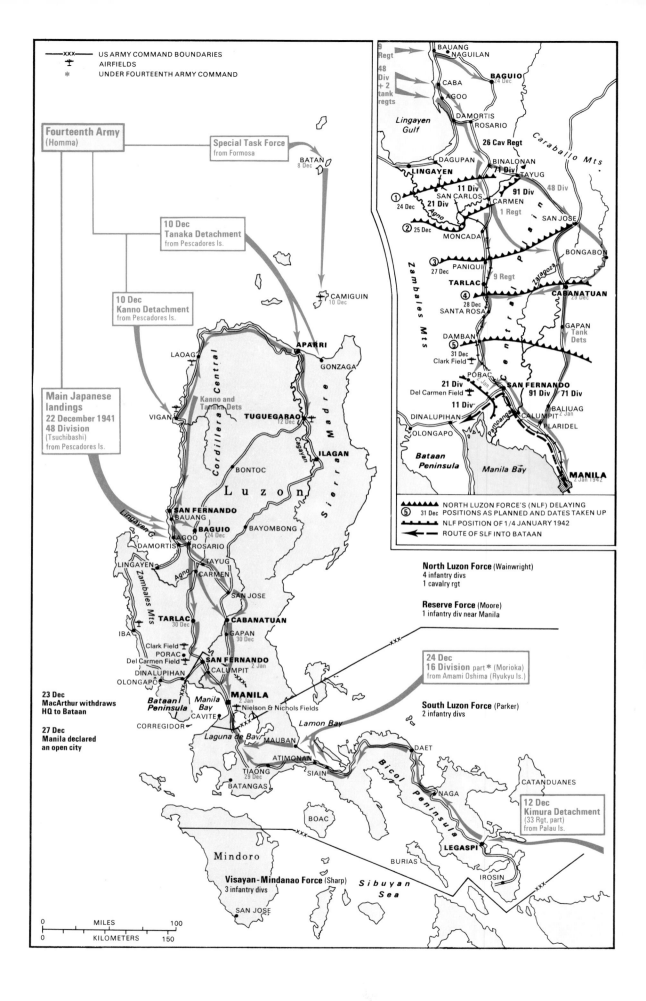

US ARMY COMMAND BOUNDARIES
AIRFIELDS
UNDER FOURTEENTH ARMY COMMAND

Fourteenth Army (Homma)

Special Task Force from Formosa

BATAN 8 Dec

10 Dec
Tanaka Detachment from Pescadores Is.

CAMIGUIN 10 Dec

10 Dec
Kanno Detachment from Pescadores Is.

APARRI

LAOAG
GONZAGA

Main Japanese landings
22 December 1941
48 Division (Tsuchibashi) from Pescadores Is.

Kanno and Tanaka Dets 12 Dec

VIGAN

TUGUEGARAO 12 Dec

Cordillera Central

Cagayan

Sierra Madre

BONTOC

ILAGAN

L u z o n

BAYOMBONG

SAN FERNANDO
BAUANG
BAGUIO 24 Dec
AGOO
ROSARIO
DAMORTIS
LINGAYEN
Lingayen G.
TAYUG
CARMEN
Agno

Zambales Mts

SAN JOSE

TARLAC 30 Dec
CABANATUAN
IBA
GAPAN 30 Dec
Clark Field
PORAC
Del Carmen Field
SAN FERNANDO 2 Jan
DINALUPIHAN
CALUMPIT
OLONGAPO

23 Dec
MacArthur withdraws HQ to Bataan

27 Dec
Manila declared an open city

Bataan Peninsula
Manila Bay
MANILA 2 Jan
Nielson & Nichols Fields
CAVITE
CORREGIDOR
Laguna de Bay
MAUBAN
Lamon Bay
TIAONG 29 Dec
ATIMONAN
SIAIN
BATANGAS

BOAC

M i n d o r o

Visayan-Mindanao Force (Sharp)
3 infantry divs

SAN JOSE

DAET

Bicol Peninsula

CATANDUANES

NAGA

12 Dec
Kimura Detachment (33 Rgt, part) from Palau Is.

LEGASPI

BURIAS

IROSIN

Sibuyan Sea

North Luzon Force (Wainwright)
4 infantry divs
1 cavalry rgt

Reserve Force (Moore)
1 infantry div near Manila

24 Dec
16 Division part * (Morioka)
from Amami Oshima (Ryukyu Is.)

South Luzon Force (Parker)
2 infantry divs

(inset top right)

BAUANG
NAGUILAN
9 Regt
48 Div + 2 tank regts
BAGUIO 24 Dec
CABA
AGOO
DAMORTIS
ROSARIO
Lingayen Gulf
26 Cav Regt
Caraballo Mts.
DAGUPAN
BINALONAN
LINGAYEN
71 Div
TAYUG
11 Div
SAN CARLOS
21 Div
① 24 Dec
91 Div
48 Div
CARMEN
1 Regt
SAN JOSE
② 25 Dec
MONCADA
Agno
Zambales Mts
BONGABON
③ 27 Dec
PANIQUI
TARLAC
④ 28 Dec
SANTA ROSA
9 Regt
CABANATUAN 29 Dec
Zaragoza
GAPAN
Tank Dets
DAMBAN
⑤ 31 Dec
Clark Field
PORAC
Del Carmen Field
21 Div
SAN FERNANDO
91 Div 71 Div
2 Jan
11 Div
DINALUPIHAN
BALIUAG
CALUMPIT 2 Jan
PLARIDEL
OLONGAPO
Pampanga
Bataan Peninsula
Manila Bay
MANILA 2 Jan 1942

▲▲▲▲ **NORTH LUZON FORCE'S (NLF) DELAYING**
⑤ 31 Dec **POSITIONS AS PLANNED AND DATES TAKEN UP**
━┿━┿━ **NLF POSITION OF 1/4 JANUARY 1942**
━ ▬ **ROUTE OF SLF INTO BATAAN**

74

MAP left: *The Japanese attack on Luzon.*
MAP below right: *The protracted struggle for Bataan.*

The Fall of the Philippines

In addition to neutralizing the US Pacific Fleet, Japan's early-war strategy called for the quick elimination of all American, British and Dutch military strongholds in the Far East. Since by far the biggest concentration of American military power in the Western Pacific – 31,000 regular troops, 100,000 local conscripts and about 150 combat aircraft, all under the command of General Douglas MacArthur – was based in the Philippines, it is hardly surprising that the Japanese should have begun bombing targets in the Philippines within hours of their attack on Pearl Harbor. What *is* surprising is the state of unpreparedness of the now-forewarned defenders. The raiders caught most of the US and Filipino warplanes on the ground and within 48 hours had destroyed 67 percent of them. In the following days, while the air raids continued, detachments of Japanese troops began coming on shore at widely scattered points on Luzon in order to seize airfields and other important facilities in preparation for a large-scale invasion.

The invasion itself began on 22 December 1941 when 43,000 men of General Masaharu Homma's 14th Army landed on Luzon at Lingayen Gulf, 150 miles northeast of Manila. Two days later an additional 7000 men landed on the southern part of the island at Lamon Bay. MacArthur's outmatched defending force was barely able even to slow the Japanese as they drove south from Lingayen Gulf to Manila. By 2 January 1942 Homma had taken the Philippine capital, and MacArthur was falling back toward Bataan, the narrow peninsula that forms the northern arm of Manila Bay. There, fighting along shortened lines, the US-Filipino forces put up such a savage defense that by mid-February they had inflicted 7000 casualties on their attackers and had all but halted the Japanese advance.

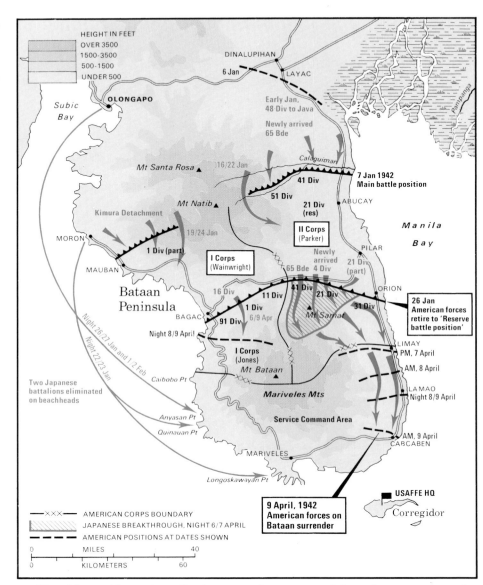

Yet this could not last, for it was obvious that MacArthur's forces, unlike the Japanese, could neither be re-supplied nor reinforced. On 12 March 1942 President Roosevelt ordered MacArthur to turn his Philippine command over to Lieutenant General Jonathan Wainwright and to assume command of the Allied forces in Australia. Thus it fell to Wainwright to try to stem the final Japanese offensive, which began on 3 April. Sick, demoralized and vastly outnumbered, the Americans on Bataan could hold out for only 6 days before surrendering.

A remnant of American troops on the island fortress of Corregidor, just off Bataan's southern tip, fought on for another month. But on 5 May the Japanese succeeded in putting powerful forces on shore at the island's eastern end. They overran the Americans' main defense line the following day, and Wainwright was then compelled to make the final surrender. While Japan celebrated the conquest of this last American foothold in the Western Pacific, 89,000 American and Filipino soldiers were marched off to a long, pitiless captivity.

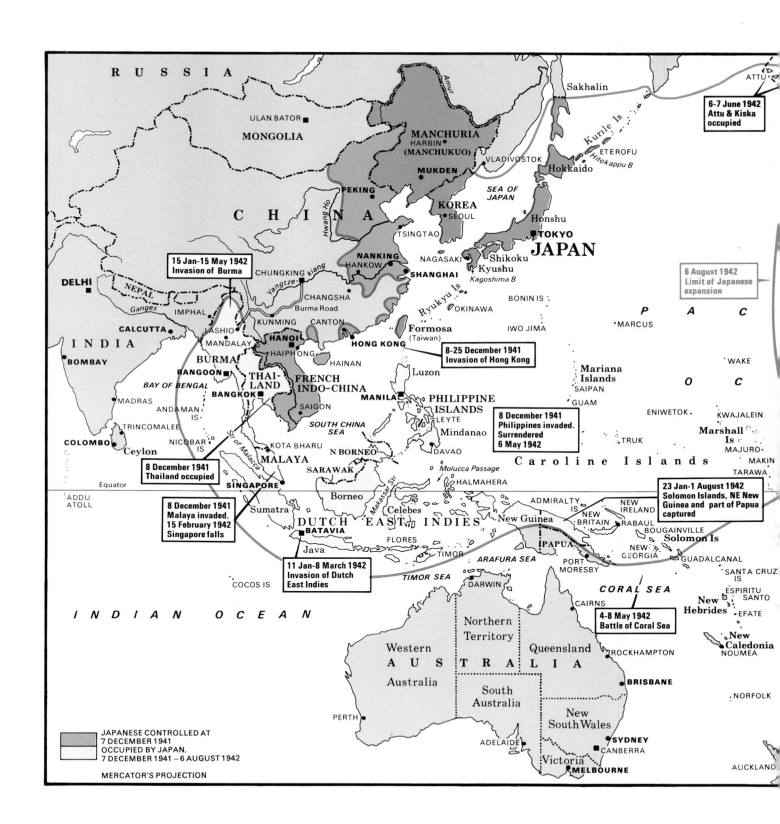

RUSSIA

ULAN BATOR ■

MONGOLIA

MANCHURIA
HARBIN ●
(MANCHUKUO)

Amur

Sakhalin

ATTU

6-7 June 1942
Attu & Kiska
occupied

MUKDEN ●

VLADIVOSTOK ●

Kurile Is

ETEROFU

Hitokappu B

Hokkaido

PEKING ●

C H I N A

KOREA
● SEOUL

SEA OF
JAPAN

Honshu

TSINGTAO ●

NAGASAKI

TOKYO

JAPAN

Shikoku
Kyushu

6 August 1942
Limit of Japanese
expansion

15 Jan-15 May 1942
Invasion of Burma

CHUNGKING

NANKING
HANKOW

SHANGHAI

Kagoshima B

P   A   C

DELHI

NEPAL

Yangtze-kiang

Hwang Ho

CHANGSHA
Burma Road

Ryukyu Is

OKINAWA

BONIN IS

● MARCUS

Ganges

IMPHAL

CALCUTTA

KUNMING

CANTON

Formosa
(Taiwan)

IWO JIMA

O   C

LASHIO

I N D I A

MANDALAY

BURMA

HANOI
HAIPHONG

HONG KONG

HAINAN

Luzon

8-25 December 1941
Invasion of Hong Kong

Mariana
Islands

● WAKE

BOMBAY ●

RANGOON ■

THAI-
LAND

FRENCH
INDO-CHINA

SAIPAN

SAIGON

MANILA ■

PHILIPPINE
ISLANDS

GUAM

ENIWETOK ●

KWAJALEIN

BAY OF BENGAL

BANGKOK ■

MADRAS ●

ANDAMAN
IS

SOUTH CHINA
SEA

LEYTE

Mindanao

8 December 1941
Philippines invaded.
Surrendered
6 May 1942

● TRUK

Marshall
Is

MAJURO ●

MAKIN

TRINCOMALEE ●

NICOBAR
IS

KOTA BHARU

DAVAO ●

TARAWA

COLOMBO

Ceylon

Str of Malacca

MALAYA

N BORNEO

SARAWAK

Molucca Str

HALMAHERA

C a r o l i n e   I s l a n d s

Equator

8 December 1941
Thailand occupied

SINGAPORE ■

Borneo

Celebes

Makassar Str

23 Jan-1 August 1942
Solomon Islands, NE New
Guinea and part of Papua
captured

ADDU
ATOLL

8 December 1941
Malaya invaded.
15 February 1942
Singapore falls

Sumatra

DUTCH   EAST   INDIES

BATAVIA ■

Java

New Guinea

FLORES

ADMIRALTY
IS

NEW
IRELAND

NEW
BRITAIN

RABAUL

PAPUA

NEW
GEORGIA

BOUGAINVILLE

Solomon Is

GUADALCANAL

11 Jan-8 March 1942
Invasion of Dutch
East Indies

ARAFURA SEA

PORT
MORESBY

SANTA CRUZ
IS

COCOS IS

TIMOR SEA

TIMOR

DARWIN ●

CORAL SEA

ESPIRITU
SANTO

New
Hebrides

EFATE

I N D I A N   O C E A N

Northern
Territory

CAIRNS ●

4-8 May 1942
Battle of Coral Sea

New
Caledonia

NOUMEA

Western

A U S T

Queensland

ROCKHAMPTON ●

NORFOLK ●

Australia

R A L I A

South
Australia

BRISBANE

PERTH ●

New
South Wales

● SYDNEY

ADELAIDE ●

CANBERRA ■

AUCKLAND

Victoria

MELBOURNE

JAPANESE CONTROLLED AT
7 DECEMBER 1941
OCCUPIED BY JAPAN,
7 DECEMBER 1941 – 6 AUGUST 1942

MERCATOR'S PROJECTION

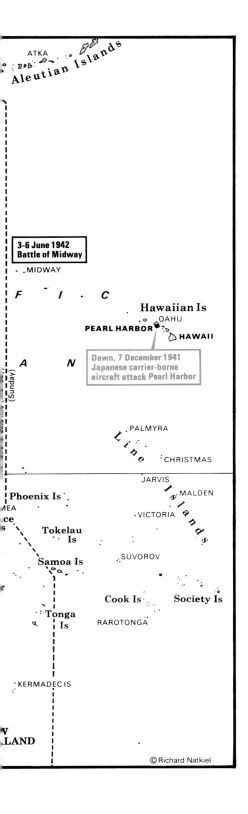

Japan Triumphant

The conquest of the Philippines was but one of a series of dazzling victories won by Japan in the first six months of the Pacific War. A few minutes before the attack on Pearl Harbor (although, thanks to the International Date Line, technically on 8 December 1941) Japanese troops landed in Malaya: in a little over two months they would conquer the entire colony, including Singapore. It would take them longer to expel UK and Chinese forces from Burma: until 15 May 1942. In the meantime they had dealt the British other severe blows, sinking HMS *Prince of Wales* and *Repulse*, Britain's two heaviest naval units in the Far East, on 10 December and capturing Hong Kong on the 25th. From the Americans they had taken Guam and Wake Islands in December, and on 11 January 1942 a Japanese submarine succeeded in disabling USS *Saratoga* for several months, thus reducing US operational fleet carrier strength in the Pacific to three.

On the same day that *Saratoga* was torpedoed, the Japanese began their invasion of the oil-rich Dutch East Indies, the most important economic prize on their agenda of conquest. To defend this vast area the overall commander of the ABDA (American, British, Dutch and Australian) force, General Sir Archibald Wavell, had something over 100,000 scattered troops, but their effectiveness would be largely dependent on what little air and naval support could be provided by approximately 200 obsolete Dutch warplanes and a six-cruiser Allied naval flotilla commanded by Dutch Rear Admiral Karel Doorman.

The Japanese plan of attack on the Indies was three-pronged. A Western Force defended by six cruisers, a light carrier and numerous destroyers was responsible for conquering western Borneo, eastern Sumatra and, ultimately western Java. A Central Force was responsible for the conquest of eastern Borneo. And an Eastern Force,

Above: *Japanese soldiers rejoice at early victories.*
MAP left: *The early Japanese attacks.*

supported by four cruisers and 14 destroyers, was responsible for taking the Celebes, Amboina, Timor, Bali and, finally, eastern Java. Not directly participating, but standing by if needed, were Admiral Nagumo's six fleet carriers.

Against this concentration of power Doorman's ABDA naval flotilla could do little. An attempt by four World War I US destroyers to interfere with the Japanese landing at Balikpapan, Borneo, on 23–4 January was unsuccessful. By early February the Japanese, now with complete control of the air, had bombed the cruiser USS *Marblehead* out of action and by the 15th had forced the remaining ABDA units to retire to the Java Sea. Here, on the 19th, in a minor naval engagement in the Lombok Straits, ABDA ships were again unsuccessful in their effort to prevent the invasion of Bali. On the 27th Japanese bombers sank USS *Langley*, an old carrier now converted to a seaplane tender.

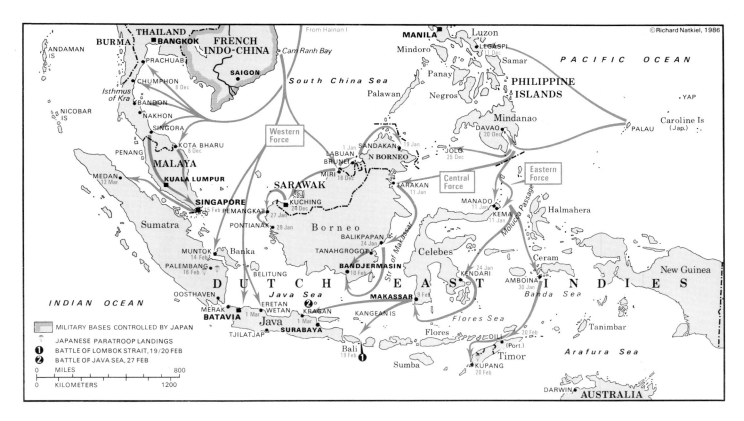

MAP: *The Japanese offensive to capture the oil-rich territories of the East Indies.*

That same day Doorman learned of a large Eastern Force convoy headed for Java, and he sortied what was left of his flotilla to intercept it. In the ensuing battle of the Java Sea, the Dutch cruisers *De Ruyter* and *Java* were sunk and the British cruiser *Exeter* was damaged, while the Japanese suffered only light damage to one destroyer. Two days later, on 1 March, Japanese ships and aircraft finished off all of the remaining ABDA cruisers – USS *Houston*, HMS *Exeter* and HMAS *Perth*. By 8 March the invasion of Java had been completed and all organized resistance in the Indies had come to an end.

Nagumo's carriers were now free to enter the Indian Ocean, where, by 9 April, they had sunk a British light carrier, two cruisers and 136,000 tons of merchant shipping, as well as bombing Colombo and Trincomalee. This was, in fact, the high water mark of the Imperial Japanese Navy's success in World War II. Although none could have foreseen it at the time, the tide was about to turn.

The Battle of the Coral Sea

In April 1942 the Japanese completed plans for a complex operation in the Coral Sea designed to reduce the United States' access to Australia and to pave the way for a possible future invasion of that continent. A large body of troops would set out from Rabaul, New Britain, to land at Port Morseby and dislodge the Australians from southern New Guinea. At the same time a smaller force would head for Tulagi, in the Solomon Islands, with the object of setting up an airbase there. Two independent task forces were to provide the troop transports with naval and air cover: Rear Admiral Goto's Covering Group, centered on the light carrier *Shoho*, would stay close to the Port Moresby Invasion Group, while Vice Admiral Takagi's powerful Carrier Strike Group, which included the fleet carriers *Zuikaku* and *Shokaku*, would circle around the Coral Sea and enter it from the east, surprising any US warships that might have come into the area and cutting off their escape route.

In fact the Americans, who had learned of the Japanese plan, did mean to interfere. Admiral Chester W Nim-

itz, CincpacFleet, ordered all available Allied units – the US fleet carriers *Lexington* and *Yorktown*, plus three cruisers and some destroyers – to rendezvous in the Coral Sea as quickly as possible. They did so on 4 May 1942, one day after the Japanese had landed on Tulagi. During the next three days the opposing carrier fleets vainly sought one another. Then, on the 7th, several things happened at once. Rear Admiral Frank J Fletcher, commander of the Allied fleet, detached the cruisers and some of the destroyers, under Rear Admiral John Crace, RN, to attack the Port Moresby Invasion Group. The Japanese mistook this squadron (Task Force 44) for the main force and bombed it heavily, but Crace adroitly extricated his ships after inflicting some damage. Meantime, aircraft from the US carriers located *Shoho* and, in short order, sank her. Yet still the two opposing groups of fleet carriers had not made contact. (For a while the Japanese thought they had, but the American targets, which they sank in a massive air attack, proved only to be the oiler *Neosho* and the destroyer *Sims*.)

The fleet carriers finally came to grips the next day, 8 May. In the ensuing exchange of air attacks, during which none of the opposing ships ever saw one another, *Yorktown* and *Sho-*

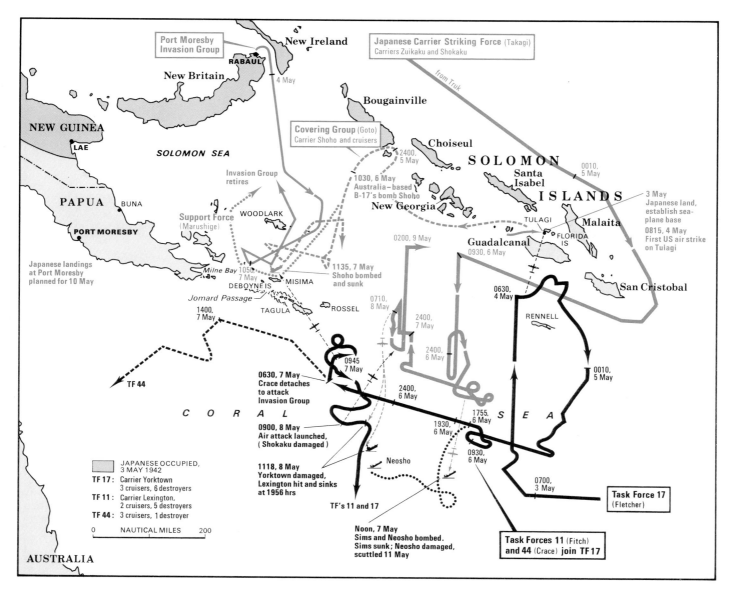

Port Moresby
Invasion Group

New Ireland

New Britain

RABAUL

4 May

Japanese Carrier Striking Force (Takagi)
Carriers Zuikaku and Shokaku

from Truk

NEW GUINEA

LAE

Bougainville

SOLOMON SEA

Covering Group (Goto)
Carrier Shoho and cruisers

2400,
5 May

Choiseul

S O L O M O N

Santa
Isabel

0010,
5 May

Invasion Group
retires

1030, 6 May
Australia-based
B-17's bomb Shoho

I S L A N D S

3 May
Japanese land,
establish sea-
plane base

PAPUA

BUNA

New Georgia

TULAGI

Malaita

0815, 4 May
First US air strike
on Tulagi

Support Force
(Marushige)

WOODLARK

Guadalcanal

FLORIDA
IS

0930, 6 May

PORT MORESBY

0200, 9 May

Japanese landings
at Port Moresby
planned for 10 May

Milne Bay 1050
7 May

MISIMA

1135, 7 May
Shoho bombed
and sunk

San Cristobal

DEBOYNE IS

0710,
8 May

0630,
4 May

RENNELL

Jomard Passage

1400,
7 May

TAGULA

ROSSEL

2400,
7 May

0010,
5 May

TF 44

0945
7 May

2400,
6 May

0630, 7 May
Crace detaches
to attack
Invasion Group

2400,
6 May

1755,
6 May

1930,
6 May

S E A

0900, 8 May
Air attack launched,
(Shokaku damaged)

C O R A L

0930,
6 May

0700,
3 May

1118, 8 May
Yorktown damaged,
Lexington hit and sinks
at 1956 hrs

Neosho

Task Force 17
(Fletcher)

JAPANESE OCCUPIED,
3 MAY 1942

TF's 11 and 17

TF 17: Carrier Yorktown
3 cruisers, 6 destroyers

TF 11: Carrier Lexington,
2 cruisers, 5 destroyers

TF 44: 3 cruisers, 1 destroyer

Noon, 7 May
Sims and Neosho bombed.
Sims sunk; Neosho damaged,
scuttled 11 May

Task Forces 11 (Fitch)
and 44 (Crace) **join TF 17**

0   NAUTICAL MILES   200

AUSTRALIA

kaku were both damaged, and *Lexington* was so heavily damaged that she had to be abandoned. Japanese aircraft losses were especially severe.

Both sides claimed victory in the Coral Sea, but at the time the full significance of what had happened could not have been easy to assess. New Guinea may have been saved, for the alarmed Port Moresby Invasion Group turned tail and headed back for Rabaul, and in fact no similar invasion attempt was ever made. On the other hand, the sinking of *Shoho* in no way compensated the Americans for the loss of *Lexington*. At the battle's end the number of fully operational US fleet carriers in the Pacific was reduced to two, as opposed to Japan's five. Yet it was just this perceived disproportion that now suggested to the Japanese that the time was ripe for an all-out

effort finally to obliterate US naval power in the Pacific. Thus, unforeseeably, the Battle of the Coral Sea affected the decision, already under consideration, that brought Japan to the disaster of Midway.

MAP above: *The Battle of the Coral Sea, the first major naval battle in history in which the opposing ships were never in visual contact.*
Below: *Flight deck scenes aboard a US carrier at Coral Sea.*

The Battle of Midway

By the middle of May 1942 the only military force between India and Hawaii capable of offering a meaningful offensive challenge to Japanese dominion was what remained of the US Pacific Fleet. It was to destroy this irritating remnant that the Japanese now proposed to occupy Midway, a provocation that, because of Midway's dangerous proximity to Pearl Harbor, would leave the Americans no choice but to commit their fleet in all-out battle.

Characteristically, the Japanese operation plan for this enterprise was at once daunting and over-elaborate. Fleet Admiral Isoroku Yamamoto would deploy an immense 162-ship armada which would include four of the six fleet carriers that Admiral Nagumo had used in the Pearl Harbor attack, three light carriers, nine battleships and numerous cruisers and destroyers, as well as 12 transports carrying 5000 troops. Although the bulk of this force, consisting of five separate groups, would converge on Midway, a smaller second force (made up of two groups) would head north to occupy Kiska and Attu in the Aleutians. (One object of this diversion was to split the US naval forces and/or outflank them.)

Although the Americans could not begin to match the overwhelming Japanese preponderance in matériel, they had at least two advantages. First, having broken the Japanese fleet code, they were well informed about Yamamoto's movements. Second, contrary to Japanese belief, they could deploy not two, but three fleet carriers, since they had been able to repair the heavy damage done to *Yorktown* in the Coral Sea in a miraculous 48 hours.

The small American Carrier Striking Force that sortied from Pearl Harbor to the defense of Midway late in May 1942 was under the overall command of Rear Admiral Frank J Fletcher, whose flagship, *Yorktown*, was the basis of Task Force 17. Sub-ordinate to Fletcher was Rear Admiral Raymond Spruance, commander of Task Force 16, which included *Enterprise* and *Hornet*. Their immediate, and most dangerous, opposition would be two advance prongs of Yamamoto's combined fleet – Nagumo's First Carrier Striking Force (centered on the fleet carriers *Akagi*, *Kaga*, *Hiryu* and *Soryu*) and Yamamoto's Main Body, which included seven battleships and a light carrier.

On the morning of 4 June the Japanese began their assault on Mid-

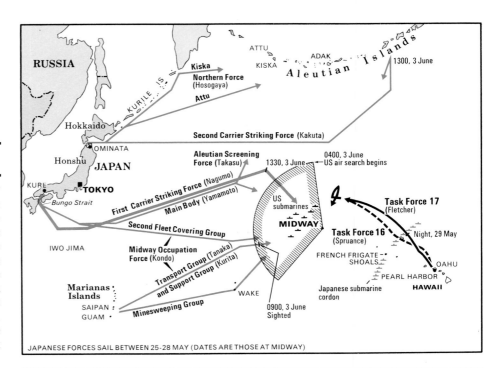

JAPANESE FORCES SAIL BETWEEN 25-28 MAY (DATES ARE THOSE AT MIDWAY)

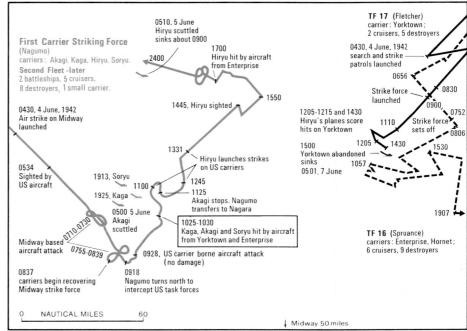

MAPS above: *The Battle of Midway showing the complicated Japanese plan with its rash dispersal of forces and the tracks of the carrier groups during the engagement.*

Above right: *Fire fighting and repair parties at work aboard the* Yorktown *after the first Japanese air attack.*

way with a 108-plane raid. The relatively few Midway-based warplanes that survived this attack then attempted a counterattack. Although the Zeros flying Combat Air Patrol over the Japanese carriers easily brushed aside this attempt, it was clear that at least one more raid on Midway would be needed to eliminate the remaining US aircraft. Thus the Japanese were in the midst of arming with high-explosive bombs appropriate for land targets when a reconnaissance plane reported the distressing news that US carriers were nearby. As the Japanese

frantically tried to re-arm with armor-piercing bombs and torpedoes the first US carrier strikes began coming in. At first they were beaten off with heavy loss, but then a dive bomber attack by planes of *Yorktown* and *Enterprise* broke through, and within minutes *Akagi*, *Kaga* and *Soryu* were all aflame and sinking. *Hiryu* retaliated with a strike that heavily damaged *Yorktown* (she was torpedoed by a Japanese submarine the next day and sank on the 7th), but then *Hiryu* in her turn was sunk by *Enterprise*'s dive bombers. Early on 5 May Yamamoto

ordered a general retirement from Midway, but not soon enough to avoid the cruiser *Mikuma* being sunk by dive bombers from *Hornet*.

Midway had dramatically altered the balance of naval power in the Pacific. Once the torpedo-damaged *Saratoga* was repaired, and when *Wasp* came into the Pacific from the Atlantic, the US Pacific Fleet would be able to deploy four fleet carriers; but now only new construction could raise the Japanese total above two. And any race for new construction was one American industry was bound to win.

Operation Torch and Tunisia

On 8 November 1942 the British and Americans undertook their first large-scale joint operation of World War II. This was Operation TORCH, a series of landings in French North Africa that were designed to cut off the escape route of German General Erwin Rommel's Afrika Korps, now in retreat after its defeat by the British at El Alamein in late October. The Allied landings were made in three areas. US troops under US General George S Patton went on shore at several points around Casablanca in Morocco, while in Algeria US and British troops under US General Lloyd Fredendall landed at Oran, and another Anglo-American force under US General Charles Ryder landed at Algiers. In overall command was US General Dwight D Eisenhower.

Earlier diplomatic efforts to persuade the local Vichy French not to oppose these landings had fallen short of complete success, and there was some sporadic fighting around Casablanca and Oran. But by 11 November all serious French resistance had ceased, and the Allied forces began to move east to attack the Germans in northern Tunisia. By early December the spearhead of this movement, the forces that had landed at Algiers, now designated the First Army and placed under the command of British General Sir Kenneth Anderson, had bogged down short of the Tunisian border, because of massive logistical problems and some spirited counterattacks by German armor. While the Allies tried to reinforce the stalled First Army, Field Marshal Albert Kesselring was also rapidly reinforcing his Wehrmacht troops in Tunisia from Sicily. Thus, when the Allies finally did manage to make their way into Tunisia early in 1943 they found themselves faced by a highly formidable, well-entrenched opposition.

In mid-February, taking advantage of poor disposal of First Army troops southwest of Tunis, the German Fifth Army launched a savage attack in the vicinity of Kasserine and inflicted 6500 casualties on the Americans and 4000 on the British at the Battle of the Kasserine Pass. Had the Germans followed up this success they might have produced a disaster for the Allies. As it was, the Allied forces in Tunisia, now under the field command of General Sir Harold Alexander, were soon able to resume their offensive, Anderson's First Army advancing from the west, while General Sir Bernard Montgomery's Eighth Army attacked from the south. By mid-April the German defensive perimeter had been compressed to an arc running from a little west of Bizerta to the southern base of the Cape Bon Peninsula, and the Axis air and sea supply lines to Tunisia had been effectively interdicted. During the first week of May the First Army succeeded in cracking the German line, and shortly thereafter the Eighth Army broke through in the south. By 7 May the Americans had occupied Bizerta and the British, Tunis. The remaining 250,000 Axis soldiers in Tunisia, whom Hitler had adamantly refused to evacuate while it was still possible, surrendered a week later. In all, the campaign had cost the Allies some 66,000 casualties, but this was deemed acceptable for exposing the whole German-occupied Mediterranean coast of Europe to potential invasion.

Right: *Landing craft bring supplies and reinforcements ashore at Oran during the early stages of Operation TORCH.*
MAP below: *The Allied landings in North Africa and the initial advances toward Tunisia.*

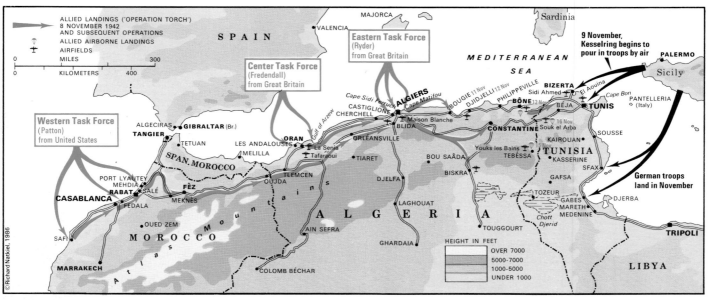

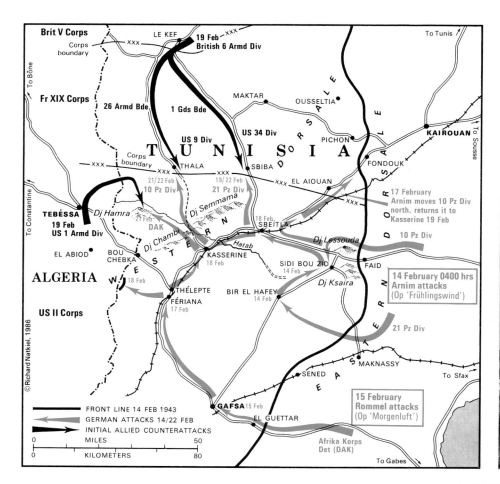

© Richard Natkiel, 1986

Brit V Corps
Corps boundary
Fr XIX Corps
To Bône
To Constantine

LE KEF
19 Feb
British 6 Armd Div
To Tunis

26 Armd Bde
1 Gds Bde
MAKTAR
OUSSELTIA

US 9 Div
US 34 Div
PICHON
KAIROUAN
To Sousse

T U N I S I A

Corps boundary
THALA
SBIBA
EL AIOUAN
FONDOUK

21/22 Feb
10 Pz Div
19/22 Feb
21 Pz Div

17 February
Arnim moves 10 Pz Div
north, returns it to
Kasserine 19 Feb

TEBÉSSA
19 Feb
US 1 Armd Div
Dj Hamra
21 Feb
DAK
Dj Semmama
18 Feb.
SBEITLA
10 Pz Div

EL ABIOD
BOU CHEBKA
Dj Chambi
KASSERINE
18 Feb
SIDI BOU ZID
14 Feb
FAID

ALGERIA
Hatab
Dj Lessouda
18 Feb

W
18 Feb
THÉLEPTE
FÉRIANA
17 Feb
BIR EL HAFEY
14 Feb
Dj Ksaira

14 February 0400 hrs
Arnim attacks
(Op 'Frühlingswind')

US II Corps
21 Pz Div

SENED
MAKNASSY
To Sfax

15 February
Rommel attacks
(Op 'Morgenluft')

GAFSA
15 Feb
EL GUETTAR

Afrika Korps
Det (DAK)
To Gabes

FRONT LINE 14 FEB 1943
GERMAN ATTACKS 14/22 FEB
INITIAL ALLIED COUNTERATTACKS

0 ――――― 50
MILES
0 ――――― 80
KILOMETERS

MAP left: *The Battle of Kasserine.*
Below: *General Patton (left) explains
his dispositions to the Supreme
Commander General Eisenhower at a
meeting in March 1943.*

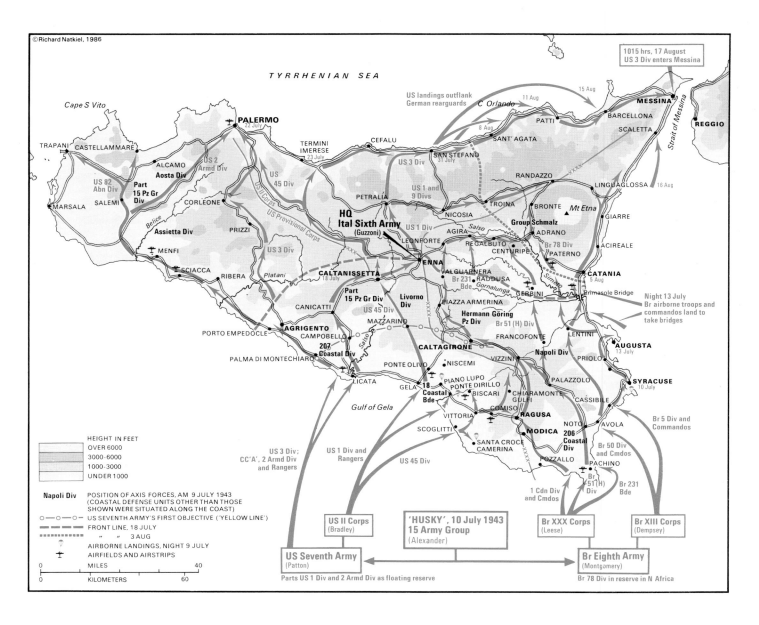

© Richard Natkiel, 1986

TYRRHENIAN SEA

Cape S Vito

1015 hrs, 17 August
US 3 Div enters Messina

US landings outflank
German rearguards

MESSINA

REGGIO

TRAPANI
CASTELLAMMARE
PALERMO
22 July
TERMINI
IMERESE
23 July
CEFALU
SAN STEFANO
31 July
SANT' AGATA
C Orlando
11 Aug
8 Aug
15 Aug
PATTI
BARCELLONA
SCALETTA
Strait of Messina

ALCAMO
US 2
Armd Div
US
45 Div
US 3 Div
RANDAZZO
LINGUAGLOSSA
16 Aug

US 82
Abn Div
SALEMI
Part
15 Pz Gr
Div
Aosta Div
CORLEONE
PETRALIA
US 1 and
9 Divs
NICOSIA
TROINA
BRONTE
Mt Etna
GIARRE

MARSALA
Assietta Div
PRIZZI
HQ
Ital Sixth Army
(Guzzoni)
LEONFORTE
AGIRA
Salso
Group Schmalz
ADRANO
ACIREALE

MENFI
SCIACCA
RIBERA
Belice
Platani
ENNA
REGALBUTO
CENTURIPE
Br 78
Div
PATERNO
CATANIA
5 Aug

US 3 Div
CALTANISSETTA
18 July
VALGUARNERA
Br 231
Bde
RADDUSA
Gornalunga
GERBINI
Simeto
Primosole Bridge
Night 13 July
Br airborne troops and
commandos land to
take bridges

CANICATTI
Part
15 Pz Gr Div
Livorno
Div
US 45 Div
PIAZZA ARMERINA
Hermann Göring
Pz Div
Br 51 (H) Div

PORTO EMPEDOCLE
AGRIGENTO
CAMPOBELLO
MAZZARINO
Salso
CALTAGIRONE
Napoli Div
FRANCOFONTE
LENTINI
AUGUSTA
13 July

PALMA DI MONTECHIARO
207
Coastal Div
VIZZINI
PRIOLO
PALAZZOLO
SYRACUSE
10 July

LICATA
PONTE OLIVO
NISCEMI
GELA
18
Coastal
Bde
PIANO LUPO
PONTE DIRILLO
BISCARI
CHIARAMONTE
GULFI
COMISO
RAGUSA
NOTO
CASSIBILE
AVOLA
Br 5 Div and
Commandos

Gulf of Gela
VITTORIA
SCOGLITTI
SANTA CROCE
CAMERINA
MODICA
206
Coastal
Div
PACHINO
POZZALLO
Br 50 Div
and Cmdos
Br 231
Bde

US 3 Div;
CC'A', 2 Armd Div
and Rangers
US 1 Div and
Rangers
US 45 Div
1 Cdn Div
and Cmdos
Br
51 (H)
Div

HEIGHT IN FEET
OVER 6000
3000-6000
1000-3000
UNDER 1000

Napoli Div — POSITION OF AXIS FORCES, AM 9 JULY 1943
(COASTAL DEFENSE UNITS OTHER THAN THOSE
SHOWN WERE SITUATED ALONG THE COAST)
○—○—○ US SEVENTH ARMY'S FIRST OBJECTIVE ('YELLOW LINE')
FRONT LINE, 18 JULY
" " 3 AUG
AIRBORNE LANDINGS, NIGHT 9 JULY
AIRFIELDS AND AIRSTRIPS

MILES   40
KILOMETERS   60

US II Corps
(Bradley)

'HUSKY', 10 July 1943
15 Army Group
(Alexander)

Br XXX Corps
(Leese)

Br XIII Corps
(Dempsey)

US Seventh Army
(Patton)
Parts US 1 Div and 2 Armd Div as floating reserve

Br Eighth Army
(Montgomery)
Br 78 Div in reserve in N Africa

The Invasion of Sicily

In January 1943, even before the fighting in Tunisia had entered its final phase, Allied leaders were debating what to do after North Africa had been secured. Although the Americans persisted (as they had since early 1942) in recommending an early invasion of France, the British felt such a large enterprise to be premature and recommended that further operations in the Mediterranean be undertaken first. British opinion prevailed, and thus was born the plan for Operation HUSKY, an invasion of Sicily.

HUSKY would be the largest amphibious operation thus far attempted. Some 80,000 troops, with 7000 vehicles, 600 tanks and 900

artillery pieces were to be landed in 48 hours. General Sir Bernard Montgomery's British Eighth Army would land on the southeastern tip of the island and drive straight north to Messina. General George S Patton's American Seventh Army would land in the vicinity of the Gulf of Gela and cover Montgomery's left flank during the drive north. In overall command would be British General Sir Harold Alexander. The opposition to be overcome would consist of nine divisions of the Italian Sixth Army and about 30,000 Germans belonging to the crack Hermann Göring Panzer and 15th Panzer Grenadier Divisions. D-Day was set for 10 July 1943.

Although the preliminary airborne assaults that were supposed to prepare the way for the landings were so

bungled as to be a near fiasco, the Axis defenders were nevertheless caught by surprise, and not only did the main bodies of troops get on shore successfully, but fierce German counterattacks on 11–12 July failed to dislodge them. Yet the Germans, soon reinforced by an additional 50,000 troops, did succeed in slowing Montgomery's northward advance to such a degree that Alexander finally acceded to Patton's request that the Seventh Army be detached from Montgomery's flank and embark on a broad encircling maneuver that would take the Seventh all the way to Palermo, on Sicily's northwest coast. Patton moved very fast, and when he arrived in Palermo on 22 July he found that the Germans there were already in the process of retreating eastward towards Messina.

MAP left: *The Allied invasion and capture of Sicily.*
Below: *Troops of the British 51st Highland Division come ashore on Sicily at the start of the fighting for the island.*

MAP *left:* Overview of the Italian campaign showing the various defense lines with which the Germans slowed the Allied advance.

Map labels:
Line reached by Allied forces in Western Europe, 7 May 1945
AUSTRIA
Brenner Pass
Line reached by Russian forces. 7 May 1945
SWITZERLAND
HUNGARY
TRENTO
TREVISO
UDINE
COMO
Danube
VERONA
PADUA
TRIESTE
MILAN
Po
Adige
VENICE
Drava
Line reached by Yugoslav partisans. 7 May 1945
TURIN
PIACENZA
YUGOSLAVIA
GENOA
BOLOGNA
23 Apr
15 Jan - 8 Apr 1945
RAVENNA
FRANCE
25 Sept 1944
RIMINI
Gothic Line
FLORENCE
SAN MARINO
PESARO
Arno
4 - 26 Aug 1944
ANCONA
LEGHORN
CECINA
AREZZO
17 June
POGGIBONSI
PERUGIA
ELBA
L.Trasimeno
Corsica
Evacuated by German Forces, 18 Sept-3 Oct, 1943
ORVIETO
TERNI
15 Jan - 11 May 1944
9 June
PESCARA
Gustav Line
Allies enter Rome 4 June 1944
ROME
8 Oct 1943
28 Sept
Sardinia
Evacuated by German Forces, 18 Sept, 1943
5 June
CASSINO
FOGGIA
19 Feb
ANZIO
TERRACINA
25 Sept
BARI
14 Sept
TYRRHENIAN SEA
GAETA
Garigliano
Volturno
NAPLES
BRINDISI
Op. "Shingle" 22 Jan 1944
SALERNO
AULETTA
TARANTO
CAGLIARI
Op. "Avalanche" 9 Sept 1943
14 Sept
14 Sept
Op. "Slapstick" 9 Sept 1943
3 Sept 1943 Italy surrenders
CORIGLIANO CALABRO
9 Sept
TRAPANI
PALERMO
MESSINA
REGGIO
ENNA
17 Aug
Op. "Baytown" 3 Sept 1943
Sicily
CATANIA
23 July
LICATA
GELA
SYRACUSE
PANTELLERIA
11 June
AVOLA
ALGERIA
TUNISIA
Op. "Husky" 10 July 1943
FRONT LINE AT DATE SHOWN
US FIFTH ARMY
BRITISH EIGHTH ARMY
LINOSA
MALTA (Br.)
MILES 200
LAMPEDUSA
KILOMETERS 300
©Richard Natkiel, 1986

The Italian Campaign

The Anglo-American invasion of Italy began on 3 September 1943, the same day that Italy signed the armistice that withdrew her from the war. The Allies' opening gambit was a British Eighth Army landing on the toe of the Italian boot at Reggio di Calabria, followed by a steady drive north through Calabria. The Germans were not deceived into imagining that this represented the extent of Allied strategic planning.

A more serious blow was struck on the 9th when US General Mark W Clark's 70,000-man Anglo-American Fifth Army came on shore at Salerno, 25 miles south of Naples, in an operation code named AVALANCHE. The Germans, who already had four divisions at the ready around the Gulf of Salerno, were at first able to confine the invaders to a string of shallow beachheads and to subject them to merciless shelling. Yet during the

He followed at once. Although fighting along the way was sometimes bitter, Patton made shrewd use of his naval support, both for shore bombardment and to make amphibious 'leapfrogging' attacks behind German strongpoints. Again his progress was remarkably swift. Meantime, Montgomery had at last broken through the German lines before Catania, and his advance also began to gather momentum. On 17 August Patton arrived in Messina, two hours ahead of the British, to complete the conquest of Sicily. About 45,000 Germans and 70,000 Italians managed to escape capture by crossing the

Straits of Messina to Italy, but 157,000 others were not so fortunate.

The invasion of Sicily had considerable effects on the course of the war. It prompted Italian King Victor Emmanuel II to depose Mussolini in July and convinced the Italian government that it was time to drop out of the war. More important, it provided the Allies with the necessary staging area from which to launch an invasion of Italy. In anticipation of this inevitability the Germans were already deploying their divisions in the central and southern parts of the Italian peninsula.

MAP below: *The landings at Salerno were fiercely contested by the Germans in the hope of deterring the Allies from further amphibious operations in Europe.*
Bottom: *The 92nd Division crossing the River Arno in January 1944.*

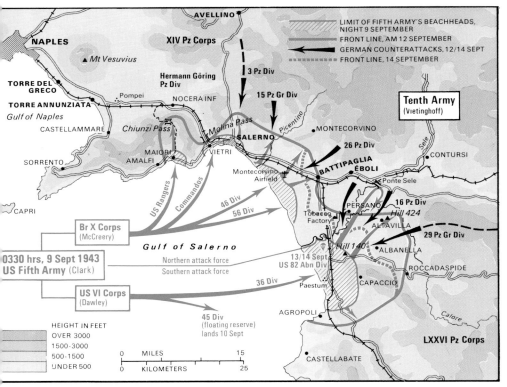

AVELLINO

NAPLES

XIV Pz Corps

Mt Vesuvius

LIMIT OF FIFTH ARMY'S BEACHHEADS, NIGHT 9 SEPTEMBER
FRONT LINE, AM 12 SEPTEMBER
GERMAN COUNTERATTACKS, 12/14 SEPT
FRONT LINE, 14 SEPTEMBER

TORRE DEL GRECO

Hermann Göring Pz Div

3 Pz Div

TORRE ANNUNZIATA
Gulf of Naples

Pompei

NOCERA INF

15 Pz Gr Div

Tenth Army
(Vietinghoff)

CASTELLAMMARE

Chiunzi Pass

Molina Pass

Picentino

SALERNO

MONTECORVINO

SORRENTO

MAIORI

VIETRI

AMALFI

Montecorvino Airfield

26 Pz Div

BATTIPAGLIA

EBOLI

CONTURSI

Sele

CAPRI

US Rangers

Commandos

46 Div

56 Div

Ponte Sele

Tobacco Factory

PERSANO

16 Pz Div

Hill 424

ALTAVILLA

29 Pz Gr Div

Br X Corps
(McCreery)

Gulf of Salerno

Hill 140

ALBANELLA

0330 hrs, 9 Sept 1943
US Fifth Army (Clark)

Northern attack force
Southern attack force

13/14 Sept
US 82 Abn Div

ROCCADASPIDE

US VI Corps
(Dawley)

36 Div

Paestum

CAPACCIO

AGROPOLI

45 Div
(floating reserve)
lands 10 Sept

Calore

HEIGHT IN FEET
OVER 3000
1500-3000
500-1500
UNDER 500

MILES   15
KILOMETERS   25

LXXVI Pz Corps

CASTELLABATE

next three days the Allies succeeded in consolidating their beachheads and moving their front a few miles inland. Between the 12th and 14th savage German counterattacks came close to undoing the whole operation, but timely reinforcements saved the day. And when, by the 16th, advance units of the Eighth Army began to near the area, German Field Marshal Albert Kesselring chose to withdraw his forces slowly northward towards a prepared chain of defensive positions, the 'Gustav Line,' that spanned the entire Italian peninsula north of Naples.

The Allies pursued the Germans until 8 October, at which time they called a rest halt along a line Volturno/Termoli, about 15 miles north of Naples. The Gustav Line now lay between 15 and 35 miles ahead of the positions occupied by the Fifth Army on the left and about 35 miles ahead of the Eighth Army's sector on the right. The advance resumed on the 12th, but now added to the difficulties posed by fierce German resistance were freezing winter rains and – especially in the west – terrain so mountainous as to slow vehicular traffic to a crawl. It took the Allies over a month and many casualties even to reach the Gustav Line, and then, except for a small British success on the extreme right, they found themselves unable to breach the line for the remainder of the year.

In January 1944 the Fifth Army launched Operation SHINGLE, an amphibious operation designed to out-flank the western end of the Gustav Line by landing the Anglo-American VI Corps north of the line at Anzio. The initial landings, beginning on 22 January, went well, but the commanding officer, US General John Lucas, was slow in leaving the beachhead and moving inland. Kesselring, on the other hand, moved very swiftly and soon surrounded the beachhead with a hastily-improvised 125,000-man army (Fourteenth Army). Although the Allies barely managed to beat off a series of powerful attacks designed to drive

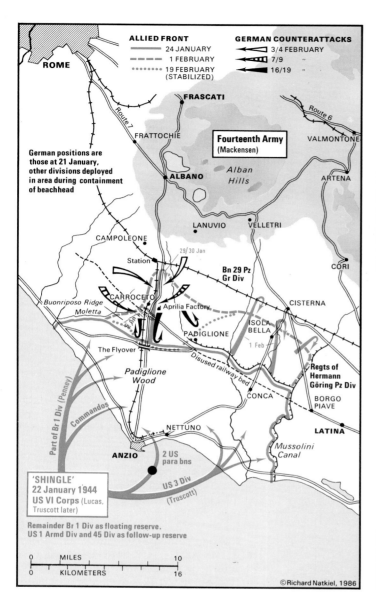

ALLIED FRONT
— 24 JANUARY
--- 1 FEBRUARY
···· 19 FEBRUARY
(STABILIZED)

GERMAN COUNTERATTACKS
◄— 3/4 FEBRUARY
◄◼◼◼ 7/9 "
◄◼◼ 16/19 "

ROME

FRASCATI

Route 7

FRATTOCHIE

Route 6

VALMONTONE

German positions are
those at 21 January,
other divisions deployed
in area during containment
of beachhead

ALBANO

Alban
Hills

Fourteenth Army
(Mackensen)

ARTENA

LANUVIO

VELLETRI

CORI

CAMPOLEONE

29/30 Jan

Station

Bn 29 Pz
Gr Div

Buonriposo Ridge
Moletta

CARROCETO

Aprilia Factory

CISTERNA

PADIGLIONE

ISOLA
BELLA

1 Feb

The Flyover

Disused railway bed

Regts of
Hermann
Göring Pz Div

Padiglione
Wood

CONCA

BORGO
PIAVE

Part of Br 1 Div (Penney)

Commandos

NETTUNO

LATINA

ANZIO

2 US
para bns

Mussolini
Canal

'SHINGLE'
22 January 1944
US VI Corps (Lucas,
Truscott later)

US 3 Div
(Truscott)

Remainder Br 1 Div as floating reserve.
US 1 Armd Div and 45 Div as follow-up reserve

MILES   0 ————— 10
KILOMETERS   0 ————— 16

©Richard Natkiel, 1986

MAP left: *The Anzio landings.*
Below: *105mm howitzers of the 598th
Field Artillery in action in Italy in
August 1944.*

them into the sea, they could not break out of the beachhead. For the next three months they were held in a state of siege, enduring incessant shelling and air raids and suffering a grisly 59,000 casualties. When, on 23 May, they finally did break out, it was only because the Gustav Line had been breached elsewhere.

Since November 1943 it had become increasingly obvious to the Allies that the area around Cassino was the most promising place for the Fifth Army to try to break through the Gustav Line. Daunting natural barriers of mountains and rivers flanked Cassino, but the town itself lay in the Liri Valley, comparatively low ground through which Autostrada 6 wound its way northwest towards Rome. Nevertheless, two considerable obstacles lay athwart this potential route

of advance: the well-defended Rapido River and the even more formidable heights of Monte Cassino, from which German small arms and artillery fire could dominate all that part of the valley.

The Allies managed to fight their way across to a few tenuously held positions on the far bank of the Rapido, though it took them most of the latter part of January 1944 and cost them many lives, but in the weeks that followed every effort they made to storm the slopes of Monte Cassino was bloodily repulsed, as were all simultaneous attempts to breach the Gustav Line elsewhere. On 15 February, acting on the mistaken idea that the 6th century Benedictine abbey that stood on the crest of Monte Cassino was being used as a German command post, the Allies bombed it to the ground. This cultur-

ally expensive deed proved to be militarily irrelevant, since the Germans were better protected in the abbey's rubble than they ever had been by the standing structure.

For the next three months the Fifth Army made no significant headway against either Monte Cassino or any other part of the line, but continuous Allied air strikes on the supply routes in the German rear slowly began to sap the defenders' strength. On 11 May the Allies launched a general offensive against the whole southwestern part of the line, from about 10 miles north of Monte Cassino to the Tyrrhenian coast. Neither the British on the right nor the Americans on the left made much progress. In the center, however, about 12 miles south of Monte Cassino, General Alphonse Juin's Free French Expeditionary

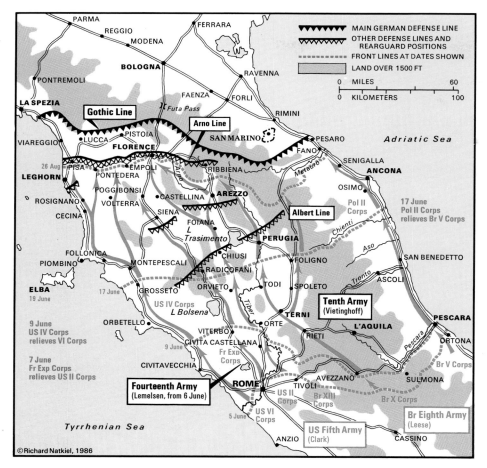

MAP top: *The Italian campaign in the summer of 1944 showing the slow Allied advance to the Gothic Line.*
Above: *B-25 Mitchell bombers of the Twelfth Air Force fly over Mount Vesuvius on their way to attack German positions near Monte Cassino.*

Corps achieved a major breakthrough. In the following days the Germans slowly began to withdraw, and on the 18th Monte Cassino at last fell to the Allies. The Allies' northward advance, so long delayed, could now proceed.

On 4 June 1944 (two days before D-Day in France) the Allies entered Rome, and by late August they were north of Arezzo and preparing to assault the Germans' final defensive position, the Gothic Line, which ran roughly east-west from a little south of La Spezia on the Tyrrhenian Sea to an approximately equal distance south of Rimini on the Adriatic. By the end of the year Fifth Army had breached this line on the west and Eighth Army, on the east, but continuing dogged German resistance, the onset of another grim winter and the general exhaustion of the Allied troops made further exploitation of these successes impossible. It was not until the following spring, during the final months of World War II in Europe, that the offensive was resumed.

During the winter General Clark had assumed overall command of the Allied armies in Italy, turning command of the Fifth Army over to US General Lucius Truscott. As before, the Fifth occupied the left of the Allied Line and the Eighth, the right. Clark began his final offensive on 9 April 1945. By the 23rd Bologna had been captured and elements of both armies had entered the eastern Po Valley. Now they diverged. The Eighth wheeled east, slicing through the crumbling German Tenth Army to take Padua, Venice and Trieste in rapid succession. Simultaneously the Fifth brushed aside the German Fourteenth Army and the somewhat notional Italian Ligurian Army in a wide-ranging advance that took the Fifth as far west as Turin and Milan by 2 May and, by 6 May, as far north as the Brenner Pass, where it met with elements of the US Seventh Army coming south from Germany. But even before that, on 29 April 1945, the formal surrender of the German forces in Italy had begun.

The Italian campaign had lasted 20 months, had cost the Allies heavily in blood and treasure and had not ended until Germany itself had been invaded and defeated. Certainly it had diverted many badly-needed German troops from other fronts, but precisely how important it was to the Allies' final victory is still a matter of debate.

MAP below: *The land fighting on Guadalcanal.*
Bottom: *Scene during a Japanese air attack on a US supply convoy off Guadalcanal in November 1942. Nearest the camera is the transport President Jackson.*

The Solomons Campaign

After the Battle of Midway the Americans were understandably eager to exploit their fortuitous victory, yet Allied grand strategy dictated that the European theater should be given priority. Thus, in the summer of 1942 most US military resources were being concentrated on preparations for the forthcoming invasion of North Africa, and little was available for operations elsewhere. Plainly, any US offensive action in the Pacific at this time would have to be limited in scale, and there was much debate about what undertaking would be most strategically effective.

In the end, it was decided that the Solomon Islands would be the most appropriate target. The Japanese had made Rabaul, New Britain, the hub of their air and naval power in the Southwest Pacific, and they were now thrusting out spokes from this hub in the form of advance airbases being built in the Solomons. If the Americans could seize these islands they would not only

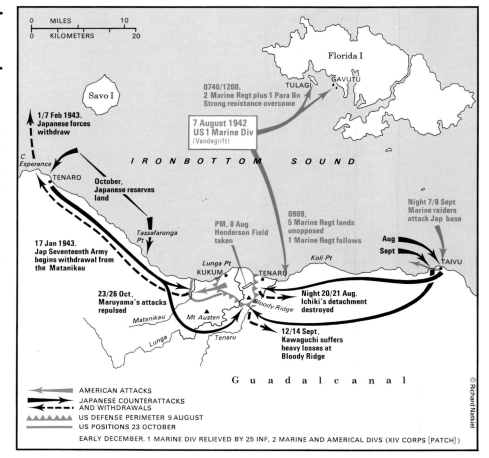

0 MILES 10
0 KILOMETERS 20

Florida I

Savo I

TULAGI   GAVUTU

0740/1200,
2 Marine Regt plus 1 Para Bn
Strong resistance overcome

1/7 Feb 1943,
Japanese forces
withdraw

7 August 1942
US 1 Marine Div
(Vandegrift)

C
Esperance

IRONBOTTOM   SOUND

TENARO

October,
Japanese reserves
land

Night 7/8 Sept
Marine raiders
attack Jap base

Tassafaronga
Pt

0909,
5 Marine Regt lands
unopposed
1 Marine Regt follows

PM, 8 Aug
Henderson Field
taken

Koli Pt

Aug
Sept

17 Jan 1943,
Jap Seventeenth Army
begins withdrawal from
the Matanikau

Lunga Pt
KUKUM

TENARU

TAIVU

Night 20/21 Aug,
Ichiki's detachment
destroyed

23/26 Oct,
Maruyama's attacks
repulsed

Bloody Ridge

Matanikau   Mt Austen

12/14 Sept,
Kawaguchi suffers
heavy losses at
Bloody Ridge

Lunga   Tenaru

G u a d a l c a n a l

© Richard Natkiel

⟶ AMERICAN ATTACKS
⟶ JAPANESE COUNTERATTACKS
---- AND WITHDRAWALS
▲▲▲ US DEFENSE PERIMETER 9 AUGUST
〰〰 US POSITIONS 23 OCTOBER

EARLY DECEMBER, 1 MARINE DIV RELIEVED BY 25 INF, 2 MARINE AND AMERICAL DIVS (XIV CORPS [PATCH])

interrupt the Japanese plan to forge a ring of bases around eastern Australia but would gain bases of their own from which to strike at Rabaul.

The informal code name Operation SHOESTRING (formally, it was WATCHTOWER), was a wry acknowledgment of the slender resources with which the hastily-mounted US invasion on the Solomons would have to be carried out. Admiral Frank J Fletcher was to be in overall tactical command, and General Alexander Vandegrift would lead the 19,000 US Marines allocated for the initial landings on the islands of Guadalcanal and Tulagi. D-Day was set for 7 August 1942.

The landing on Guadalcanal proved to be relatively easy: there were only 2200 Japanese on the island, and these were mostly construction workers. By the evening of the 7th 11,000 Marines were on shore, and the next morning they took control of Guadalcanal's airfield, thereafter called Henderson Field. The small island of Tulagi, 20 miles north of Guadalcanal, proved somewhat more difficult, the 6000 Marine invaders having to fight hard for two days before subduing the 1500 Japanese defenders. Nevertheless, the opening phases of WATCHTOWER had gone well, and by 20 August the first US planes were beginning to land on Henderson Field.

The Japanese were, however, in no way content to let this invasion pass unchallenged. Although US land-based and carrier-based aircraft soon established local daytime control of the sea, at night Japanese naval squadrons were able to land troops on Guadalcanal and to shell US installations there. By early September there were 6000 Japanese regular troops on the island, a number that swelled to 20,000 in little more than a month. Throughout the remainder of the year a series of fierce battles was fought both on Guadalcanal and on the surrounding waters (qv), and it was not until early February 1943 that the Japanese, increasingly frustrated in their efforts to supply and reinforce

their troops on Guadalcanal, finally chose to evacuate the island. In the six months of fighting they had sustained 25,000 casualties and considerable naval and air losses.

While the long battle to secure Guadalcanal was being fought, the Allies, under General Douglas MacArthur, had been enjoying equal success in Papua New Guinea. By September they had thwarted Japanese attempts both to strike at Port Moresby from bases on the northern coast and to take Milne Bay, on New Guinea's extreme eastern tip. And by the end of 1942 the Allies had established control over the whole north coast of Papua from Milne Bay to Buna. As a result, it now became possible to think in terms of launching a two-pronged offensive against Rabaul itself. MacArthur's western prong would proceed up the north coast of New Guinea to the Huon Peninsula, cross the straits to New Britain and thrust across the island to Rabaul. The eastern prong, under the direction of Admiral William Halsey, would simultaneously mount the Solomons island chain until it was in a position to close on Rabaul from the opposite direction. How difficult all this would be was perhaps not fully taken into account: it would take MacArthur a year to reach the Huon Peninsula and cross the straits, and it would take Halsey at least as long to conquer the Solomons.

Halsey initiated the second phase of the Solomons campaign on 20 June 1943 when he began the invasion of the islands of New Georgia and Rendova, northwest of Guadalcanal. It took a month and a half of savage fighting to vanquish the 10,000 Japanese defending these islands and to secure the vital airstrip at Munda, on New Georgia. Then, in a tactic that would become standard in the Pacific war, Halsey bypassed the next island to the north, Kolombangara, and landed instead on its northern neighbor, Vella Lavella. This landing (15 August) was virtually unopposed by the surprised Japanese, and the powerful Kolombangara garrison was neu-

tralized at a stroke.

Unfortunately, the remaining major Solomons target, Bougainville, only 250 air miles from Rabaul, could not be 'leapfrogged.' This island was 125 miles long, contained six airfields and was defended by 60,000 Japanese army and navy personnel. Halsey began his attack by making a diversionary landing on the island of Choiseul, southeast of Bougainville, on 28 October. Then, with Japanese attention firmly fixed on Choiseul, he made his main landing on Bougainville in the vicinity of Empress Augusta Bay on 1 November. Although caught by surprise, the Japanese soon began their counterattacks, but these were delivered piecemeal, and the 3rd Marine Division, reinforced by the Army's 37th Division on 9 November, slowly fought their way inland. By the end of the year, when MacArthur's forces already had a foothold on New Britain, Bougainville was still far from secured. But the Americans on Bougainville nevertheless held enough of the island to activate three airfields, from which they at once began to bomb Rabaul.

Yet now the physical capture of Rabaul seemed less attractive to the Allies than it had a year earlier. A hub without spokes, vulnerable to overwhelming land-based and carrier-based air attacks, Rabaul had been effectively neutralized for all important strategic purposes. The US Navy's huge island-hopping offensive across the Pacific had already begun, and it was time to unleash MacArthur for the conquest of the remainder of New Guinea. The Allies' new objective was not the single naval base of Rabaul, but the whole of the Philippine Islands. So, in the end, Rabaul was bypassed, and the Solomons campaign gradually wound down to the necessary, but strategically secondary task of rooting out the last vestiges of Japanese resistance on Bougainville. This was not finally accomplished until April 1944. By that time the drive in the Pacific was already being accelerated.

MAP 1: *The Battle of Savo Island,*
8–9 August 1942.
MAP 2: *The Battle of the Eastern*
Solomons, 24–25 August 1942.
Below: *The American carrier* Wasp
on fire and sinking after being
hit by the Japanese submarine I.19.

The Solomons Naval Campaign

While the US Army and Marines were battling their way up the islands of the Solomons chain the US Navy was engaged in an equally violent and important struggle for control of the surrounding waters. Although the American victory at Midway had put the US Pacific Fleet and the Imperial Japanese Navy on a more nearly equal footing in terms of potential power, which fleet would subsequently win the upper hand was still very much in doubt. The naval battles of the Solomons campaign put this to the test.

The first round went to the Japanese. On the night of 8–9 August 1942, 24 hours after the Marines first landed on Guadalcanal and Tulagi, a strong force of IJN cruisers surprised a group of Allied warships patrolling off Savo Island. In a dazzling demonstration of night-fighting skill, the Japanese quickly, and without loss to themselves, sank the US cruisers *Astoria*, *Quincy* and *Vincennes*, the Australian

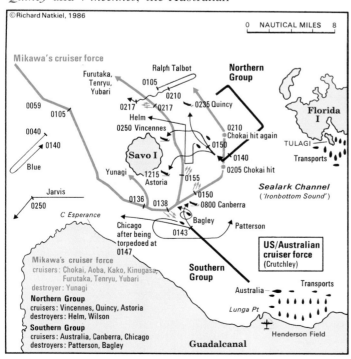

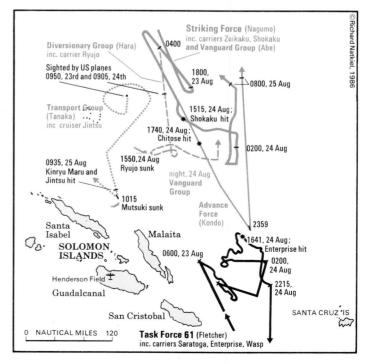

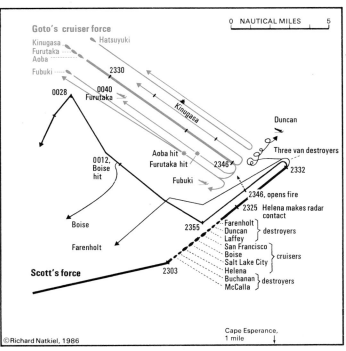

MAP 3: *The Battle of Cape Esperance, 11–12 October 1942.*
MAP 4: *The Battle of Santa Cruz, 26 October 1942.*

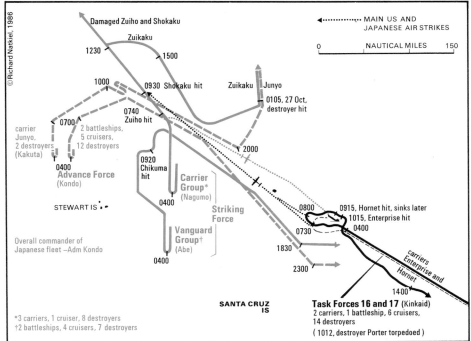

cruiser *Canberra* and a destroyer. They did not destroy any of the transports landing troops on the islands.

As US airpower on and around Guadalcanal grew, it became increasingly dangerous for Japanese ships to enter the southern Solomons area during the daylight hours, though they could and did move freely at night. In August the Japanese made one of their few challenges to US daytime superiority by sending to Guadalcanal a large convoy supported by the two remaining IJN fleet carriers, *Zuikaku* and *Shokaku*, and the light carrier *Ryujo*. This was intercepted by aircraft from the US fleet carriers *Enterprise*, *Saratoga* and *Wasp*. In the ensuing round of aerial strikes and counterstrikes on 23–5 August (the Battle of the Eastern Solomons) *Enterprise*, *Shokaku* and the IJN seaplane carrier *Chitose* were damaged, and *Ryujo* was sunk. The next day US

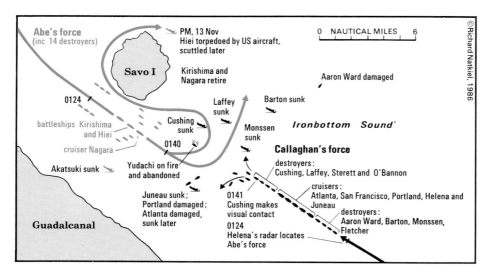

Map left:

Abe's force (inc 14 destroyers)

PM, 13 Nov
Hiei torpedoed by US aircraft, scuttled later

Savo I

0   NAUTICAL MILES   6

© Richard Natkiel, 1986

Kirishima and Nagara retire

0124

battleships Kirishima and Hiei

cruiser Nagara

Cushing sunk

0140

Aaron Ward damaged

Laffey sunk

Barton sunk

Monssen sunk

'Ironbottom Sound'

Callaghan's force

destroyers:
Cushing, Laffey, Sterett and O'Bannon

Akatsuki sunk

Yudachi on fire and abandoned

cruisers:
Atlanta, San Francisco, Portland, Helena and Juneau

0141
Cushing makes visual contact

Juneau sunk; Portland damaged; Atlanta damaged, sunk later

0124
Helena's radar locates Abe's force

destroyers:
Aaron Ward, Barton, Monssen, Fletcher

Guadalcanal

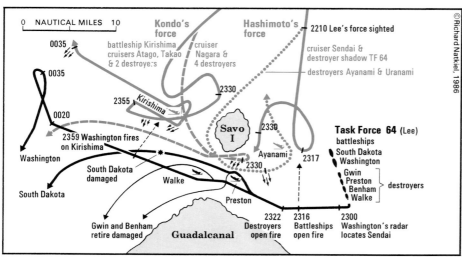

Map center:

0   NAUTICAL MILES   10

© Richard Natkiel, 1986

Kondo's force

Hashimoto's force

2210 Lee's force sighted

0035

battleship Kirishima cruisers Atago, Takao & 2 destroyers

cruiser Nagara & 4 destroyers

cruiser Sendai & destroyer shadow TF 64

0035

destroyers Ayanami & Uranami

2355   Kirishima

2330

0020

2330

Savo I

Task Force 64 (Lee)

battleships
South Dakota
Washington

2359 Washington fires on Kirishima

Washington

Ayanami

2330

2317

Gwin
Preston
Benham
Walke

destroyers

South Dakota damaged

Walke

South Dakota

Preston

2322
Destroyers open fire

2316
Battleships open fire

2300
Washington's radar locates Sendai

Gwin and Benham retire damaged

Guadalcanal

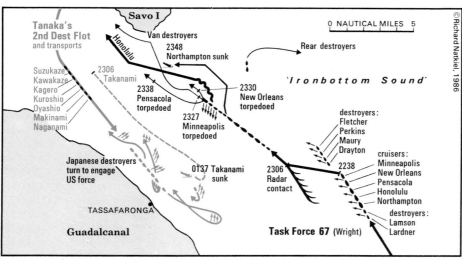

Map bottom:

Savo I

Tanaka's 2nd Dest Flot and transports

Van destroyers

0   NAUTICAL MILES   5

© Richard Natkiel, 1986

2348 Northampton sunk

Rear destroyers

Honolulu

2306 Takanami

Suzukaze
Kawakaze
Kagero
Kuroshio
Oyashio
Makinami
Naganami

2338
Pensacola torpedoed

2330
New Orleans torpedoed

'Ironbottom Sound'

2327
Minneapolis torpedoed

destroyers:
Fletcher
Perkins
Maury
Drayton

Japanese destroyers turn to engage US force

0137 Takanami sunk

2306
Radar contact

2238

cruisers:
Minneapolis
New Orleans
Pensacola
Honolulu
Northampton

TASSAFARONGA

destroyers:
Lamson
Lardner

Guadalcanal

Task Force 67 (Wright)

MAP left: *First stage of the Naval Battle of Guadalcanal on the night of 12–13 November 1942.*
MAP center: *The battle continued on the night of 13–14 November.*
MAP bottom: *The Battle of Tassafaronga, 30 November–1 December 1942.*

heavy cruiser *Furutaka* and a destroyer, and the Americans a destroyer. On 26 October, in another carrier duel (the Battle of Santa Cruz), *Hornet* was sunk and *Enterprise* was again damaged, while the Japanese sustained major damage to the carriers *Shokaku* and *Zuiho*. The two navies clashed again on 12–15 November in the sprawling nighttime Naval Battle of Guadalcanal, in which the Japanese lost the battleships *Hiei* and *Kirishima* and two destroyers, and the Americans the cruisers *Juneau* and *Atlanta* and five destroyers (both sides suffering serious damage to numerous other ships). And in a final round of fighting in the waters around Guadalcanal on the night of 30 November–1 December (the Battle of Tassafaronga) the Americans suffered heavy damage to three cruisers and lost a fourth, *Northampton*.

US troops finally secured Guadalcanal in February 1943, but the naval war raged on as the Americans slowly ascended the Solomons chain. The US cruiser *Helena* was sunk early in July in one of several naval encounters attendant to the invasion of New Georgia, and later that month the Japanese lost the cruiser *Jintsu*, and the Americans a destroyer, in the Battle of Kolombangara. Three more IJN destroyers were sunk in the Battle of Vella Gulf in August, and on the night of 2 November, in a battle that erupted when IJN warships attempted to interfere with the US landing on Bougainville at Empress Augusta Bay, the Japanese lost the cruiser *Sendai* and a destroyer, and the Americans a destroyer.

The losses and damage suffered by both sides in the Solomons naval campaign were painful in the extreme, but now that the American war industry was fully mobilized the Americans could make up their losses very much faster than the Japanese could ever hope to make up theirs. In fact, it was in this superficially even-handed war of attrition in the Solomons that the Americans finally won naval supremacy in the Pacific.

land-based aircraft so savaged the remaining Japanese force that it was obliged to retire.

Attrition in this grim naval campaign mounted steadily throughout the remainder of 1942 as each side attempted to prevent the other from re-supplying and reinforcing its troops on shore. On 31 August a Japanese submarine severely damaged *Saratoga*, and on 14 September another submarine sank *Wasp*. In the night Battle of Cape Esperance, fought on 11–12 October, the Japanese lost the

MAP right: *The US defense zones and the U-Boat campaign April–December 1941.*

Battle of the Atlantic

Well before the United States entered the war, her ships were in action against German submarines in the Atlantic. The Lend-Lease Bill, ensuring US supplies for embattled Britain, was passed in March 1941, and in the following month it was decided that the so-called Defense Zone, the waters adjacent to the American continent, would be extended to 26 degrees W, almost the longitude of Iceland. In the summer this line, where US escorts handed over their convoys to the Royal Navy, was moved further out, to mid-Atlantic. With German U-Boats preying on shipping bound to and from Britain, it was inevitable that, in time, US escorts would be mistaken for British. In September the destroyer *Greer* was unsuccessfully attacked by a U-Boat, and dropped depth charges in reply. In October the destroyer *Kearney* was damaged by a torpedo, and a few days later USS *Reuben James*, another destroyer, was sunk with heavy loss of life.

Admiral Dönitz, commanding German submarine operations, had plans prepared for a possible US entry into the war, and in December 1941 Operation DRUMROLL was born. Expecting, correctly, that the Americans would be unprepared, and aware that his submarines were hard-pressed by the British in the Eastern Atlantic, Dönitz diverted most of his forces to the US Atlantic seaboard and Gulf of Mexico where, for about six months, they waged a highly destructive war against both ocean and coastal shipping. US anti-submarine tactics were primitive, and suitable ships and aircraft were not available. Much of the coastal trade had to be transferred to the railroads, while many cargoes destined for Britain were lost almost as soon as they left harbor. In the first three months of this campaign the U-Boats sank 60 tankers in the Caribbean alone, but with the progressive introduction of a convoy system these successes diminished until in mid-

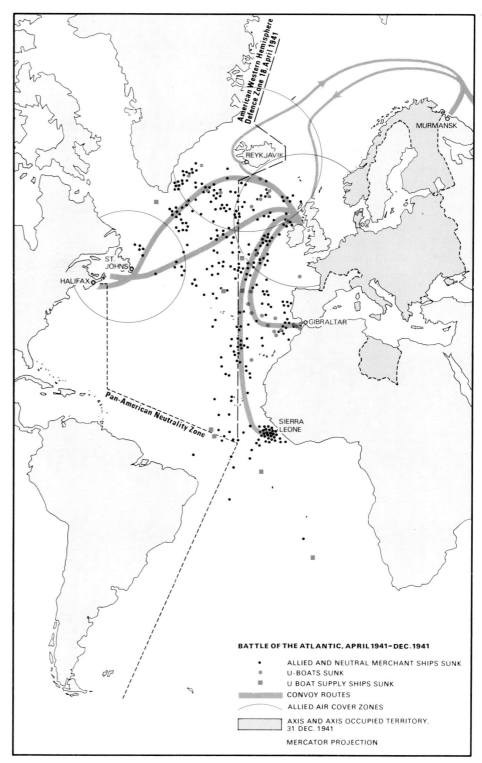

BATTLE OF THE ATLANTIC, APRIL 1941–DEC. 1941

- • ALLIED AND NEUTRAL MERCHANT SHIPS SUNK
- • U-BOATS SUNK
- ■ U BOAT SUPPLY SHIPS SUNK
- ▬ CONVOY ROUTES
- ◠ ALLIED AIR COVER ZONES
- ▭ AXIS AND AXIS OCCUPIED TERRITORY, 31 DEC. 1941

MERCATOR PROJECTION

1942 Dönitz withdrew from the area and concentrated his efforts once more in mid-Atlantic, which was out of reach of shore-based Allied aircraft.

It was not long before the Allies solved this problem. The British had introduced the idea of the escort carrier, a merchant vessel fitted with an elementary flight deck, and US industry soon fitted out such ships by the

dozen. Meanwhile, it was found that B-24 Liberators could be fitted with extra fuel tanks, enabling them to patrol mid-Atlantic waters. This air surveillance forced U-Boats to spend more of their patrol under water, making it difficult to speed hither and thither in pursuit of convoys. By the fall of 1942 it seemed that Dönitz was facing defeat, despite the heavy ship-

MAP below: *America's entry into the war brought the U-Boats to the US East Coast.*
Bottom: *Admiral Raeder, Commander in Chief of the German Navy in the early years of the war.*

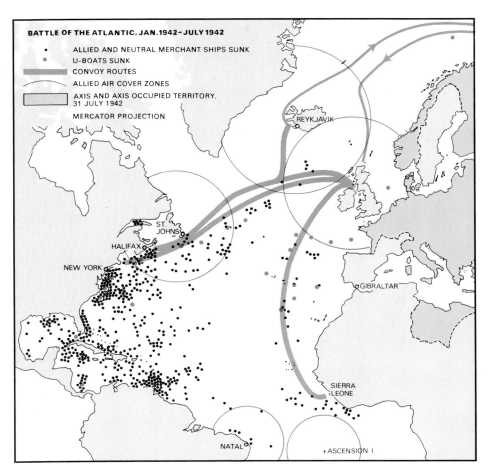

BATTLE OF THE ATLANTIC, JAN. 1942 – JULY 1942

- • ALLIED AND NEUTRAL MERCHANT SHIPS SUNK
- • U-BOATS SUNK
- ▬ CONVOY ROUTES
- ⌒ ALLIED AIR COVER ZONES
- ▭ AXIS AND AXIS OCCUPIED TERRITORY, 31 JULY 1942
- MERCATOR PROJECTION

REYKJAVIK
ST. JOHNS
HALIFAX
NEW YORK
GIBRALTAR
SIERRA LEONE
NATAL
ASCENSION I.

MAP right: *The convoy battles at their height.*
Below: *US troops land on Iceland in 1942. American forces first came to Iceland in July 1941 in a move to support the British in the Atlantic.*
Bottom: *A U-Boat victim burns.*

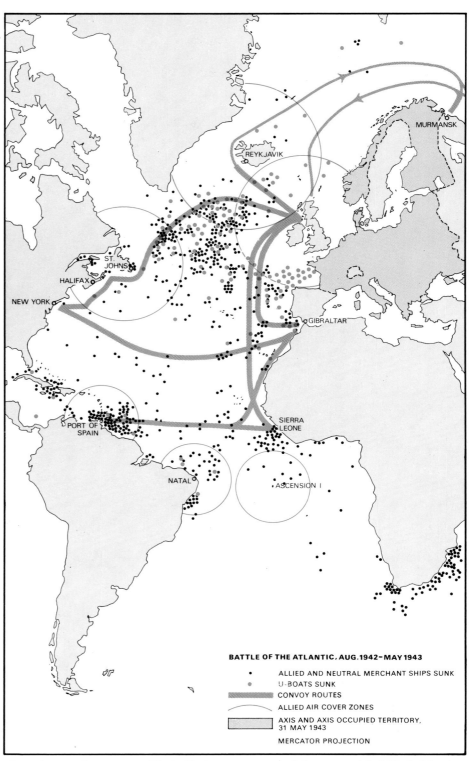

BATTLE OF THE ATLANTIC, AUG. 1942–MAY 1943

- •   ALLIED AND NEUTRAL MERCHANT SHIPS SUNK
- •   U-BOATS SUNK
-   CONVOY ROUTES
-   ALLIED AIR COVER ZONES
-   AXIS AND AXIS OCCUPIED TERRITORY, 31 MAY 1943

MERCATOR PROJECTION

ping losses he was still inflicting. American shipyards seemed likely not only to produce scores of escorts but also to build tankers and freighters faster than Dönitz could sink them.

However, the diversion of escort ships and aircraft to support the North African landings gave the Germans another chance. In early 1943, Dönitz's forces seemed about to change the course of the war, with Allied shipping losses exceeding the rate at which they could be made good, and with the U-Boat fleet, at over 300 units, six times larger than the fleet with which Germany began the war in 1939.

But the half-million tons of Allied shipping sunk in three weeks during March was virtually the peak of the German effort. Henceforth, events worked against the U-Boat crews. The Allies returned escort ships and aircraft to the Atlantic, code-breaking by the 'Ultra' specialists enabled U-Boat movements to be predicted, new centimetric radar enabled Allied aircraft to home in on U-Boats before the latter could pick them up on their own equipment, and sonar devices were improved and used with greater skill. U-Boat losses became particularly heavy close to the French bases from which they operated; they had the choice of moving on the surface and risking air attack, or of proceeding slowly underwater which, though safer, meant that the time they spent in the patrol zone had to be drastically

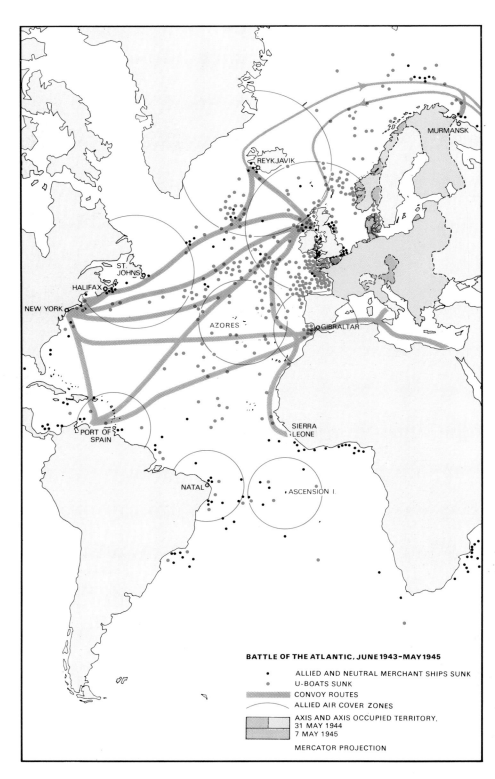

BATTLE OF THE ATLANTIC, JUNE 1943–MAY 1945

- •   ALLIED AND NEUTRAL MERCHANT SHIPS SUNK
- •   U-BOATS SUNK
- ▬▬   CONVOY ROUTES
- ◯   ALLIED AIR COVER ZONES
- ▢▢   AXIS AND AXIS OCCUPIED TERRITORY,
  31 MAY 1944
  7 MAY 1945

MERCATOR PROJECTION

reduced. In this and several other ways the U-Boats were in a no-win situation, and new technologies like the *Schnorkel* device (permitting the diesel engine to be used submerged) came too late to affect the issue. By 1945, almost all the experienced submariners had been lost, and crews were dispirited and hastily-trained.

The Battle of the Atlantic was the longest, and probably the most crucial, campaign of the war. If the maritime supply line had been cut, Britain would have been unable to continue the war and, without Britain, the Normandy landings and victory in Europe would most probably have been rendered impossible.

The Bomber Offensive

Although in 1940 it became clear that strategic bombing was not quite the deadly weapon that had been claimed, the Allies devoted many scarce resources to an air offensive over Europe which, more often than not, failed to inflict damage at all commensurate with the losses of skilled and brave aircrew that were incurred.

The decisive difficulty was that neither the British, nor even the Americans with their Norden bombsight, had the technical means to drop their bombs accurately. They had the skill and determination to take their

bombers over the targets but, except when they operated in massive numbers, they did comparatively little damage.

The British, having suffered grievously from German fighters, soon concentrated on night bombing and eventually, having realized that what they liked to call precision bombing was nothing of the sort, preferred to bomb civilian populations; setting a town on fire ('area bombing') was easier than hitting a factory or railway junction. When the US Eighth Air Force reached Britain in 1942 it was used for daylight bombing, the theory being that the heavy gun armaments of the B-24 and B-17 bombers would enable them to fight off the German fighters. However, in practice this did not work out quite as favorably as hoped, and deep raids into Germany were postponed until long-range escort fighters became available. In early 1943 the availability of P-47 Thunderbolt fighters enabled some deeper raids to be made, but it was not until the advent of the

Below: *A formation of USAAF P-38 Lightning fighters of the Fifteenth Air Force seen during operations over Yugoslavia.*
Bottom: *B-17 Flying Fortresses of the 91st Bomb Group set out for Germany in March 1944.*

MAP right: *Major targets for the Allied Combined Bomber Offensive. Prospects for the attacks were transformed by the introduction of the long range P-51 Mustang escort fighter in December 1943.*

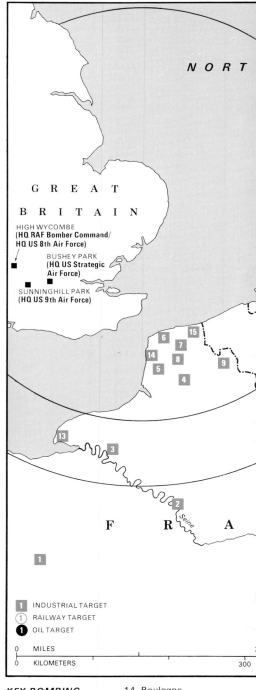

KEY BOMBING TARGETS

Industrial
1 Le Mans (aircraft)
2 Paris
3 Rouen
4 Siracourt (V-bombs)
5 Lottinghem
6 Mimovecques (V-bombs)
7 Watten
8 Wizernes (V-bombs)
9 Lille
10 Brussels (aircraft)
11 Rotterdam
12 Amsterdam (aircraft)
13 Le Havre

14 Boulogne
15 Dunkirk
16 Metz
17 Emden (U-boats)
18 Wilhelmshaven (U-boats)
19 Vegesack (U-boats)
20 Bremen (aircraft)
21 Hamburg
22 Flensburg (U-boats)
23 Kiel (U-boats)
24 Lübeck
25 Hannover
26 Brunswick
27 Magdeburg
28 Oschersleben (aircraft)
29 Dessau (aircraft)
30 Essen
31 Dortmund

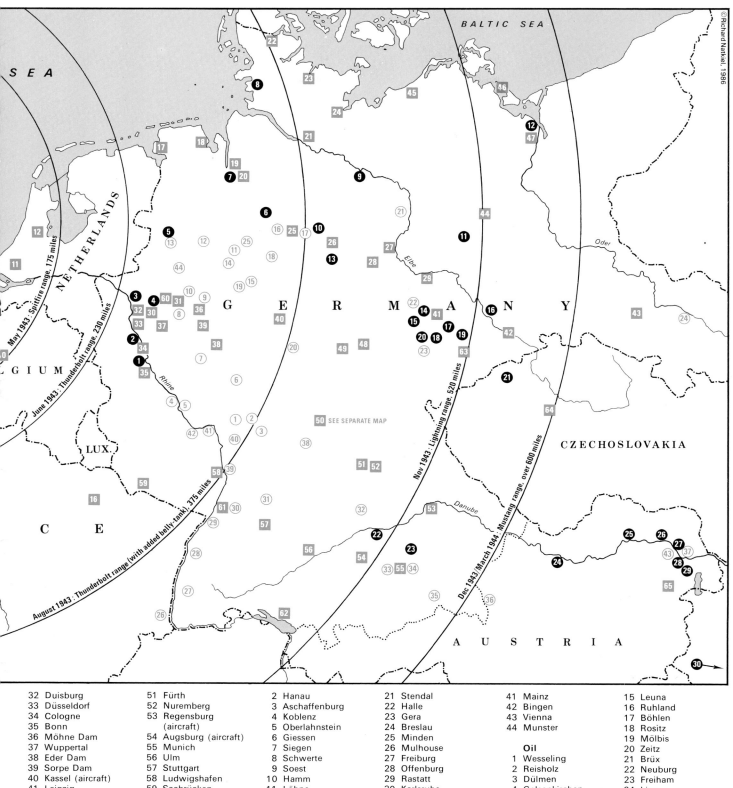

© Richard Natkiel, 1986

32 Duisburg	51 Fürth	2 Hanau	21 Stendal	41 Mainz	15 Leuna
33 Düsseldorf	52 Nuremberg	3 Aschaffenburg	22 Halle	42 Bingen	16 Ruhland
34 Cologne	53 Regensburg	4 Koblenz	23 Gera	43 Vienna	17 Böhlen
35 Bonn	(aircraft)	5 Oberlahnstein	24 Breslau	44 Munster	18 Rositz
36 Möhne Dam	54 Augsburg (aircraft)	6 Giessen	25 Minden		19 Mölbis
37 Wuppertal	55 Munich	7 Siegen	26 Mulhouse	**Oil**	20 Zeitz
38 Eder Dam	56 Ulm	8 Schwerte	27 Freiburg	1 Wesseling	21 Brüx
39 Sorpe Dam	57 Stuttgart	9 Soest	28 Offenburg	2 Reisholz	22 Neuburg
40 Kassel (aircraft)	58 Ludwigshafen	10 Hamm	29 Rastatt	3 Dülmen	23 Freiham
41 Leipzig	59 Saabrücken	11 Löhne	30 Karlsruhe	4 Gelsenkirchen	24 Linz
42 Dresden	60 Bochum	12 Osnabrück	31 Heilbronn	5 Salzbergen	25 Moosbierbaum
43 Liegnitz	61 Karlsruhe	13 Rheine	32 Treuchtlingen	6 Nienburg	26 Korneuburg
44 Munster	62 Friedrichshafen	14 Bielefeld	33 Pasing	7 Farge	27 Floridsdorf
45 Rostock	63 Chemnitz	15 Altenbecken	34 Munich	8 Heide	28 Schwechat
46 Peenemünde	64 Prague	Neuenbecken	35 Rosenheim	9 Hitzacker	29 Lobau
(V-bombs)	65 Wiener Neustadt	16 Seelze	36 Salzburg	10 Dollbergen	30 Ploesti
47 Stettin	(aircraft)	17 Hameln	37 Strasshof	11 Derben	
48 Erfurt		18 Hameln	38 Würzburg	12 Pölitz	
49 Gotha (aircraft)	**Railways**	19 Paderborn	39 Mannerheim	13 Salzgitter	
50 Schweinfurt	1 Frankfurt	20 Bebra	40 Darmstadt	14 Lützkendorf	
(ball-bearings)					

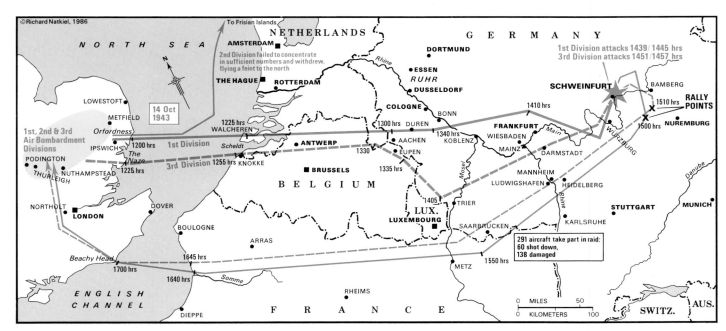

NORTH SEA

NETHERLANDS

GERMANY

To Frisian Islands

AMSTERDAM

2nd Division failed to concentrate in sufficient numbers and withdrew, flying a feint to the north

DORTMUND

1st Division attacks 1439/1445 hrs
3rd Division attacks 1451/1457 hrs

THE HAGUE

ESSEN
RUHR
DUSSELDORF

Rhine

SCHWEINFURT

BAMBERG

LOWESTOFT

ROTTERDAM

COLOGNE

METFIELD

14 Oct
1943

BONN

1410 hrs

RALLY
POINTS

1510 hrs

1st, 2nd & 3rd
Air Bombardment
Divisions

1225 hrs
WALCHEREN

Orfordness

DUREN

1300 hrs

1340 hrs

FRANKFURT

WÜRZBURG

NUREMBURG

1500 hrs

IPSWICH

1200 hrs

1st Division

Scheldt

ANTWERP

AACHEN

KOBLENZ

WIESBADEN

Main

PODINGTON

The Naze

3rd Division 1255 hrs

1330

EUPEN

MAINZ

DARMSTADT

THURLEIGH

1225 hrs

KNOKKE

1335 hrs

Mosel

MANNHEIM

Danube

NUTHAMPSTEAD

BRUSSELS

LUDWIGSHAFEN

HEIDELBERG

NORTHOLT

BELGIUM

1405

TRIER

Rhine

STUTTGART

MUNICH

LONDON

DOVER

LUX.
LUXEMBOURG

KARLSRUHE

BOULOGNE

SAARBRUCKEN

291 aircraft take part in raid:
60 shot down,
138 damaged

ARRAS

Beachy Head

1645 hrs

METZ

1550 hrs

1700 hrs

1640 hrs

Somme

ENGLISH
CHANNEL

RHEIMS

FRANCE

DIEPPE

MILES   50

KILOMETERS   100

SWITZ.

AUS.

P-51 Mustang later in the year that regular penetration attacks could be made. Meanwhile, other US Air Forces, based in the Mediterranean, joined the bomber offensive.

The dangers of operating without adequate fighter cover were illustrated by the heavy losses incurred in the 1943 daylight raids on Schweinfurt, where a ball-bearing factory, key supplier of the German arms industry, was the target. In the first raid one sixth of the Flying Fortresses were lost, and in the second a fifth of the 300-odd bombers were lost. The German fighters had clearly outgunned the bombers.

Attacks on specific targets regarded as vital to the German war effort continued alongside the attacks on German cities, with British and American operations being closely coordinated. In February 1944 German aircraft factories were the chosen target, and the Luftwaffe lost hundreds of fighter interceptors, thanks to the American P-51 escorts. But from postwar reports it is clear that such raids only interrupted German production for a few days, if that, after each attack.

However, slightly improved aiming techniques and, more important,

MAP above: *The disastrous daylight bombing raid on Schweinfurt proved that bombers could not reach a well-defended target by day without prohibitive casualties unless escorts were provided for the whole mission.*
Right: *Supplies flood ashore on Omaha Beach after D-Day.*

the deployment of masses of bombers against each objective, were beginning to ensure that specified targets could indeed be hit. This improvement was put to good use in the Normandy campaign, when railways, road bridges, and airfields were put out of action for a few all-important days. In late 1944 the assault on German cities was resumed and, apart from killing hundreds of thousands of German civilians, caused severe transport and fuel difficulties. The culmination of the so-called area-bombing technique was the burning of the city of Dresden, together with thousands of its inhabitants, in early 1945; like so much of previous strategic bombing, this Anglo-American operation produced massive civilian casualties in return for a negligible gain.

The D-Day Landings

The Allied landing in Normandy was
the most complex and perilous operation of World War II. Beaches just to
the west of Havre, and well to the west
of where the Germans had been led to
expect the blow to fall, had been
chosen. Here, the beaches were long
and broad enough to give the five
divisions of the first wave enough room
to deploy. Despite the bad weather, D-
Day began at 0200 on 6 June 1944
with the landing of airborne troops
charged with securing certain key
objectives, such as river bridges and
protective flank positions. Then came
a massed naval bombardment from a
fleet that included elderly US and
British battleships, followed by bombing. In general the naval guns were

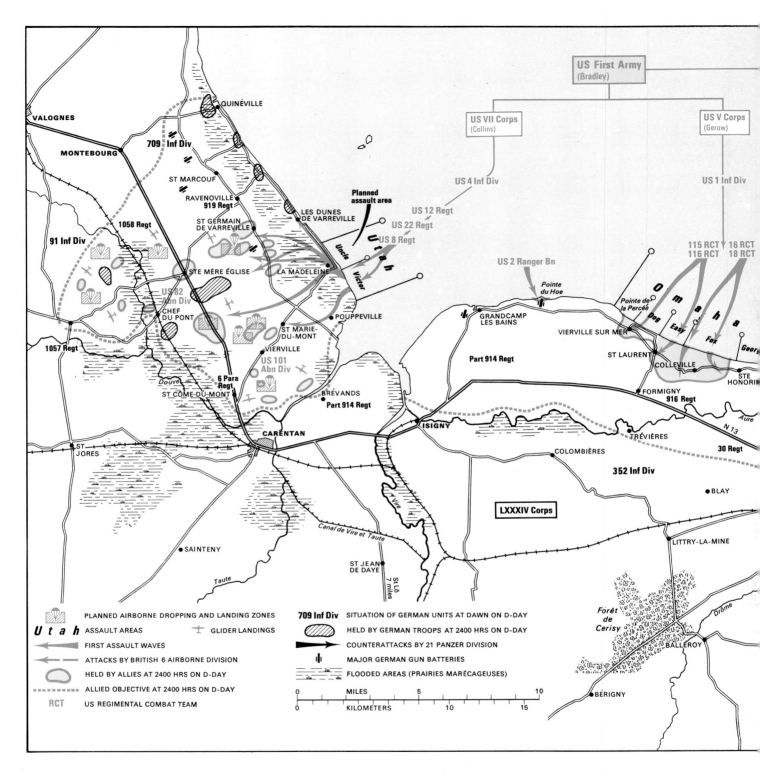

US First Army
(Bradley)

US VII Corps
(Collins)

US V Corps
(Gerow)

US 4 Inf Div

US 1 Inf Div

US 12 Regt

US 22 Regt

US 8 Regt

US 2 Ranger Bn

115 RCT 16 RCT
116 RCT 18 RCT

VALOGNES

MONTEBOURG

QUINÉVILLE

709 Inf Div

ST MARCOUF

RAVENOVILLE
919 Regt

1058 Regt

91 Inf Div

LES DUNES
DE VARREVILLE

Planned
assault area

ST GERMAIN
DE VARREVILLE

STE MÈRE ÉGLISE

LA MADELEINE

U t a h

Uncle

Victor

US 82
Abn Div

CHEF
DU PONT

POUPPEVILLE

Pointe
du Hoe

GRANDCAMP
LES BAINS

Pointe de
la Percée

O m a h a

Dog

Easy

Fox

Geor

VIERVILLE SUR MER

ST LAURENT

COLLEVILLE

STE
HONORI

1057 Regt

Douve

6 Para
Regt

ST CÔME-DU-MONT

ST MARIE-
DU-MONT

VIERVILLE

US 101
Abn Div

BRÉVANDS

Part 914 Regt

FORMIGNY
916 Regt

Part 914 Regt

ISIGNY

TRÉVIÈRES

Aure

N 13

30 Regt

ST
JORES

CARENTAN

COLOMBIÈRES

352 Inf Div

BLAY

LXXXIV Corps

Vire

SAINTENY

Canal de Vire et Taute

LITTRY-LA-MINE

St Lô
7 miles

ST JEAN
DE DAYE

Taute

Forêt
de
Cerisy

Drôme

BALLEROY

BÉRIGNY

🪂 PLANNED AIRBORNE DROPPING AND LANDING ZONES	709 Inf Div SITUATION OF GERMAN UNITS AT DAWN ON D-DAY
U t a h ASSAULT AREAS ✠ GLIDER LANDINGS	⬭ HELD BY GERMAN TROOPS AT 2400 HRS ON D-DAY
⬅ FIRST ASSAULT WAVES	▶ COUNTERATTACKS BY 21 PANZER DIVISION
⬅— ATTACKS BY BRITISH 6 AIRBORNE DIVISION	⬛ MAJOR GERMAN GUN BATTERIES
⬭ HELD BY ALLIES AT 2400 HRS ON D-DAY	≈ FLOODED AREAS (PRAIRIES MARÉCAGEUSES)
⋯ ALLIED OBJECTIVE AT 2400 HRS ON D-DAY	
RCT US REGIMENTAL COMBAT TEAM	

MILES   0   5   10

KILOMETERS 0   10   15

used against coast defense artillery, while the bombs were reserved for other, softer, defense positions.

Under the overall command of General Dwight D Eisenhower, with the British General Montgomery in local command, the US First Army under Bradley was landed to the west, on Utah and Omaha beaches, while the British Second Army under Demp-sey came ashore on Gold, Juno, and Sword beaches. They were preceded by specialized engineer groups which blew up the beach obstacles that form-ed part of the German fortified 'At-lantic Wall.' The landing craft them-selves carried artillery and rocket launchers, and these provided close fire support as the infantry landed. Thanks to all this shelling and bomb-ing, the landing itself went well, and the infantry was able to move off the beaches and dig itself into its initial positions. Only on Omaha Beach, where the amphibious tanks that were intended to support the infantry sank in rough seas, was there difficulty, and morale here was restored by the end of the day. After the five assault divi-sions, another six followed.

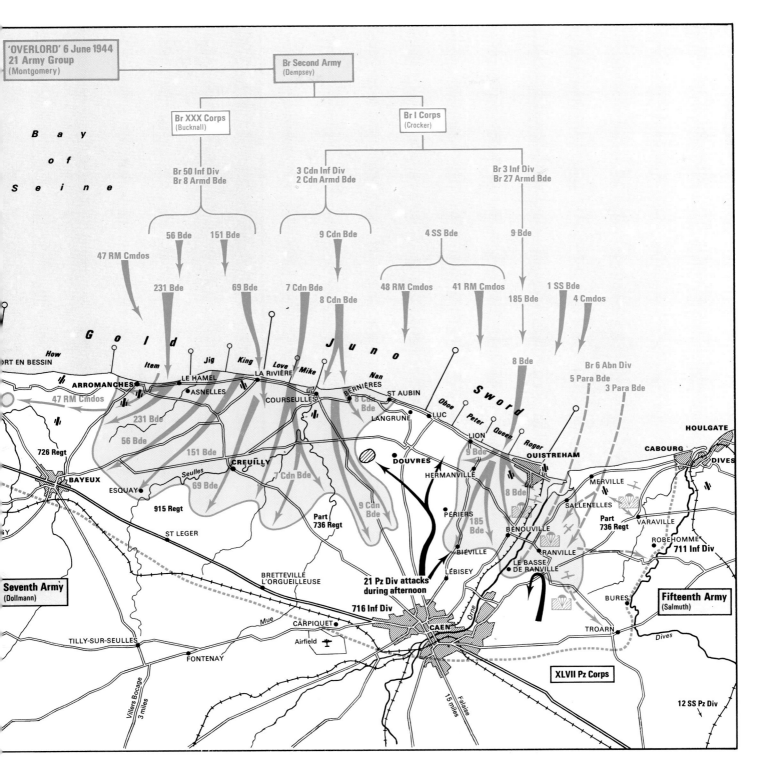

'OVERLORD' 6 June 1944
21 Army Group
(Montgomery)

Br Second Army (Dempsey)

Br XXX Corps (Bucknall)

Br I Corps (Crocker)

Br 50 Inf Div
Br 8 Armd Bde

3 Cdn Inf Div
2 Cdn Armd Bde

Br 3 Inf Div
Br 27 Armd Bde

56 Bde   151 Bde

9 Cdn Bde

4 SS Bde   9 Bde

47 RM Cmdos

231 Bde   69 Bde

7 Cdn Bde

48 RM Cmdos   41 RM Cmdos   1 SS Bde   4 Cmdos

8 Cdn Bde

185 Bde

8 Bde

Br 6 Abn Div
5 Para Bde
3 Para Bde

Bay of Seine

Gold

How   Item   Jig   King   Love   Mike   *Juno*   Nan   *Sword*

PORT EN BESSIN   LE HAMEL   LA RIVIÈRE   BERNIÈRES   ST AUBIN   Oboe   Peter   Queen   Roger   HOULGATE

ARROMANCHES   ASNELLES   COURSEULLES   8 Cdn Bde   LANGRUNE   LUC   LION   OUISTREHAM   CABOURG   DIVES

47 RM Cmdos   231 Bde   DOUVRES   9 Bde   8 Bde   MERVILLE

726 Regt   56 Bde   151 Bde   HERMANVILLE   SALLENELLES   Part 736 Regt   VARAVILLE

BAYEUX   Seulles   CREULLY   69 Bde   7 Cdn Bde   PÉRIERS   185 Bde   ROBEHOMME   711 Inf Div

ESQUAY   9 Cdn Bde   BÉNOUVILLE   BURES

915 Regt   Part 736 Regt   BIÉVILLE   RANVILLE   LE BASSE DE RANVILLE

ST LEGER   LÉBISEY   **21 Pz Div attacks during afternoon**

Seventh Army (Dollmann)   BRETTEVILLE L'ORGUEILLEUSE   **716 Inf Div**   **Fifteenth Army** (Salmuth)

TILLY-SUR-SEULLES   Mue   CARPIQUET   CAEN   TROARN   Dives

FONTENAY   Airfield   Orne   **XLVII Pz Corps**

Villers Bocage 3 miles   Falaise 15 miles   **12 SS Pz Div**

The landing, Operation OVER-LORD, was essentially designed to solve three problems: landing troops against heavy artillery fire, then getting the infantry and, more difficult, the tanks and artillery, off the beaches and over or around the tank traps and ditches which blocked the way inland, and finally ensuring a continuous supply not only of reinforcements but of supplies of all kinds.

Allied shelling and bombing helped to solve the first task, and specialized tanks solved the second. Not only did the Allies have tanks that could float ashore with the first wave of infantry, but there were also tanks that could flail the ground to explode mines, blow up concrete bunkers with very heavy mortar projectiles, or lay roads and bridges. For the long-term supply of the troops, until a port could be captured, there was 'Mulberry,' a prefabricated system of hollow concrete structures that could be floated to the shore, then sunk to form an artificial harbor. Later, the vital fuel supply was assured by 'Pluto' (Pipe Line Under The Ocean), which was laid from Britain to the French coast.

Invading Southern France

In 1944 the Allies were in agreement about the desirability of launching, simultaneously with the landings in Normandy, a diversionary attack against German forces in the Mediterranean theater. The British wished to drive northward out of Italy, whereas the Americans preferred an attack on southern France; this latter was also favored by the French and by the Russians.

The American preference was adopted. The aim of the operation was to attract and destroy as many German troops as possible, and also to capture the ports of Toulon and Marseilles, which would be useful entries into France for fresh troops and supplies from the United States.

Not surprisingly, the intention to start this operation at the same time as the Normandy landings could not be fulfilled, because all available landing craft were committed to the main venture. The operation accordingly began in mid-August, when the US Seventh Army under General Alexander M Patch landed on the beaches of the French Riviera west of Cannes. The next day the Free French First Army under General de Lattre de Tassigny landed not far from St Tropez with the aim of capturing Marseilles and Toulon.

Helped by a preliminary drop by an Anglo-American airborne division, which blocked the roads along which any German counterattack would come, the Seventh Army went on shore with only about 200 casualties and, almost 100,000-strong, faced quite weak German forces. Most German forces had been drawn out of southern France, either to Italy or toward Normandy, and although on paper there were eleven German divisions available, in reality the French and Americans were not faced with overwhelming opposition. Many of the German units were kept busy by the French

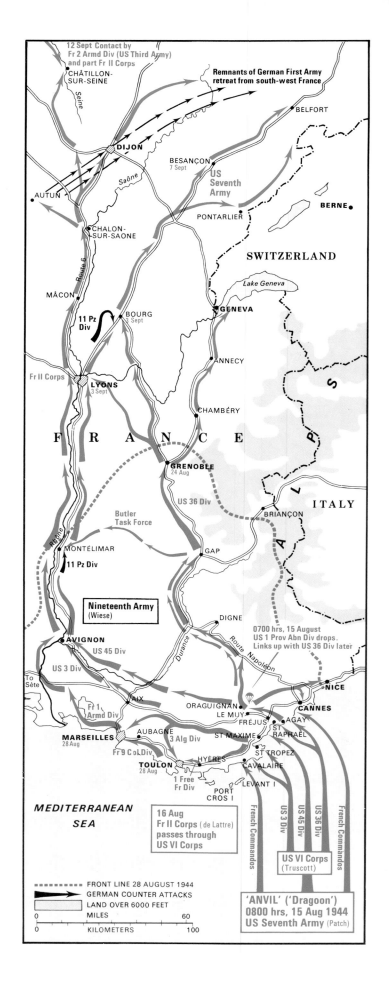

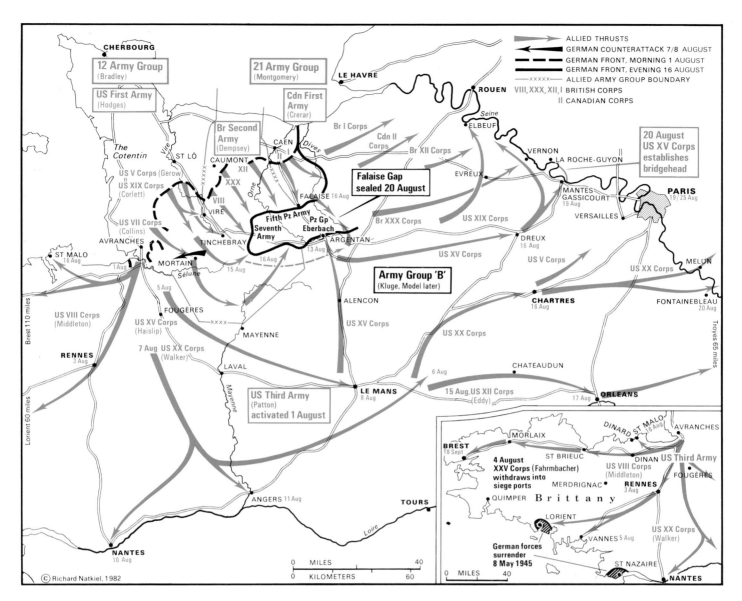

Map labels (above map - The Allied break-out from Normandy, July–August 1944):

ALLIED THRUSTS
GERMAN COUNTERATTACK 7/8 AUGUST
GERMAN FRONT, MORNING 1 AUGUST
GERMAN FRONT, EVENING 16 AUGUST
XXXX ALLIED ARMY GROUP BOUNDARY
VIII, XXX, XII, I BRITISH CORPS
II CANADIAN CORPS

CHERBOURG

12 Army Group
(Bradley)

US First Army
(Hodges)

21 Army Group
(Montgomery)

LE HAVRE

ROUEN

Cdn First
Army
(Crerar)

Seine
ELBEUF

VERNON

LA ROCHE-GUYON

20 August
US XV Corps
establishes
bridgehead

The Cotentin

ST LÔ

Br Second
Army
(Dempsey)

CAUMONT

CAEN

Dives

Br I Corps

Cdn II
Corps

Br XII Corps

EVREUX

MANTES
GASSICOURT
19 Aug

PARIS
19/25 Aug

VERSAILLES

US V Corps (Gerow)
US XIX Corps
(Corlett)

Vire

XII

XXX

Orne

VIII

VIRE

FALAISE 16 Aug

Falaise Gap
sealed 20 August

Br XXX Corps

US XIX Corps

DREUX
16 Aug

US V Corps

MELUN

US XX Corps

US VII Corps
(Collins)

AVRANCHES

TINCHEBRAY

Fifth Pz Army
Seventh
Army

Pz Gp
Eberbach

ARGENTAN

13 Aug

US XV Corps

Army Group 'B'
(Kluge, Model later)

CHARTRES
16 Aug

FONTAINEBLEAU
20 Aug

ST MALO
16 Aug

1 Aug

MORTAIN

Sélune

16 Aug

15 Aug

ALENCON

Troyes 65 miles

Brest 110 miles

5 Aug

FOUGÈRES

US VIII Corps
(Middleton)

US XV Corps
(Haislip)

xxxx

MAYENNE

US XV Corps

US XX Corps

CHATEAUDUN

RENNES
3 Aug

7 Aug US XX Corps
(Walker)

LAVAL

Mayenne

6 Aug

15 Aug, US XII Corps
(Eddy)

17 Aug

ORLEANS

Lorient 60 miles

US Third Army
(Patton)
activated 1 August

LE MANS
8 Aug

ANGERS 11 Aug

TOURS

Loire

NANTES
10 Aug

© Richard Natkiel, 1982

0   MILES   40
0   KILOMETERS   60

Inset map (The invasion of the South of France / Brittany):

DINARD ST MALO
16 Aug
AVRANCHES

MORLAIX

BREST
18 Sept

ST BRIEUC

DINAN

US Third Army

4 August
XXV Corps (Fahrmbacher)
withdraws into
siege ports

MERDRIGNAC

US VIII Corps
(Middleton)

RENNES
3 Aug

FOUGÈRES

QUIMPER

Brittany

LORIENT

VANNES 5 Aug

US XX Corps
(Walker)

German forces
surrender
8 May 1945

ST NAZAIRE

NANTES

0   MILES   40

MAP above: *The Allied break-out from Normandy, July–August 1944.*
MAP left: *The invasion of the South of France.*

Resistance, while others consisted of Russian prisoners of war who had elected to fight, not very enthusiastically, for the Germans.

The Americans moved northward against the German Nineteenth Army, which offered little resistance, and then went north along the Rhône to link up with Patton's US Third Army, which was moving south-eastward

from Paris. Patch's progress had been fast, thanks to the diversionary attacks of the French Resistance on the German forces which were intended to block his path. Meanwhile the French First Army, helped by massive French civilian resistance within the cities, took Toulon and Marseilles within days. Marseilles was captured before the end of August and the French then joined up with the US Seventh Army to form the US 6th Army Group.

All in all, this was a very successful, though secondary, campaign. It achieved its objectives with small loss partly because the Germans were quick to withdraw, but partly because the landing operation was exemplary, benefitting from the experience of amphibious operations which the Allies had been steadily accumulating since 1942.

Normandy

Within a few weeks of the successful D-Day landings, the Allies had sufficient troops and supplies ashore to begin the next stage of their campaign, the breakout from the coast. The plan involved an attack by the 21st Army Group of British, Canadian and Polish units against the German defenses around Caen. Since a breakthrough here would imperil the whole German position, it was expected that enemy reserves would be thrown into the battle. With the German reserves thus committed, the US 12th Army Group under Bradley would be able to batter a way through the enemy line and launch its armored divisions into the French interior. Allied air superiority, which on D-Day had ensured that not

MAP right: *The German disaster around Falaise.*
MAP below: *The American breakthrough at Avranches which brought the stubborn German defense in Normandy to an end.*

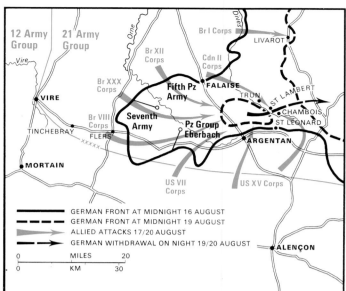

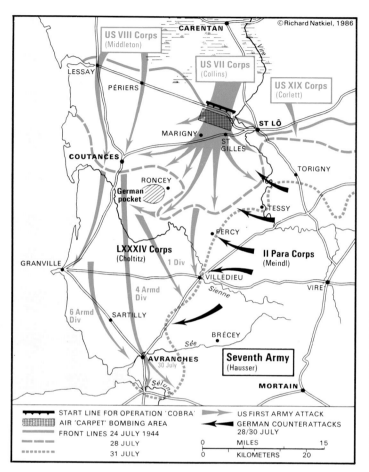

a single aircraft was lost to the Luftwaffe, was to be exploited to the full.

Action began on 7 July with a heavy bombing of Caen, followed by saturation bombing of the nearby German defenses ten days later. The first bombing merely destroyed the French town, making it almost impassable for the British tanks, while the second bombing ploughed the Normandy fields without achieving its aim of blasting a safe path for the British armor; the enemy tanks and artillery that were believed to be in the area had withdrawn in good time, only to reappear and inflict heavy punishment when the British armored columns came up. By the end of July this costly battle was still continuing; the British seemed no nearer to a breakthrough but at least they had drawn four Panzer divisions to their sector.

Bradley's forces had captured Cherbourg late in June, but the port was so wrecked as to be unserviceable. On 25 July, taking advantage of the German preoccupation with the British around Caen, the Americans began a massive attack southward from St Lô. The US infantry attacked on a four-mile front, and thanks to close radio coordination between ground and air, the heavy air attacks which accompanied this offensive were relatively successful. Almost 2000 bombers were used, as well as fighter-bombers; the material damage they inflicted was less than these numbers might suggest, but they kept the enemy in a useful state of confusion. Thanks to this, George S Patton's Third Army was able to break through a gap at Avranches and, dividing its armored forces, make rapid advances

Above: *British Sherman tanks in the village of Reviers in Normandy in June 1944.*
MAP above right: *The 'broad front' Allied advance from the Seine to Belgium and eastern France.*

into Brittany in the west and toward Paris in the east.

Hitler, who was facing a critical situation not only in Normandy but on the Russian front as well, sacked his commander (von Rundstedt) and appointed Kluge in his place. Kluge, however, soon found that Hitler had his own ideas on how to conduct this campaign, and was ordered to concentrate his forces against Avranches, with the aim of cutting off the US advance at its apparent source. Soon the six German divisions found them-

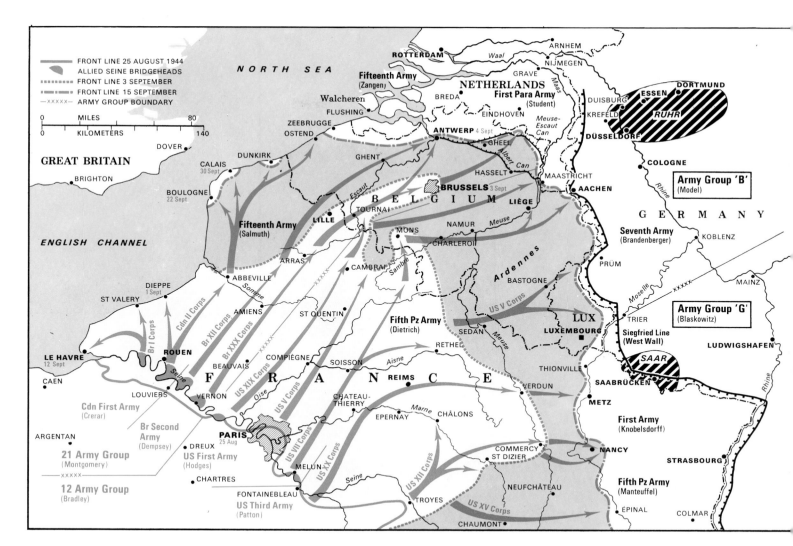

Advance to the Rhine

selves between Patton's units and, to the north, the Allied bridgehead, which was expanding southwards from the coast. When Patton diverted his XV Corps northward against Kluge, capturing Argentan at the same time as the Canadian First Army moved south toward Falaise, the German position was desperate, with troops, tanks and vehicles crammed on to narrow roads and making perfect targets for air attacks by US Thunderbolts and British Typhoons. In the end, despite a strong rearguard action by a Panzer division, the Germans lost the greater part of fifteen divisions when the Allies closed in at Falaise, a military disaster which virtually sealed the fate of the German presence in France.

The Falaise operation marked the end of the Battle of Normandy. The Allies turned to pin remaining German divisions against the Seine, while Patton's armored divisions continued their swift advance toward Paris.

After their disaster at Falaise and their failure to hold a line along the Seine, the German forces in France were in confused retreat before the victorious Allies who were in confused advance. The latter had no clear plan for this stage of the campaign, which had turned out more successfully than they had hoped. Some generals favored a mass advance on a narrow front which might take the Allies well inside Germany before winter, while others preferred a step-by-step advance on a broad front which, though slower, seemed less risky. In fact, the German defense line, the so-called *Westwall*, was not as strong as the Allies believed and it seems likely that a swift, narrow advance would have been successful. But General Eisenhower, who bore the heavy responsibility of making this decision, chose the safer option.

One of his problems, which not all his subordinate generals quite understood, was that the early termination of the Normandy campaign had left the Allies with over two million men to feed, not to speak of half a million vehicles to fuel, and no large port was yet available. The Canadians had taken a few French channel ports, but these were not enough. A period of slow advance therefore had much to recommend it.

At the end of August the British 21st Army Group and the US 12th Army Group began their advance from the Seine toward Belgium. This carried them as far as Antwerp, captured in early September, but German forces on the other side of the Scheldt prevented this great port being of immediate use to the Allies. At this point, with Belgium liberated, the problem became one of bridges, for the Netherlands was crisscrossed by rivers and canals. On 17 September US airborne divisions were dropped to secure river crossings near Nij-

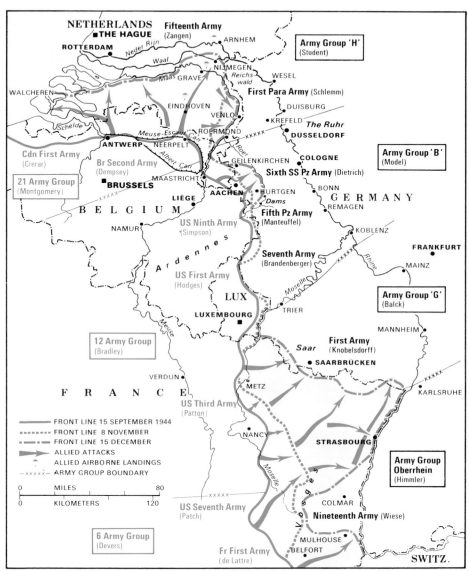

megen and Eindhoven, while a British airborne division landed near Arnhem to secure a Rhine crossing. The two US drops were successful, but the British failed heroically after landing too far from the target bridge.

With the failure of the Arnhem operation it was no longer possible to hope for a fast advance into Germany by the northern flank of the Allied armies. There was no alternative to the slow approach on a broad front. However, by early November the Scheldt was cleared of Germans, so

MAP above: *The Allied advance September–December 1944.*
Right: *Bradley, Eisenhower and Patton.*

that Antwerp could become the much-needed supply port. Meanwhile, Bradley's 12th Army Group was reinforced and Allied troops, from Nijmegen in the north down to Switzerland in the south, were poised on Germany's frontier. Their advance would take them to the Rhine, which the Germans would surely defend desperately.

Below left: *British paratroops in Arnhem. Despite the success of the American airborne units at Eindhoven and Nijmegen, Arnhem proved to be 'a bridge too far.'*
MAP below right: *The German plan for the Ardennes offensive.*

Bottom: *American prisoners taken during the first German advances of the Battle of the Bulge.*

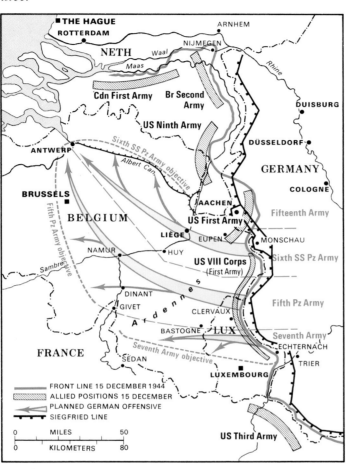

At first there was panic, enabling the Germans to break the front in several places. But here, as would be the case many times in this six-week struggle, panic and confusion on the part of some was compensated by unexpected heroism and steadfastness by others. The US First Army at this time witnessed a number of discreditable episodes, but also found the courage and skill to hold back the Germans for several vital days. In the prevailing terrain, and especially in the snowy weather, bridges and crossroads were all-important, and American units, often quite small, managed to hold these for far longer than the Germans had expected.

This slowing of the German schedule gave the Allied command time to recover its poise and redeploy its formations. The German advance had created a salient (the 'bulge'), and the urgent task of the Anglo-American armies was to stop this bulge getting any bigger. General Eisenhower placed all troops that were north of the bulge under the British General Montgomery, even though most of them were American, while south of the bulge Patton's Third Army was to swing northward and tackle the flank of the

Battle of the Bulge

Just as the Allied armies in December 1944 were beginning the struggle to break through the defense system known as the *Westwall*, Hitler was urging his unenthusiastic generals into a massive counteroffensive which almost succeeded, and was to be virtually the German forces' last throw in their effort to stem the Allies' advance from the west.

The weakest parts of the Allied line were the 100-odd miles in the Ardennes, where very broken terrain, forests, and scarcity of roads made troop movements difficult. This did not seem likely territory for a German counterblow, and the American troops there were not only thin on the ground but, for the most part, were

not regarded as first-rate units. Some were resting and re-equipping after gruelling battles, while others were inexperienced new arrivals.

Hitler's plan was to assemble what amounted to Germany's last effective reserves and, with ten armored divisions and fourteen others, make several surprise breakthroughs in the Ardennes. Once this was achieved, two Panzer armies would advance and converge on Antwerp, so vital to the Allies. As so many times previously, Hitler's concept was reckless but, at first, favored by good luck. In this case the luck consisted in the weather, which was so bad that Allied reconnaissance and attack aircraft could hardly operate. Thus the German blow, when it fell, was a surprise. The US VIII Corps suddenly found itself assaulted by eight Panzer divisions.

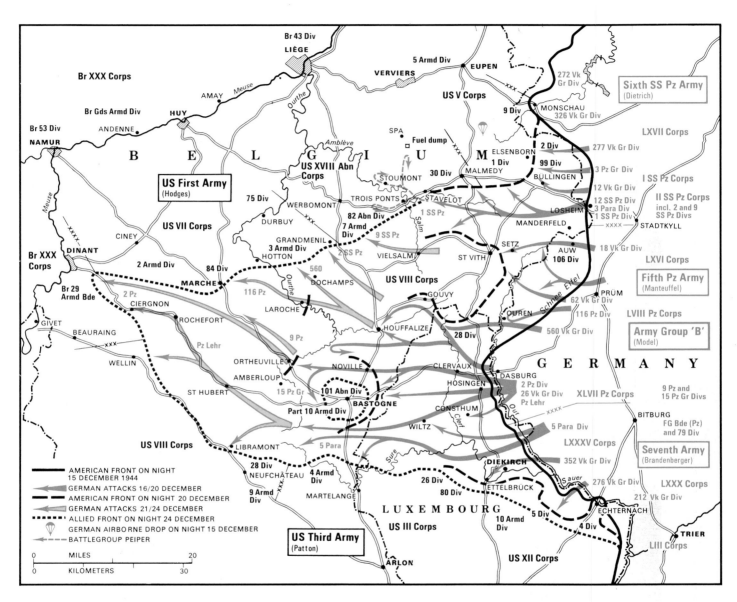

Br XXX Corps

Br Gds Armd Div

Br 53 Div

NAMUR

B E L G I U M

US First Army
(Hodges)

US VII Corps

Br XXX Corps

DINANT

Br 29 Armd Bde

2 Pz

CIERGNON

GIVET

BEAURAING

WELLIN

ST HUBERT

US VIII Corps

LIBRAMONT

28 Div

NEUFCHÂTEAU

9 Armd Div

MARTELANGE

US Third Army
(Patton)

ARLON

LUXEMBOURG

US III Corps

AMAY

HUY

ANDENNE

CINEY

MARCHE

2 Armd Div

84 Div

ROCHEFORT

Pz Lehr

ORTHEUVILLE

AMBERLOUP

15 Pz Gr

Br 43 Div

LIÈGE

Meuse

Ourthe

Amblève

US XVIII Abn Corps

75 Div

WERBOMONT

DURBUY

GRANDMENIL
3 Armd Div
HOTTON

560

DOCHAMPS

116 Pz

LAROCHE

Ourthe

9 Pz

NOVILLE

101 Abn Div

BASTOGNE

Part 10 Armd Div

5 Para

4 Armd Div

VERVIERS

5 Armd Div

SPA

Fuel dump

STOUMONT

30 Div

TROIS PONTS

82 Abn Div
7 Armd Div

9 SS Pz

2 SS Pz

GOUVY

HOUFFALIZE

28 Div

CLERVAUX

HOSINGEN

CONSTHUM

WILTZ

Clerf

Sure

26 Div

80 Div

10 Armd Div

EUPEN

US V Corps

9 Div

MONSCHAU

ELSENBORN
1 Div
MALMEDY

99 Div

BULLINGEN

STAVELOT

1 SS Pz

Salm

MANDERFELD

LOSHEIM

SETZ

VIELSALM

ST VITH

US VIII Corps

AUW
106 Div

OUREN

Schnee Eifel

DASBURG

2 Pz Div
26 Vk Gr Div
Pz Lehr

5 Para Div

DIEKIRCH

ETTELBRUCK

Sauer

5 Div

4 Div

TRIER

US XII Corps

Sixth SS Pz Army
(Dietrich)

272 Vk Gr Div

LXVII Corps

326 Vk Gr Div

277 Vk Gr Div

3 Pz Gr Div

I SS Pz Corps

12 Vk Gr Div
12 SS Pz Div
3 Para Div
1 SS Pz Div

II SS Pz Corps
incl. 2 and 9
SS Pz Divs

STADTKYLL

18 Vk Gr Div

LXVI Corps

Fifth Pz Army
(Manteuffel)

PRÜM

62 Vk Gr Div

LVIII Pz Corps

116 Pz Div

560 Vk Gr Div

Army Group 'B'
(Model)

G E R M A N Y

9 Pz and
15 Pz Gr Divs

XLVII Pz Corps

BITBURG

FG Bde (Pz)
and 79 Div

LXXXV Corps

Seventh Army
(Brandenberger)

352 Vk Gr Div

276 Vk Gr Div

LXXX Corps

212 Vk Gr Div

ECHTERNACH

LIII Corps

AMERICAN FRONT ON NIGHT 15 DECEMBER 1944
GERMAN ATTACKS 16/20 DECEMBER
AMERICAN FRONT ON NIGHT 20 DECEMBER
GERMAN ATTACKS 21/24 DECEMBER
ALLIED FRONT ON NIGHT 24 DECEMBER
GERMAN AIRBORNE DROP ON NIGHT 15 DECEMBER
BATTLEGROUP PEIPER

MILES   20

KILOMETERS   30

German advance. Superb staff work by Patton's subordinates enabled his units to rush northward, where they engaged in a bloody struggle against German armor. Meanwhile, the British placed themselves at Dinant, blocking the way to the Meuse and enabling the US First and Ninth armies to gather themselves for the counteroffensive.

The Germans were further impeded by their failure to capture Bastogne, a key road junction that was held against heavy odds by the US 101st Airborne Division. The defense

of this town, and General Anthony McAuliffe's reply of 'Nuts!' to a formal German invitation to surrender, quite justifiably became one of the epics of American military history.

In the last week of December the weather changed, and this finally ended German hopes. The slushy ground became frozen hard, and the skies cleared to enable the Allies to exploit their air superiority. The weak Luftwaffe bombed Allied airfields but with little success and, like the German ground forces, soon began to

MAP above: *The German offensive in the Ardennes.*
Right: *A German Mark V Panther tank moves along a typical woodland road in the Ardennes.*

suffer from fuel shortages. After December it was really a question of mopping up, but the difficult terrain and German tenacity meant that the bulge was not completely pushed back until February.

MAP below: *The attacks of the US Third and First Armies against the Bulge.*
Below right: *General Anthony McAuliffe, hero of the defense of Bastogne.*

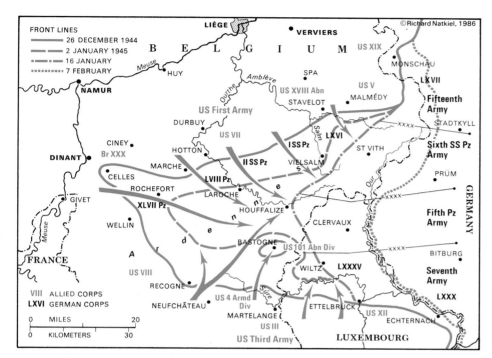

Crossing the Rhine

After the failure of the German counteroffensive in the Ardennes, it was clear that Germany's best chance lay in surrender. However, Hitler had his own ideas. The wide Rhine, paralleling Germany's western frontier, was still defensible, and he intended to fight on. He still hoped for a last-minute miracle, namely a quarrel between the Russians, advancing on the Eastern Front, and the western powers, advancing on the Rhine.

Eisenhower's plan was to push back the remaining Germans from the western side of the Rhine, and then to attack along its whole length. Numerous crossing attempts were to be made, in the expectation that one or two would succeed by sheer energy and unexpectedness, and others by overwhelming use of artillery and infantry resources. First moves came

in the south, where the US 6th Army Group with French support captured Colmar, south of Strasbourg, in early February 1945, and pushed the Germans on to the other side of the Rhine. In the north, using massive artillery support, the British and Canadians advanced out of the Netherlands into and beyond the Reichswald forest.

Then on 23 February the US Ninth Army, using assault boats to cross the flooded Roer Valley, defeated stiff German resistance in hard-fought battles and advanced to the west bank of the river. Further south, the US First Army, which was fighting its way toward Cologne, Bonn and Koblenz, discovered that the Rhine bridge at Remagen was still intact, the Germans having kept it open for the benefit of their last retreating troops. The bridge was captured by a rapid assault which left the few defenders too little time to explode the demolition charges, and the Allies found themselves in posses-

sion of a heavy-traffic bridge across the river. Unfortunately, successive levels of the American command were unwilling to take the initiative of using this unexpected prize, and it was not until the news reached the headquarters of the 12th Army Group that orders were given to pass all available troops and supplies over the bridge as rapidly as possible. This enabled a bridgehead to be established on the eastern bank, and the US engineers took advantage of this to build several temporary bridges. So, when German heavy artillery and bombs finally put the Remagen bridge out of service, it was too late. The Rhine had been passed and remained passable.

Then, on 24 March, Patton's Third Army forced a crossing at Oppenheim against slight resistance, and the same day, in the north, an Anglo-American assault carried the Rhine at Wesel, opening the way for an advance on the Ruhr and Berlin.

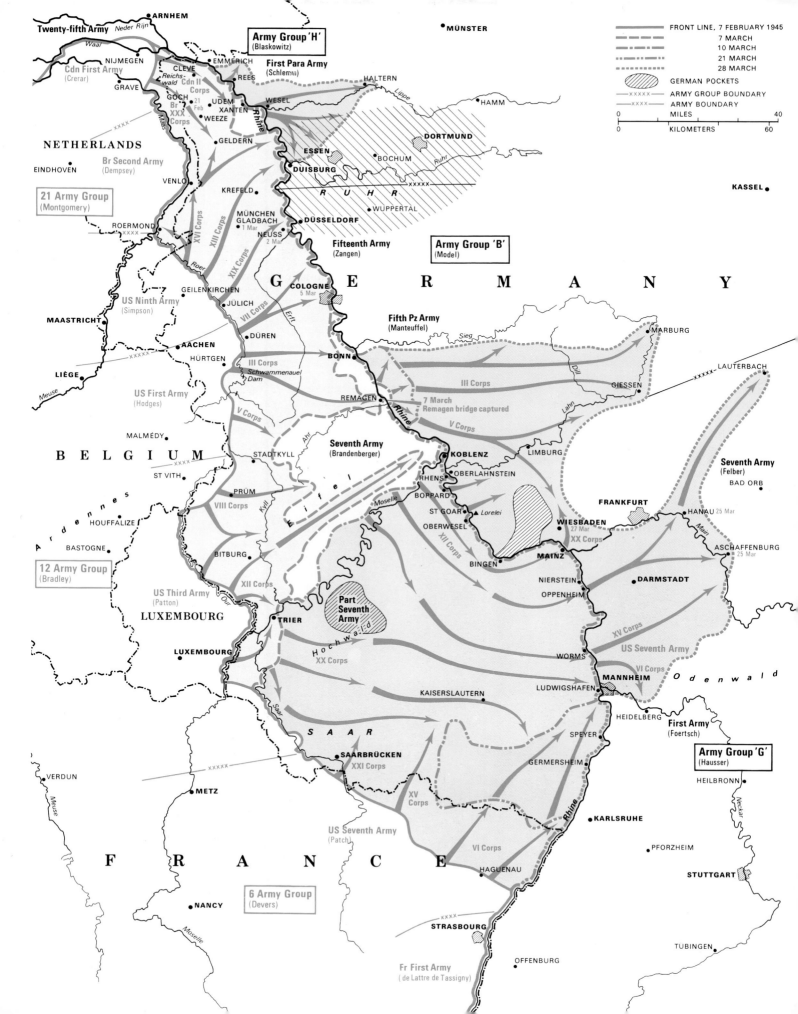

ARNHEM
Twenty-fifth Army   Neder Rijn
NIJMEGEN
Waal   MÜNSTER
Cdn First Army
(Crerar)   CLEVE   EMMERICH
Reichs-   Cdn II   REES   HALTERN
wald   Corps
GOCH   UDEM   Lippe
GRAVE   Br   21   XANTEN   WESEL   HAMM
XXX   Feb   WEEZE   Rhine
NETHERLANDS   Corps
GELDERN   DORTMUND   Army Group 'H'
(Blaskowitz)
EINDHOVEN   Br Second Army
(Dempsey)   VENLO   ESSEN   First Para Army
(Schlemm)   BOCHUM   KASSEL
DUISBURG
KREFELD   R U H R
21 Army Group   MÜNCHEN   Ruhr
(Montgomery)   GLADBACH   WUPPERTAL
1 Mar   G   E   DÜSSELDORF   R   M   A   N   Y
ROERMOND   NEUSS
2 Mar   Fifteenth Army
XVI Corps   XIII Corps   (Zangen)   Army Group 'B'
(Model)
US Ninth Army   XIX Corps   COLOGNE
(Simpson)   GEILENKIRCHEN   5 Mar
MAASTRICHT   JÜLICH   Erft   Fifth Pz Army   MARBURG
VII Corps   (Manteuffel)
AACHEN   DÜREN   BONN   Sieg   GIESSEN   LAUTERBACH
HÜRTGEN   III Corps   Dill
LIÈGE   Schwammenauel   REMAGEN   III Corps
Meuse   Dam   Rhine   7 March   Lahn   Limburg
US First Army   V Corps   Remagen bridge captured   V Corps
(Hodges)   Ahr   KOBLENZ   LIMBURG   Seventh Army
MALMÉDY   Seventh Army   (Felder)
STADTKYLL   (Brandenberger)   RHENS   OBERLAHNSTEIN   BAD ORB
BELGIUM   Eifel   BOPPARD   FRANKFURT
ST VITH   Moselle   ST GOAR   Lorelei   WIESBADEN   HANAU 25 Mar
PRÜM   XII Corps   27 Mar
HOUFFALIZE   VIII Corps   Kyll   OBERWESEL   XX Corps   ASCHAFFENBURG
BASTOGNE   BITBURG   BINGEN   MAINZ   25 Mar
Ardennes   XII Corps   NIERSTEIN   DARMSTADT
12 Army Group   Our   OPPENHEIM
(Bradley)   US Third Army   Part   XV Corps
(Patton)   Seventh   Odenwald
LUXEMBOURG   Army   WORMS   US Seventh Army
LUXEMBOURG   TRIER   Hochwald   VI Corps
XX Corps   LUDWIGSHAFEN   MANNHEIM
Saar   KAISERSLAUTERN   HEIDELBERG   First Army
(Foertsch)
SAAR   SPEYER   Army Group 'G'
(Hausser)
VERDUN   SAARBRÜCKEN   GERMERSHEIM   HEILBRONN
METZ   XXI Corps   XV
Corps   Rhine   KARLSRUHE
F   R   A   N   C   E   PFORZHEIM
US Seventh Army   HAGUENAU   STUTTGART
(Patch)   VI Corps   Neckar
NANCY   6 Army Group
(Devers)   TÜBINGEN
Moselle   STRASBOURG
Fr First Army   OFFENBURG
(de Lattre de Tassigny)

FRONT LINE, 7 FEBRUARY 1945
7 MARCH
10 MARCH
21 MARCH
28 MARCH
GERMAN POCKETS
XXXXX   ARMY GROUP BOUNDARY
XXXX   ARMY BOUNDARY
MILES   40
0
0   KILOMETERS   60

Breakthrough to the Elbe

Once across the Rhine, the Allied armies found themselves facing scattered remnants of the Wehrmacht. Apart from a few surviving paratroop and SS units, these for the most part consisted of the last offerings of the conscription machine: elderly men, youths and boys, and the unfit. Nevertheless, resistance was sometimes sharp, although the Germans had no chance of achieving anything except perhaps a few extra days of life for the Third Reich.

In the Ruhr industrial region, the German command hoped to hold enough cities to drag the Allies into protracted street fighting. In order to foil these German delaying tactics, the US First and Ninth Armies encircled the region, and then just three corps were sent in to capture the cities while the main bulk of the Allied forces continued eastward. Eventually the German Army Group B, inside the Ruhr, was forced to surrender and its commander, Field Marshal Walther Model, committed suicide after refusing to obey an impracticable order to break out of the encirclement. About 400,000 German troops were captured here.

The Allied troops hurrying eastward were directed toward Berlin, but for a number of reasons they never reached that destination. The most important factor in this change of plan were intelligence reports suggesting that the Germans intended to set up a so-called national redoubt in the mountains of Bavaria where, it was thought, they could conduct a guerrilla war for years. Eisenhower decided to forestall this possibility by diverting the US Third and Seventh Armies to the south. It was also thought that at this stage of the war, with no really battleworthy German armies to seek out and destroy, there was no point in risking casualties from last-ditch resistance by a drive on to Berlin. In any case, by the existing inter-Allied agreements any territory won by the western allies beyond the Elbe and the Harz Mountains had to be handed back to Russian control at the end of the war. So, despite the entreaties of General William Simpson, commander of the US Ninth Army which had won a bridgehead over the Elbe, Eisenhower decided to go no further than the Elbe and it was on this river, at Torgau, east of Leipzig, that the American and Russian armies met on 24 July. Six days later Hitler was dead and Berlin in Russian hands. German units in the north surrendered to the British on Luneberg Heath, south of Hamburg, on 5 May, while simultaneously German forces east of the Elbe, preferring American captivity to Russian, surrendered to General Simpson. Germany's capitulation followed on 7 May, and the war in Europe was over. The USA had sent about three million men to this theater, of whom about 465,000 became casualties (121,000 were killed). The British and Canadians contributed another million and suffered about 184,000 casualties.

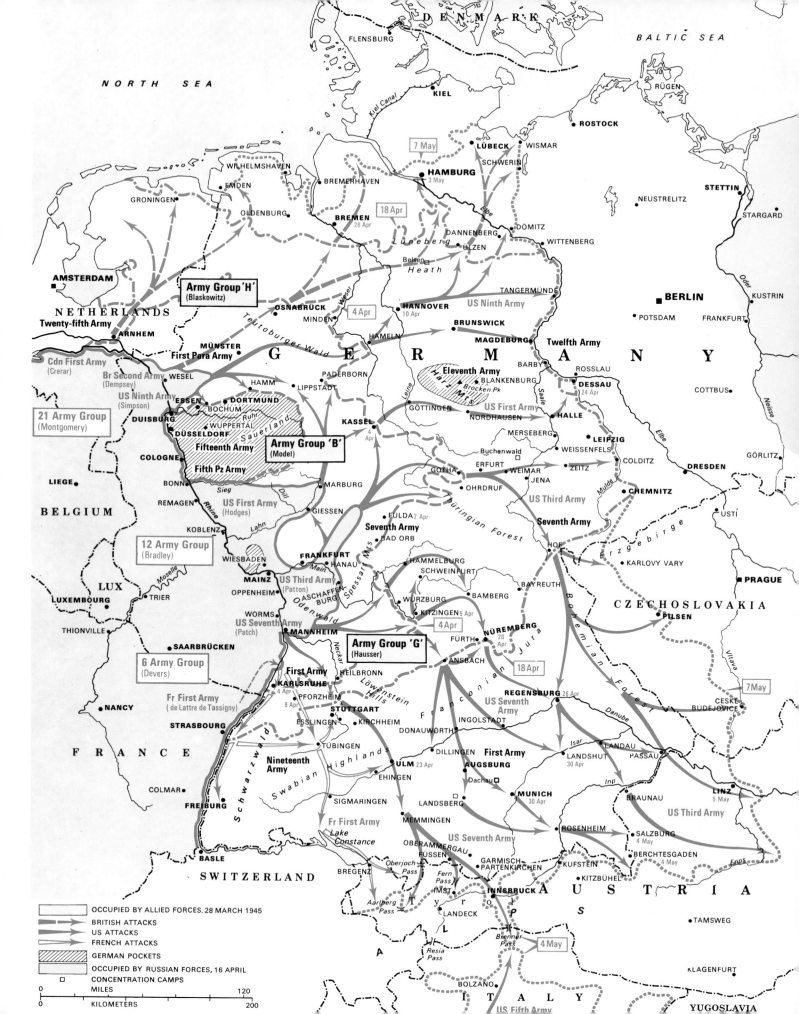

DENMARK

BALTIC SEA

NORTH SEA

FLENSBURG

KIEL

Kiel Canal

RÜGEN

ROSTOCK

WISMAR

STETTIN

WILHELMSHAVEN

BREMERHAVEN

7 May

LÜBECK

SCHWERIN

NEUSTRELITZ

STARGARD

EMDEN

BREMEN
26 Apr

HAMBURG
3 May

DANNENBERG

DÖMITZ

GRONINGEN

OLDENBURG

18 Apr

Lüneberg

ÜLZEN

WITTENBERG

Oder

KUSTRIN

AMSTERDAM

NETHERLANDS

Twenty-fifth Army

ARNHEM

Army Group 'H'
(Blaskowitz)

OSNABRÜCK

4 Apr

Belsen □
Heath

TANGERMÜNDE

BERLIN

POTSDAM

FRANKFURT

MINDEN

HANNOVER
10 Apr

US Ninth Army

BRUNSWICK

MAGDEBURG

Twelfth Army

BARBY

ROSSLAU

Cdn First Army
(Crerar)

Br Second Army
(Dempsey)

WESEL

MÜNSTER

First Para Army

HAMELN

Eleventh Army
Harz Mts
BLANKENBURG
Brocken Pk

DESSAU
24 Apr

COTTBUS

Neisse

HAMM

LIPPSTADT

PADERBORN

GÖTTINGEN

US First Army

HALLE

US Ninth Army
(Simpson)

ESSEN

BOCHUM

DORTMUND

KASSEL
4 Apr

NORDHAUSEN

MERSEBERG

LEIPZIG

21 Army Group
(Montgomery)

DUISBURG

WUPPERTAL
Ruhr
Sauerland

WEISSENFELS

COLDITZ

GÖRLITZ

DÜSSELDORF

Fifteenth Army

Army Group 'B'
(Model)

MARBURG

Buchenwald □

ERFURT

WEIMAR

ZEITZ

Elbe

Mulde

CHEMNITZ

DRESDEN

COLOGNE

Fifth Pz Army

BONN

Sieg

GOTHA

JENA

USTÍ

LIEGE

REMAGEN

Rhine

Dill

GIESSEN

OHRDRUF

US Third Army

BELGIUM

KOBLENZ

Lahn

FULDA
2 Apr

Thüringian Forest

Erzgebirge

KARLOVY VARY

PRAGUE

12 Army Group
(Bradley)

WIESBADEN

FRANKFURT

Seventh Army

BAD ORB

HOF

CZECHOSLOVAKIA

LUX

MAINZ

Moselle

HANAU

Seventh Army

LUXEMBOURG

TRIER

OPPENHEIM

US Third Army
(Patton)

ASCHAFFEN-
BURG

HAMMELBURG

SCHWEINFURT

Spessart Mts

BAYREUTH

PILSEN

THIONVILLE

WORMS

Odenwald

WÜRZBURG

BAMBERG

Bohemian Forest

NÜREMBERG
20 Apr

US Seventh Army
(Patch)

MANNHEIM

KITZINGEN
5 Apr

4 Apr

Army Group 'G'
(Hausser)

FÜRTH

Franconian Jura

18 Apr

First Army

HEILBRONN

ANSBACH

6 Army Group
(Devers)

SAARBRÜCKEN

KARLSRUHE
4 Apr

PFORZHEIM
8 Apr

*Löwenstein
Hills*

REGENSBURG
26 Apr

CESKE
BUDEJOVICE

7 May

Fr First Army
(de Lattre de Tassigny)

STUTTGART

ESSLINGEN

KIRCHHEIM

US Seventh
Army

INGOLSTADT

Danube

PASSAU

NANCY

STRASBOURG

Schwarzwald

TÜBINGEN

DONAUWORTH

DILLINGEN

First Army

AUGSBURG

LANDSHUT
30 Apr

LANDAU

Isar

LINZ
5 May

FRANCE

Nineteenth
Army

*Swabian
Highlands*

ULM 23 Apr

EHINGEN

Dachau □

Inp

BRAUNAU

COLMAR

FREIBURG

SIGMARINGEN

LANDSBERG

MUNICH
30 Apr

ROSENHEIM

US Third Army

*Lake
Constance*

Fr First Army

MEMMINGEN

SALZBURG
4 May

BASLE

OBERAMMERGAU

US Seventh Army

GARMISCH-
PARTENKIRCHEN

KUFSTEIN

BERCHTESGADEN
4 May

Enns

SWITZERLAND

BREGENZ

*Oberjoch
Pass*

FÜSSEN

*Fern
Pass*

KITZBÜHEL

TAMSWEG

*Aarlberg
Pass*

IMST

INNSBRUCK

AUSTRIA

LANDECK

T y r o l

A l p s

*Brenner
Pass*

4 May

KLAGENFURT

*Resia
Pass*

BOLZANO

ITALY

US Fifth Army

YUGOSLAVIA

	OCCUPIED BY ALLIED FORCES, 28 MARCH 1945
	BRITISH ATTACKS
	US ATTACKS
	FRENCH ATTACKS
	GERMAN POCKETS
	OCCUPIED BY RUSSIAN FORCES, 16 APRIL
□	CONCENTRATION CAMPS

0   MILES   120

0   KILOMETERS   200

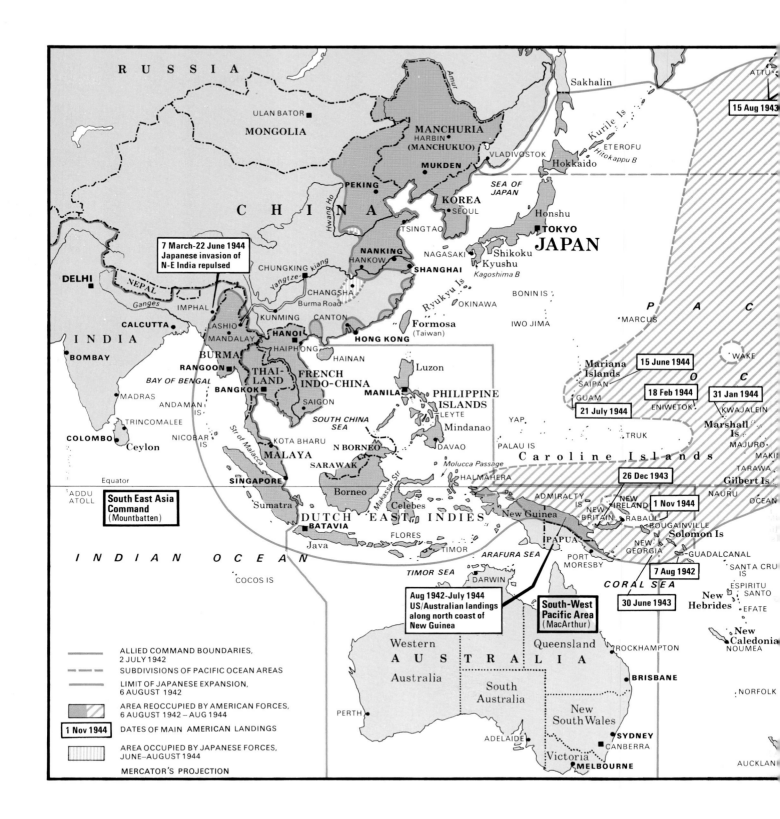

RUSSIA

ULAN BATOR

MONGOLIA

MANCHURIA
HARBIN
(MANCHUKUO)
MUKDEN
VLADIVOSTOK

PEKING

C H I N A

Amur

Sakhalin

ATTU

15 Aug 1943

Kurile Is
ETEROFU
Hitokappu B

Hokkaido

SEA OF
JAPAN

KOREA
SEOUL

Honshu

TOKYO

JAPAN

Shikoku

7 March-22 June 1944
Japanese invasion of
N-E India repulsed

Hwang Ho

CHUNGKING

Yangtze-kiang

CHANGSHA

Burma Road

KUNMING

NANKING
HANKOW

SHANGHAI

TSINGTAO

NAGASAKI

Kyushu

Kagoshima B

DELHI

NEPAL

Ganges

IMPHAL

CALCUTTA

INDIA

BOMBAY

CANTON

HONG KONG

Ryukyu Is

OKINAWA

Formosa
(Taiwan)

BONIN IS

IWO JIMA

P
A
C
I

MARCUS

WAKE

O

C

LASHIO
MANDALAY

HANOI

HAIPHONG

HAINAN

Luzon

BURMA

RANGOON

BAY OF BENGAL

THAI-
LAND

BANGKOK

FRENCH
INDO-CHINA

SAIGON

MANILA

PHILIPPINE
ISLANDS

LEYTE

Mindanao

YAP.

Mariana
Islands

SAIPAN

GUAM

15 June 1944

18 Feb 1944

21 July 1944

ENIWETOK

31 Jan 1944

KWAJALEIN

Marshall
Is

MAJURO

MAKI

MADRAS

ANDAMAN
IS

TRINCOMALEE

COLOMBO

Ceylon

NICOBAR
IS

Str of Malacca

KOTA BHARU

MALAYA

SINGAPORE

SOUTH CHINA
SEA

N BORNEO

SARAWAK

Davao

PALAU IS

TRUK

Caroline Islands

TARAWA

Gilbert Is

Equator

ADDU
ATOLL

South East Asia
Command
(Mountbatten)

Sumatra

DUTCH

BATAVIA

Java

Borneo

Celebes

Makassar Str

Molucca Passage

HALMAHERA

E A S T   I N D I E S

FLORES

TIMOR

26 Dec 1943

ADMIRALTY
IS

New Guinea

NEW
IRELAND

NEW
BRITAIN

RABAUL

NAURU

OCEAN

1 Nov 1944

BOUGAINVILLE

Solomon Is

NEW &
GEORGIA

GUADALCANAL

SANTA CRU
IS

INDIAN   OCEAN

COCOS IS

TIMOR SEA

DARWIN

ARAFURA SEA

PAPUA

PORT
MORESBY

7 Aug 1942

CORAL SEA

30 June 1943

ESPIRITU
SANTO

New
Hebrides

EFATE

Aug 1942-July 1944
US/Australian landings
along north coast of
New Guinea

South-West
Pacific Area
(MacArthur)

Western

A U S T R A L I A

Australia

South
Australia

New
Caledonia

NOUMEA

ROCKHAMPTON

Queensland

BRISBANE

NORFOLK

PERTH

ADELAIDE

New
South Wales

SYDNEY
CANBERRA

Victoria

MELBOURNE

AUCKLAN

ALLIED COMMAND BOUNDARIES,
2 JULY 1942

SUBDIVISIONS OF PACIFIC OCEAN AREAS

LIMIT OF JAPANESE EXPANSION,
6 AUGUST 1942

AREA REOCCUPIED BY AMERICAN FORCES,
6 AUGUST 1942 – AUG 1944

1 Nov 1944   DATES OF MAIN AMERICAN LANDINGS

AREA OCCUPIED BY JAPANESE FORCES,
JUNE–AUGUST 1944

MERCATOR'S PROJECTION

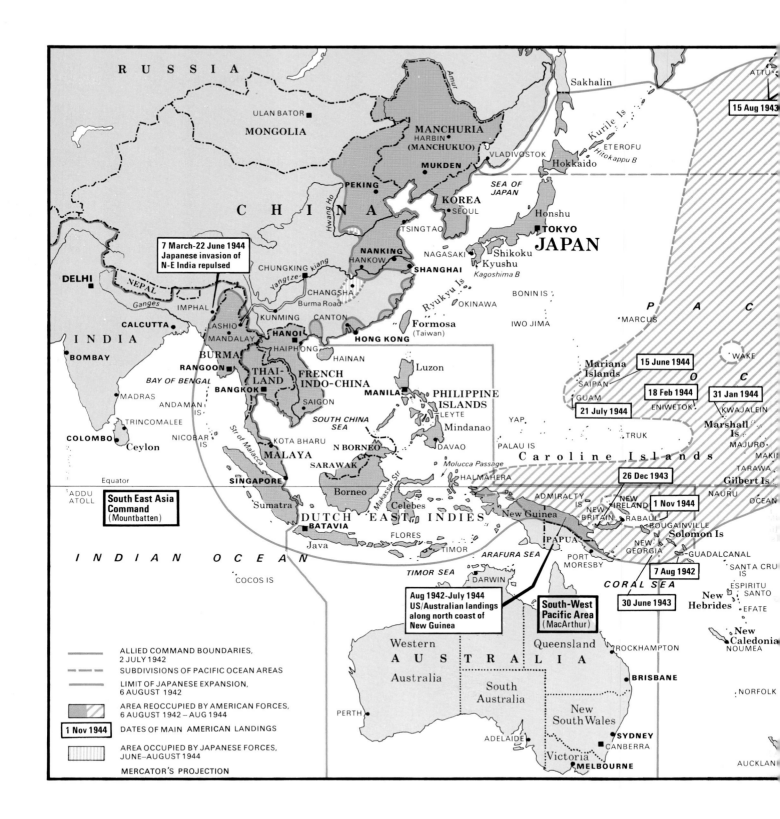

118

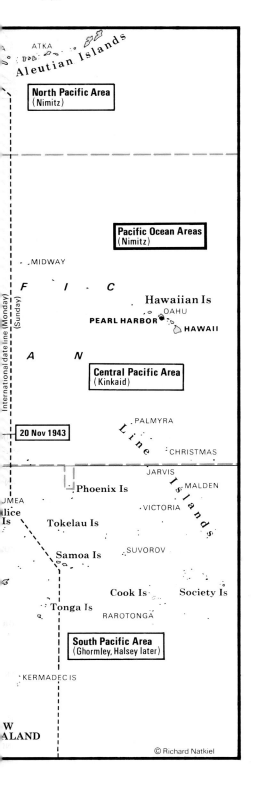

© Richard Natkiel

Counteroffensive in the Pacific

The defeat of the Japanese Navy at Midway, followed by the hard-fought victories at Guadalcanal and the naval engagements in the Solomons, meant that at the end of 1942 the Americans were ready to push back the Japanese tide. While British Commonwealth forces managed to hold back the Japanese on the Burma-India frontier, the Americans envisioned two lines of attack in the Pacific. In the Southwest Pacific, American and Australian forces under General Douglas MacArthur would concentrate on forcing back the Japanese in New Guinea, thereby lifting the threat to Australia and eventually winning a stepping stone for further advances. In the wider expanses of the Pacific, profiting from

the radically changed naval balance of power following the destruction of Japanese aircraft carriers at Midway and the arrival of newly-built carriers for the US fleets, successive landings would be made in a strategy which became known as 'island-hopping.'

'Island-hopping' meant that, as one island after another fell to US amphibious assaults, the Americans would acquire airfields and bases that, in due course, would bring Japan into convenient bombing range. Meantime, it was expected that the series of island battles would wear down the Japanese forces. An additional feature was that those islands which the Japanese had fortified into strongpoints could be merely by-passed and left to wither from supply shortages. This strategy, it was thought, would shorten the war by bringing the Japanese homeland under attack earlier than would the alternative strategy of a methodical

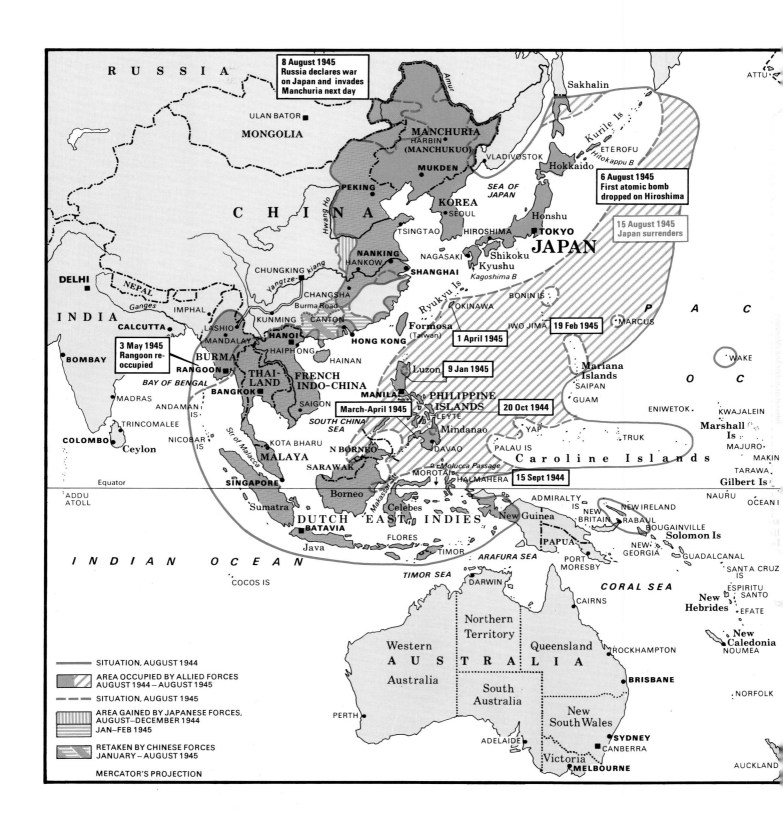

8 August 1945
Russia declares war on Japan and invades Manchuria next day

6 August 1945
First atomic bomb dropped on Hiroshima

15 August 1945
Japan surrenders

3 May 1945
Rangoon re-occupied

1 April 1945

19 Feb 1945

9 Jan 1945

March–April 1945

20 Oct 1944

15 Sept 1944

R U S S I A

MONGOLIA

ULAN BATOR

MANCHURIA
HARBIN
(MANCHUKUO)

MUKDEN

VLADIVOSTOK

Sakhalin

Hokkaido

Kurile Is

ETEROFU
Hitokappu B

PEKING

KOREA
SEOUL

SEA OF
JAPAN

Honshu

TOKYO

ATTU

C H I N A

Hwang Ho

TSINGTAO

HIROSHIMA

JAPAN

NANKING
HANKOW

CHUNGKING

SHANGHAI
NAGASAKI

Shikoku
Kyushu
Kagoshima B

DELHI

NEPAL

Ganges

CHANGSHA

Burma Road

Yangtze-kiang

CANTON

Ryukyu Is

OKINAWA

BONIN IS

P A C

MARCUS

INDIA

IMPHAL

KUNMING

Formosa
(Taiwan)

1 April 1945

IWO JIMA

19 Feb 1945

CALCUTTA

LASHIO
MANDALAY

HANOI
HAIPHONG

HONG KONG

HAINAN

Luzon

9 Jan 1945

Mariana
Islands
SAIPAN

WAKE

O C

BOMBAY

BURMA

RANGOON

THAI-
LAND

BANGKOK

FRENCH
INDO-CHINA

SAIGON

MANILA

PHILIPPINE
ISLANDS

LEYTE

20 Oct 1944

GUAM

ENIWETOK

KWAJALEIN

Marshall
Is
MAJURO

BAY OF BENGAL

MADRAS

ANDAMAN
IS

March–April 1945

SOUTH CHINA
SEA

Mindanao

YAP

TRUK

MAKIN

TRINCOMALEE

NICOBAR
IS

Str of Malacca

KOTA BHARU

N BORNEO

DAVAO

PALAU IS

Molucca Passage

MOROTAI

15 Sept 1944

HALMAHERA

Caroline Islands

TARAWA

Gilbert Is

COLOMBO

Ceylon

MALAYA

SARAWAK

Equator

NAURU

OCEAN I

ADDU
ATOLL

SINGAPORE

Sumatra

DUTCH

BATAVIA

Java

E A S T

Borneo

Celebes

FLORES

Makassar

I N D I E S

New Guinea

PAPUA

TIMOR

ARAFURA SEA

PORT
MORESBY

ADMIRALTY
IS

NEW
BRITAIN
RABAUL

NEW IRELAND

BOUGAINVILLE

NEW
GEORGIA

Solomon Is

GUADALCANAL

SANTA CRUZ
IS

ESPIRITU
SANTO

New
Hebrides

EFATE

New
Caledonia
NOUMEA

I N D I A N   O C E A N

COCOS IS

TIMOR SEA

DARWIN

CORAL SEA

CAIRNS

NORFOLK

Northern
Territory

Western
Australia

Queensland

ROCKHAMPTON

A U S T R A L I A

Australia

South
Australia

New
South Wales

BRISBANE

PERTH

ADELAIDE

Victoria

SYDNEY
CANBERRA

MELBOURNE

AUCKLAND

SITUATION, AUGUST 1944

AREA OCCUPIED BY ALLIED FORCES
AUGUST 1944 – AUGUST 1945

SITUATION, AUGUST 1945

AREA GAINED BY JAPANESE FORCES,
AUGUST–DECEMBER 1944
JAN–FEB 1945

RETAKEN BY CHINESE FORCES
JANUARY – AUGUST 1945

MERCATOR'S PROJECTION

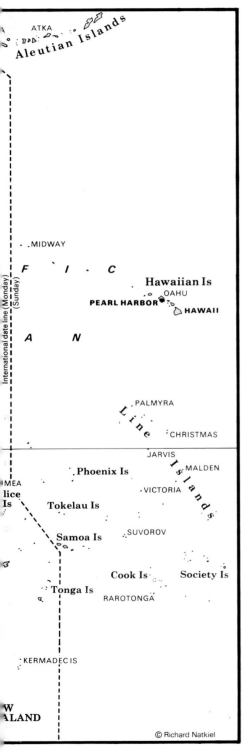

recapturing, starting with New Guinea, of all the territories overrun by the Japanese. It did mean, though, that the liberation of important territories like the Philippines and the East Indies would be postponed. However, a final decision as to which of the two alternatives should have priority could be put off until 1944. For the time being, thanks to the flood of supplies and equipment reaching the US forces, the two strategies could both be pursued simultaneously.

In November 1943 an early am-phibious landing at Tarawa, though eventually successful, inflicted enormous casualties on the US Marines as the Japanese fought, almost literally, to the last man. Evidently 'island-hopping' would be costly but, beginning with Tarawa, the Americans continually learned from experience and found ways to reduce their casualty rates. In particular, Tarawa showed them that for island landings a new concept of landing craft, the tracked landing vehicle, was needed, to cope with the reefs.

New Guinea

The Japanese made a last attempt to capture Port Moresby in summer 1942, but their overland drive was blocked by Australian forces. Then, Australian and US units laid an airstrip at Milne Bay, as a prelude to offensive operations. Meanwhile, despite the tangled, mountainous, disease-ridden and practically unmapped terrain, US and Australian troops advanced over the Owen Stanley Range to the north coast to capture Buna and Sanananda.

This advance, while blocking a threat to Australia, was regarded as part of the Allied counteroffensive and was intended to form one prong of an attack on Japanese-held Rabaul, the other prong being an island-hopping advance from the direction of the Solomon Islands. As things turned out, however, it was later decided merely to encircle Rabaul and thereby avoid the heavy casualties that could

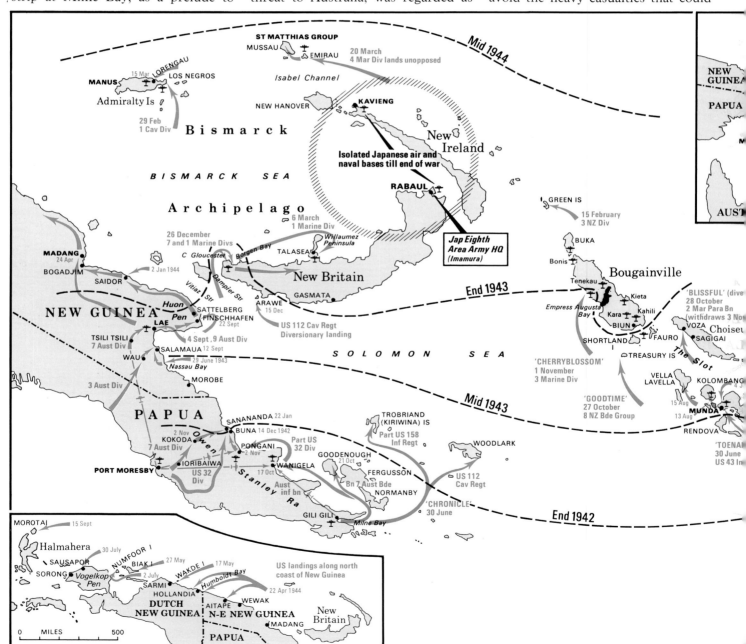

MAP below left: *The Australian and American offensives in the Solomons and New Guinea.*
MAP below right: *The attacks made during the Gilbert and Marshall Islands campaigns.*

be expected in a direct assault. But this initial strategy determined the shape of the New Guinea campaign, and its development into an attack on New Britain.

Preparatory moves had been made earlier, often making use of airborne landings. An Australian brigade airlifted to Wau had established a for-

ward base for assaults on the Japanese garrisons at Salamaua and Lae. Further east, US forces had landed to capture the Trobriand and Woodlark islands.

In September 1943 the 9th and 7th Australian Divisions, with the help of an airdrop by a US parachute regiment, captured Lae and Salamaua. The Australians then set off for Madang, which they captured in April. Lesser Japanese garrisons were killed or dispersed at the same time. These successes cleared the way for landings in New Britain, made by US Marines and an armored cavalry regiment in December. At this point it was decided to isolate, rather than capture, Rabaul, so forces were despatched to take the Admiralty and St Matthias islands, in order to complete the encirclement. Following this stabilization of the situation, most of the American forces moved to new campaigns, leaving the Australians the task of containing the Japanese in eastern New Britain.

There still remained strong Japanese forces in western New Guinea. In fact, the Japanese command, aware of the strategic importance of this area, devoted considerable resources, although not many men, to strengthening their position here. General MacArthur decided to bypass the Japanese Eighteenth Army, which among other things was defending itself against the Australians in the Madang area, and to strike much further west at the Japanese Second Army, which was holding Dutch New Guinea. Landings were made, heavy fighting followed which resulted in severe Japanese casualties but relatively few American, and by the end of July 1944 MacArthur's troops had reached the western tip of New Guinea. When, a few days later, the Australians defeated a final desperate counteroffensive by the Japanese Eighteenth Army, the New Guinea campaign, one of the most grueling of the entire war, came to an end. MacArthur could now turn his attention to the Philippines and keep his famous promise, 'I shall return.'

The Marshall Islands

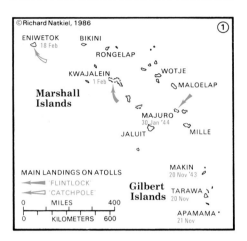

Enjoying almost overwhelming air and naval superiority, the Americans could pick and choose their island targets in the Pacific counteroffensive. The Gilbert Islands were an early priority because, once they were captured, the Marshalls could be tackled and the Japanese fleet base at Truk put under threat. In November 1943 Tarawa, with its coral strongpoint of Betio, was captured at very heavy cost, while the neighboring island of Makin was taken with relatively few losses.

With the main Gilbert islands secure, the Americans pressed on to the Marshalls, 500 miles to the northwest. The intention was not to capture all the islands of the group, but simply those which had good airfields. A preliminary and unopposed landing was made on Majuro, which provided a useful harbor. Then, at the beginning of February, Kwajalein Atoll, where the main Japanese strength was concentrated, was assaulted. Benefitting from the lessons of Tarawa, the preliminary area bombardment was replaced by close-range bombardment of specified targets, and nearby small islands were captured to serve as gun platforms for flanking artillery support. The defenders, without air or naval support, soon fell victim to the American infantry. Of the 8000 Japan-

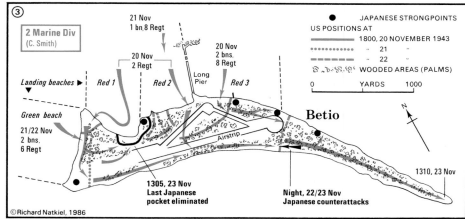

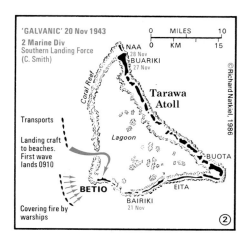

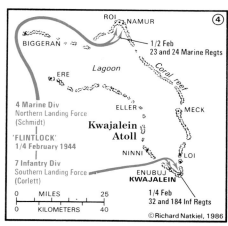

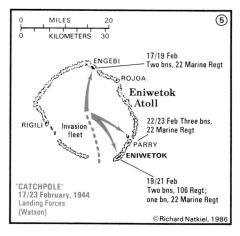

ese, 7870 were killed, but of the 41,000 US troops involved, less than 350 lost their lives. Two smaller nearby islands, Roi and Namur, were also captured.

The more distant Eniwetok Atoll, which promised a hard fight, could now be assaulted six weeks ahead of schedule, and was entrusted to the reserves that had been unused on Kwajalein. The American landing craft entered the Eniwetok lagoon and, on different days, came ashore first at Engebi, where the two Marine battalions encountered little opposition, then at Eniwetok, where another two battalions needed two days of heavy fighting to clear out the defenders, and finally at Parry, where two other battalions met stiff opposition. For the most part, the Japanese fought to the last man, many of them being killed by flamethrowers as they sheltered in their concrete bunkers.

While all this was happening, the Japanese Combined Fleet was lying at Truk, in the Caroline Islands, unable to intervene because it was almost totally bereft of air cover. It was attacked by aircraft of the US Fifth Fleet, managed to escape, but sacrificed a large number of precious merchant ships in doing so. Evidently Truk was now too dangerous as a base, and the Japanese fleet retired to the Philippines. This retreat from Truk enabled the US command to stick to its plan of by-passing the Carolines in favor of an immediate campaign against the Marianas.

MAPS top: *The Tarawa landings and details of the fighting on Betio.*
MAP center: *The landings on Kwajalein.*
MAP above: *The landings at Eniwetok.*

The Marianas

About 1000 miles nearer to Japan than the Marshalls, the Marianas Islands were the next objective of the Americans. These were not coral islands, but rocky, and the three largest of them, Guam, Saipan, and Tinian, were suitable for the construction of airfields from which the new B-29 Superfortress bombers could attack Japan itself.

In mid-June 1944, after heavy preliminary bombing by carrier aircraft of the Fifth Fleet, over 500 US ships arrived off Saipan with about 127,000 troops. Following a feint attack by reserve regiments, the main attack was made in two separate thrusts, each by a Marine division, on each side of Afetna Point. Although there were about 30,000 Japanese on Saipan instead of the 20,000 anticipated, the Americans crossed the island within three days, splitting the Japanese forces into two parts.

The southern part was easily dealt with by a single infantry battalion, and the remaining infantry joined the Marines in the drive against the northern defenders. In this, the infantry moved slower than the Marines, which spared them the high casualty rate suffered by the latter but aroused some ill-feeling on the part of the Marine commanders. As the Japanese were pushed up into the narrower part of the island their position became

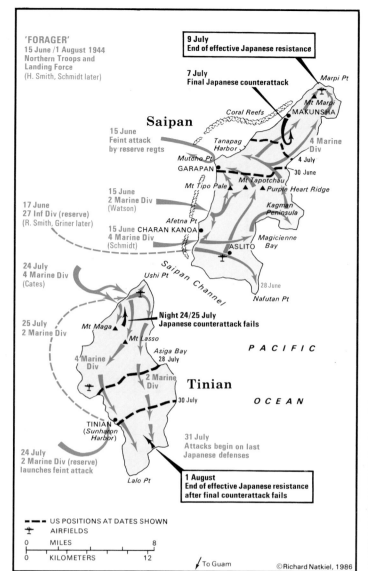

Saipan map labels:

'FORAGER'
15 June/1 August 1944
Northern Troops and
Landing Force
(H. Smith, Schmidt later)

9 July
End of effective Japanese resistance

7 July
Final Japanese counterattack

Marpi Pt

Mt Marpi
MAKUNSHA

Coral Reefs

Saipan

15 June
Feint attack
by reserve regts

Tanapag
Harbor

4 Marine
Div

4 July
30 June

Mutcho Pt
GARAPAN

Mt Tipo Pale   Mt Tapotchau
Purple Heart Ridge

17 June
27 Inf Div (reserve)
(R. Smith, Griner later)

Kagman
Peninsula

15 June
2 Marine Div
(Watson)

Afetna Pt

15 June CHARAN KANOA
4 Marine Div
(Schmidt)

Magicienne
Bay

ASLITO

Saipan Channel

28 June

Nafutan Pt

24 July
4 Marine Div
(Cates)

Ushi Pt

PACIFIC

Night 24/25 July
Japanese counterattack fails

25 July
2 Marine Div

Mt Maga

Mt Lasso

Asiga Bay
28 July

OCEAN

4 Marine
Div

2 Marine
Div

Tinian

30 July

24 July
2 Marine Div (reserve)
launches feint attack

TINIAN
(Sunharon
Harbor)

31 July
Attacks begin on last
Japanese defenses

Lalo Pt

1 August
End of effective Japanese resistance
after final counterattack fails

US POSITIONS AT DATES SHOWN
AIRFIELDS

0   MILES   8
0   KILOMETERS   12

To Guam
©Richard Natkiel, 1986

Guam map labels:

'FORAGER'
21 July/10 August 1944
Southern Troops and
Landing Force
(Geiger)

10 August
End of effective
Japanese resistance

Mt Machanao

PACIFIC OCEAN

1 Marine Bde
FINAGUAYAC

Pati Pt

UPI

0829, 21 July
3 Marine Div
(Turnage)

TAGUAC

3 Marine
Div

6 Aug

LULOG

Mt Santa Rosa

Tumon
Bay

DEDEDO

77 Inf Div

Asan Pt Adelup Pt

Mt Barrigada

CABRAS I

AGANA

1 Aug

Orote
Peninsula
29 July

Piti Navy Yard

ASAN

Mt Chachao
Mt Alutom
Mt Tenjo

0830, 21 July
1 Prov Marine
Bde (Shepherd)
Followed later by
77 Inf Div (reserve)
(Bruce)

Apra
Harbor

AGAT

Bangi Pt   Mt Alifan

Guam

MATA

Coral Reef

Mt Lamlan

INARAJAN

UMATAC

JAPANESE COUNTERATTACKS
ON NIGHT OF 25/26 JULY
AIRFIELD

Ajayan
Pt

Last Japanese soldier surrendered in 1972

0   MILES   10
0   KILOMETERS   15

©Richard Natkiel, 1986

MAP above: *The campaigns on Tinian and Saipan.*
Top right: *A P-47 Thunderbolt fighter destroyed on the ground by a Japanese attack during the fighting for Saipan.*
MAP above right: *The fighting for Guam.*

hopeless. A final suicidal counterattack was pushed back by the US infantry and resistance more or less ceased, with 2000 Japanese consenting to be captured. American dead, at a little more than 3000, were only one ninth of the Japanese killed.

After Saipan came Guam, where the Japanese had 13,000 soldiers and over 5000 sailors. American landing tactics again involved the separate landing of two Marine divisions, one on each side of a coastal objective, this time the Orote Peninsula. The two divisions, after some fighting, managed to link up to create a wide bridgehead before turning northward against the main Japanese strength. The Japanese retreated only slowly, launching determined counterattacks at every opportunity, and held out until they were pushed to the very tip of the island at Mount Machanao. Again, the Japanese dead at 17,300 were about nine times the American loss. Some of the Japanese, rejecting both suicide and capture, hid in the jungle and reappeared after the war was over, in one case 27 years after the Japanese surrender.

While the struggle for Guam was in progress, other landings were made on Tinian. Here the tactics of the two Marine divisions were different. One was used to make a feint attack while the other landed on two beaches in the northern extremity of the island, where it was joined by the division that had made the feint. The Japanese had only about 9000 men on the island, and their night counterattack on the beachheads was weak. The Marines then pushed south until the defenders were crammed into the southern end of the island, where resistance ceased at the beginning of August. This time the Japanese killed, at 6000, were twenty times more numerous than the American dead.

The American engineers moved fast, and before the end of October long-range Superfortress bombers were operating from the newly-built airfields of the Marianas.

Battle of the Philippine Sea

After the Americans captured the Marshall Islands, the Japanese naval command planned an operation designed to lure American aircraft carriers into heavy attacks by Japan's few remaining naval air squadrons. This was set in motion when the US Task Force 58 was covering the American landings in the Marianas.

Following reports that the Japanese 1st Mobile Fleet, having been joined by another force from the south, was steaming toward the Marianas, Admiral Raymond Spruance, commanding the US Fifth Fleet, postponed the landings on Guam and concentrated west of Tinian. The Japanese, meanwhile, divided their force into an advance group with three carriers and a main group of six carriers about a hundred miles astern. Admiral Ozawa, commanding the Japanese 1st Mobile Fleet, hoped that the smaller leading group would attract the Americans' carrier aircraft and leave the main group free to

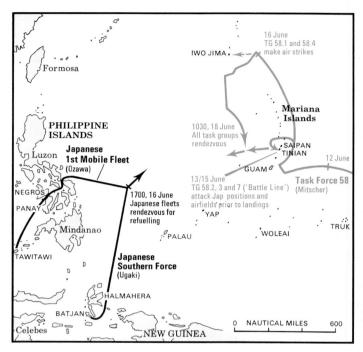

MAP above: *The approach of the fleets to the Battle of the Philippine Sea.*

MAPS below: *The two days of fighting. The Japanese attempted to use the longer range of their aircraft, but most were shot down.*

launch a crushing blow by bombers and torpedo aircraft. However, by unwisely radioing for maximum support by shore-based aircraft, Ozawa revealed to the Americans the position of his main force.

On the morning of 19 June, as Ozawa was flying off his strike aircraft, an American submarine torpedoed his newest carrier, which blew up. A few hours later another submarine sank a second carrier. The Japanese aircraft were easily detected by radar as they approached the US forces, and were soon dealt with, although some later attacks using a new torpedo bomber, the Tenzan, did break through and, if they had been carried out by more experienced crews, would have caused serious damage to the American ships. At the end of 19 June the Japanese carrier aircraft, which had begun with about 400 planes, had carried out four unsuccessful strikes and were left with less than one hundred serviceable aircraft.

Ozawa moved northwest to refuel, and for a time the Americans lost contact. But the following day in mid-afternoon a US reconnaissance aircraft spotted the Japanese ships, which

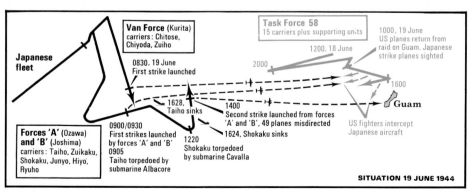

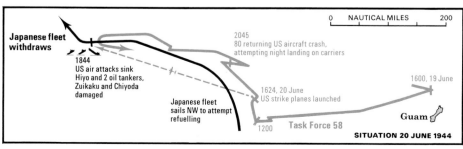

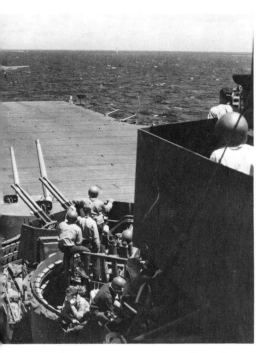

The Leyte Landings

In July 1944 President Roosevelt made the choice between two possible lines of attack for the final offensive against Japan. He chose General MacArthur's proposal for the immediate recapture of the Philippines, with concurrent invasions of Iwo Jima and Okinawa, two islands strategically placed between the northern tip of the Philippines and southern Japan.

As a preliminary, aircraft of the US Third Fleet attacked Japanese bases in the Philippines. These attacks attracted surprisingly little opposition from Japanese fighters so, rightly concluding that the hostile air strength was less than expected, MacArthur brought forward the landing from the planned 20 December to 20 October, a change very smoothly executed by his staff.

In early October Third Fleet aircraft attacked Okinawa and Formosa in order to weaken the ability of the Japanese to launch air strikes from

by that time were 300 miles distant from the American carriers. This meant that the American aircraft caught up with their targets only in the evening, but despite fading light and strong fighter defenses they succeeded in sinking or damaging the surviving Japanese carriers of the main group. Ozawa was able to escape with his remaining ships to Okinawa, while the US aircraft attempted to find and then make night landings on their carriers before their fuel ran out. Being inexperienced in both these techniques, many of them failed, but most of the crews of the eighty aircraft lost during the night were saved.

At this stage of the war, loss of trained aircrew was more damaging than the loss of the aircraft themselves, and in this respect also the Americans won a clear victory. They had lost in these operations about 130 aircraft, but only 76 aircrew. The Japanese, on the other hand, had lost 400 carrier aircraft and several hundred aircrew. Although the Battle of Midway remained the most important naval battle of the Pacific War, this battle was significant because it finished Japan as a naval air power.

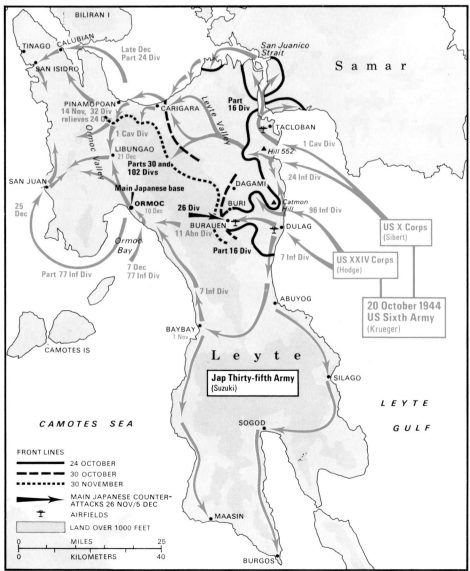

these islands. In the process, the American forces destroyed over 600 Japanese aircraft.

The invasion was directed at Leyte, one of the medium-sized islands of the Philippine group, located between the larger islands of Samar and Mindanao. About 700 ships of the US Seventh Fleet carried the 200,000 men of the invasion force, who began landing on 20 October on the eastern side of the island. One landing was made south of Tacloban and the other, simultaneously, a little farther south near Dulag. Thanks to the large number of craft available, 132,000 men were ashore by nightfall, and they moved inland before the Japanese could concentrate against them.

Defending the Philippines as a whole, General Tomoyuki Yamashita had about 350,000 men at his disposal. Some of these were needed to deal with the Filipino guerrillas, and the rest were distributed through the islands. On Leyte itself the Japanese had only one division, totalling about 16,000 men, and by the end of the month the Americans had occupied most of the northern part of the island. But by this time Yamashita had ordered his Thirty-Fifth Army to move to Leyte, and 35,000 men were landed before the Americans cut the Japanese sea communications here.

The Japanese strategy was to concentrate in the mountainous central part of the island, out of range of the elderly US battleships whose heavy guns could be so destructive against coastal strongpoints. The stubborn Japanese resistance in this area was aided by heavy rainfall, which brought the American advance almost to a halt in November. A main Japanese base at Ormoc, covered by enemy troop concentrations in the nearby mountains, was attacked by the US XXIV Corps, but held out until the US 77th Division landed in an outflanking movement. The capture of Ormoc was followed by a link-up at Libungao of the two US prongs.

Cut off, the Japanese resisted a little longer, but by the end of December, short of food, they were disorganized and weak. Meanwhile, a beachhead on the neighboring island of Samar had been established. Although there remained on Leyte a few scattered bands of Japanese, to all intents and purposes the island was in American hands from January 1945, opening the way for an attack on the largest island, Luzon. In the Leyte operations the Japanese lost about 70,000 men, more than four times the US casualties. Thus the high ratio of Japanese to American casualties continued, despite the general rule that attack is more costly than defense. The Japanese practice of fighting to the very end, together with overwhelming US air superiority, explains this.

Top left: *General MacArthur wades ashore on his famous, long-awaited return to the Philippines.*
Top: *A landing ship moves carefully in toward the beach at Leyte.*
Above: *The Japanese cruiser* Kumano *heavily damaged by air attack while retiring after the Battle off Samar in the aftermath of the Leyte Gulf operations.*
MAP above right: *Overview of the three sectors of the Leyte Gulf battle.*

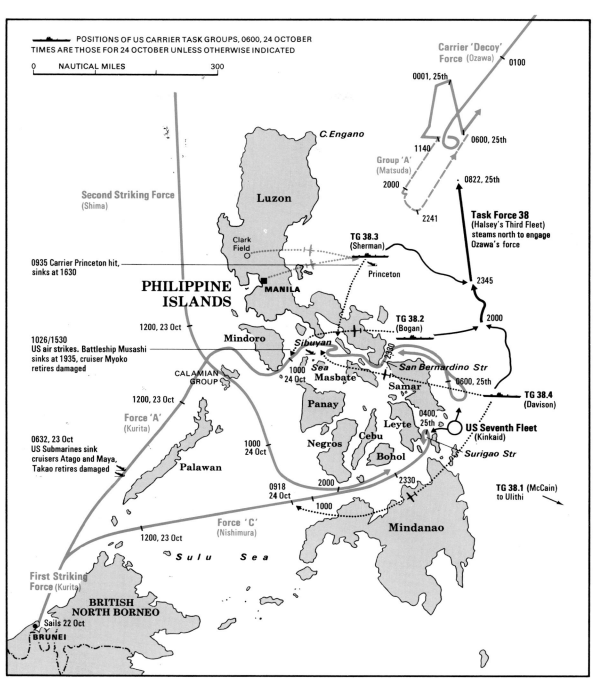

POSITIONS OF US CARRIER TASK GROUPS, 0600, 24 OCTOBER
TIMES ARE THOSE FOR 24 OCTOBER UNLESS OTHERWISE INDICATED

0   NAUTICAL MILES   300

Carrier 'Decoy'
Force (Ozawa)   0100

0001, 25th

1140

0600, 25th

Group 'A'
(Matsuda)

2000

2241

0822, 25th

Task Force 38
(Halsey's Third Fleet)
steams north to engage
Ozawa's force

2345

2000

C. Engano

Second Striking Force
(Shima)

Luzon

Clark
Field

TG 38.3
(Sherman)

Princeton

0935 Carrier Princeton hit,
sinks at 1630

PHILIPPINE
ISLANDS

MANILA

TG 38.2
(Bogan)

1200, 23 Oct

Mindoro

Sibuyan

San Bernardino Str

0600, 25th

TG 38.4
(Davison)

1026/1530
US air strikes. Battleship Musashi
sinks at 1935, cruiser Myoko
retires damaged

1000
24 Oct

Sea
Masbate

Samar

0400,
25th

1200, 23 Oct

CALAMIAN
GROUP

Panay

Leyte

US Seventh Fleet
(Kinkaid)

Force 'A'
(Kurita)

1000
24 Oct

Negros

Cebu

Bohol

Surigao Str

0632, 23 Oct
US Submarines sink
cruisers Atago and Maya,
Takao retires damaged

Palawan

TG 38.1 (McCain)
to Ulithi

0918
24 Oct

2000

2330

1000

1200, 23 Oct

Force 'C'
(Nishimura)

Mindanao

S u l u   S e a

First Striking
Force (Kurita)

BRITISH
NORTH BORNEO

Sails 22 Oct

BRUNEI

Battle of Leyte Gulf

At the time of the Leyte landings the Japanese had few naval aircraft left, and even fewer experienced crews. For what was to be their last fleet action, they relied heavily, therefore, on gunfire and in fact the Battle of Leyte Gulf was the last classical naval battle, with opposing surface ships actually in sight of each other.

The Japanese plan was to send in a carrier force which, although mustering very few aircraft, would play a vital role by attracting American attacks. While the US air strength was thus engaged, two other Japanese groups would pass from west to east through the Philippines and fall upon the US invasion fleet off Leyte, which, if the decoy proved successful, would be without the air cover normally provided by the US fleet carriers. These two groups were Kurita's main striking force, steaming northward from Borneo, and a southern force consisting of two groups, Shima's and Nishimura's, acting independently. It was a well-thought-out plan, which made

the best use of Japanese strength in battleships and cruisers. Should these ships catch the invasion fleet unprotected the Americans would face a disastrous situation.

The operation started badly for the Japanese, because while US submarines soon detected and reported the striking forces, sinking two heavy cruisers in addition, they failed to spot Ozawa's decoy force. It was only when the US carrier *Princeton* was damaged by shore aircraft, and Ozawa scraped together thirty carrier aircraft to attack the rest of US Task Group 38.3,

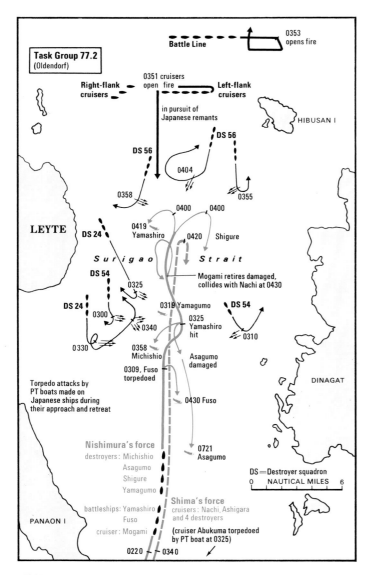

Task Group 77.2
(Oldendorf)

Battle Line
0353 opens fire

0351 cruisers open fire

Right-flank cruisers
Left-flank cruisers

in pursuit of Japanese remants

HIBUSAN I

DS 56
DS 56
0404
0358
0355
0400 0400

LEYTE
0419 Yamashiro
0420 Shigure

DS 24

Mogami retires damaged, collides with Nachi at 0430

Surigao   Strait

DS 54
0325
0319 Yamagumo

DS 24   0300
0340
0325 Yamashiro hit
DS 54
0310

0330
0358 Michishio

Asagumo damaged

0309, Fuso torpedoed

DINAGAT

0430 Fuso

Torpedo attacks by PT boats made on Japanese ships during their approach and retreat

0721 Asagumo

Nishimura's force
destroyers: Michishio
Asagumo
Shigure
Yamagumo

battleships: Yamashiro
Fuso

cruiser: Mogami

PANAON I

DS = Destroyer squadron
0   NAUTICAL MILES   6

Shima's force
cruisers: Nachi, Ashigara
and 4 destroyers

(cruiser Abukuma torpedoed
by PT boat at 0325)

0220 — 0340

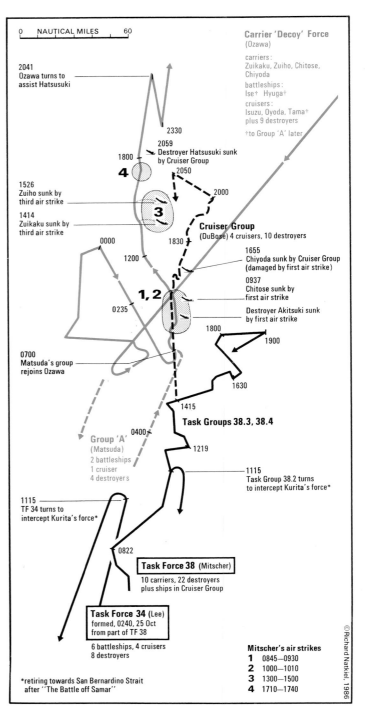

MAP left: *The Surigao Strait action.*
MAP right: *The Battle off Samar in which Admiral Kurita inexplicably failed to win an important victory.*
Bottom left: *Torpedo boats played a decisive part in harrying the Japanese squadron advancing through the Surigao Strait before it was finally turned back by Admiral Oldendorf's battleships. PT.131 is shown.*
MAP below: *Halsey's action with the Japanese decoy force.*

0   NAUTICAL MILES   60

Carrier 'Decoy' Force
(Ozawa)

carriers:
Zuikaku, Zuiho, Chitose,
Chiyoda
battleships:
Ise†, Hyuga†
cruisers:
Isuzu, Oyoda, Tama†
plus 9 destroyers

†to Group 'A' later

2041
Ozawa turns to assist Hatsusuki

2330

2059
Destroyer Hatsusuki sunk by Cruiser Group
1800
4
2050
2000

1526
Zuiho sunk by third air strike
3
1830

1414
Zuikaku sunk by third air strike

Cruiser Group
(DuBose) 4 cruisers, 10 destroyers

0000
1200
1655
Chiyoda sunk by Cruiser Group
(damaged by first air strike)

0937
Chitose sunk by first air strike
1, 2
0235

Destroyer Akitsuki sunk by first air strike

1800
1900

0700
Matsuda's group rejoins Ozawa

1630

1415

Task Groups 38.3, 38.4

1219
1115
Task Group 38.2 turns to intercept Kurita's force*

Group 'A'
(Matsuda)
2 battleships
1 cruiser
4 destroyers

0400

1115
TF 34 turns to intercept Kurita's force*

0822

Task Force 38 (Mitscher)
10 carriers, 22 destroyers
plus ships in Cruiser Group

Task Force 34 (Lee)
formed, 0240, 25 Oct
from part of TF 38
6 battleships, 4 cruisers
8 destroyers

*retiring towards San Bernardino Strait
after "The Battle off Samar"

Mitscher's air strikes
1 0845—0930
2 1000—1010
3 1300—1500
4 1710—1740

© Richard Natkiel, 1986

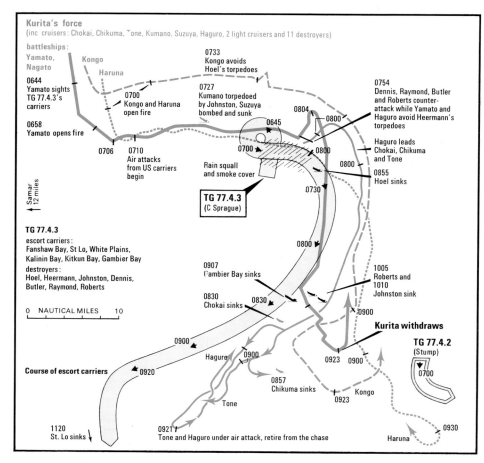

Kurita's force
(inc cruisers: Chokai, Chikuma, Tone, Kumano, Suzuya, Haguro, 2 light cruisers and 11 destroyers)

battleships:
Yamato, Nagato
Kongo
Haruna

0644 Yamato sights TG 77.4.3's carriers

0658 Yamato opens fire

0706
0710 Air attacks from US carriers begin

0700 Kongo and Haruna open fire

0727 Kumano torpedoed by Johnston, Suzuya bombed and sunk

0733 Kongo avoids Hoel's torpedoes

0645

0700

Rain squall and smoke cover

TG 77.4.3 (C Sprague)

0804
0800
0800
0730

0754 Dennis, Raymond, Butler and Roberts counter-attack while Yamato and Haguro avoid Heermann's torpedoes

Haguro leads Chokai, Chikuma and Tone

0855 Hoel sinks

Samar 12 miles

TG 77.4.3
escort carriers:
Fanshaw Bay, St Lo, White Plains, Kalinin Bay, Kitkun Bay, Gambier Bay
destroyers:
Hoel, Heermann, Johnston, Dennis, Butler, Raymond, Roberts

0 NAUTICAL MILES 10

0907 Gambier Bay sinks

0830
0830 Chokai sinks

1005 Roberts and 1010 Johnston sink

0900

Course of escort carriers

0900

0920

Hagure

0900

0923 0900

Kurita withdraws

TG 77.4.2 (Stump)
0700

0857 Chikuma sinks

Kongo

0923

Tone

1120 St. Lo sinks

0921 Tone and Haguro under air attack, retire from the chase

Haruna

0930

that the Americans realized that there were Japanese to the north of them. By the time the decoy force was spotted, Kurita's main force was already under heavy air attack, his giant battleship *Musashi* being sunk. Kurita was wise enough to turn back temporarily, causing the commander of the US Third Fleet, Admiral William F Halsey, to conclude that Ozawa was the main threat. Halsey ordered his ships northward in pursuit, therefore, leaving the invasion fleet in the care of a handful of small escort carriers and destroyers.

However, the US Seventh Fleet's cruisers and old battleships remained off the Surigao Strait, and during the night of 24–25 October Shima's and Nishimura's forces were attacked first by motor torpedo boats, then by destroyers, and finally found themselves under the radar-guided guns of the US battleships and cruisers. The battleship *Fuso* succumbed to torpedoes, while her sister *Yamashiro* was annihilated by gunfire.

But as dawn broke, despite their heavy losses in the Surigao Strait, the Japanese seemed poised for the victory they had planned. Kurita's striking force emerged from the San Bernardino Strait and was almost within gun-range before the US escort carriers knew that they were under threat. The Japanese opened fire at 17 miles, and the carrier *Gambier Bay* was soon sinking. However, smokescreens and self-sacrificial torpedo attacks by the few US destroyers in the vicinity hindered Kurita, who decided to withdraw northward.

Why Kurita, just when he was placed to win a crushing victory, abandoned the whole enterprise, has never been satisfactorily answered. Depression following the news of the Surigao Strait defeat, combined with physical tiredness, may well have been the main reason, but Kurita never convincingly explained his actions. Meanwhile, Halsey's carriers were pursuing the Japanese decoy force and off Cape Engaño their air attacks accounted for three enemy carriers. Halsey then hurriedly turned south, having heard that the Japanese main striking force was threatening the US invasion fleet. The chance of finishing off the decoy force was therefore missed but, nevertheless, Japanese losses in these engagements had been crushing.

Luzon

Having conquered Leyte, General MacArthur turned his attention to the main island of the Philippines, Luzon. Some 850 ships were provided by the US Seventh Fleet to convey 200,000 men from Leyte to the Lingayen Gulf. Supported by gunfire from Seventh Fleet battleships, and by aircraft from Halsey's Third Fleet, the landings were made in two thrusts, each by two divisions. On the way in, however, the ships were subjected to severe attacks by suicide pilots who would have caused really crucial losses had they not, in the Japanese martial tradition, directed themselves against warships rather than the more vulnerable troop-ships.

General Yamashita had divided his defending Fourteenth Army into three parts, with the largest part in the north. He made no attempt to defend the beaches, knowing that his men would be crushed by naval gunfire. Instead, he intended to fight a stubborn campaign in the interior, retiring eventually into the mountains. The first US landings were made on 6 January, and by 23 January one corps had reached the Clark Field airbase. The US Eighth Army, which had been sent to clear the southern islands, was then diverted to Luzon, where it captured Olongapo and cut off the Bataan Peninsula. Yamashita, however, had made sure that few of his forces would be left in that peninsula. Other US divisions were landed south of Manila, the intention being to advance on that capital from north and south.

Yamashita, wisely preferring to conserve his strength, did not intend to fight for Manila, but his subordinate there, an admiral commanding 18,000 sailors, decided that a heroic last stand would be more seemly than a withdrawal. So, for the first and only time in the Pacific campaign, American troops were forced into a major urban battle, fighting from street to street and house to house. This strug-

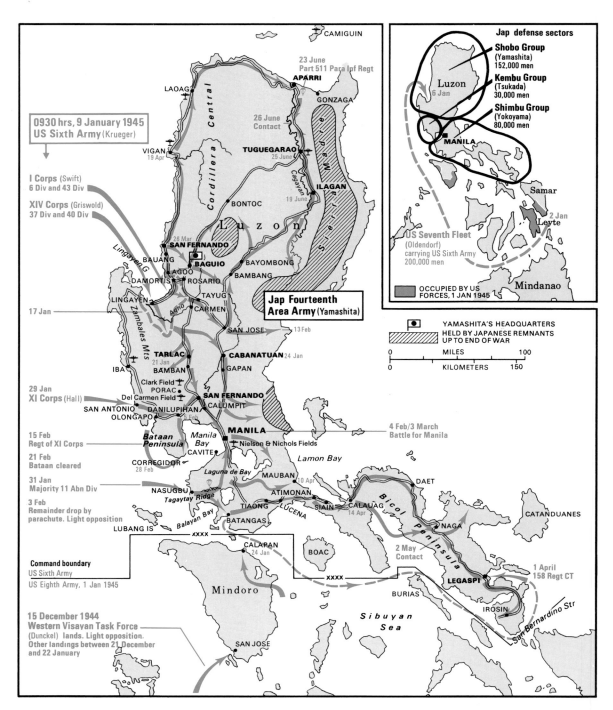

0930 hrs, 9 January 1945
US Sixth Army (Krueger)

I Corps (Swift)
6 Div and 43 Div

XIV Corps (Griswold)
37 Div and 40 Div

17 Jan

29 Jan
XI Corps (Hall)

15 Feb
Regt of XI Corps

21 Feb
Bataan cleared

31 Jan
Majority 11 Abn Div

3 Feb
Remainder drop by
parachute. Light opposition

Command boundary
US Sixth Army
US Eighth Army, 1 Jan 1945

15 December 1944
Western Visayan Task Force
(Dunckel) lands. Light opposition.
Other landings between 21 December
and 22 January

Jap Fourteenth
Area Army (Yamashita)

4 Feb/3 March
Battle for Manila

CAMIGUIN

23 June
Part 511 Para Inf Regt
APARRI

LAOAG
GONZAGA

26 June
Contact

VIGAN
19 Apr

TUGUEGARAO
25 June

ILAGAN
19 June

BONTOC

Luzon

SAN FERNANDO
26 Mar

BAUANG
AGOO
DAMORTIS
ROSARIO
BAGUIO
BAYOMBONG
BAMBANG

Lingayen G.

LINGAYEN
TAYUG
CARMEN
SAN JOSE
13 Feb

IBA
TARLAC
21 Jan
BAMBAN
CABANATUAN 24 Jan
GAPAN

Clark Field
PORAC
Del Carmen Field
SAN FERNANDO
CALUMPIT

SAN ANTONIO
DANILUPIHAN
OLONGAPO

Bataan
Peninsula

MANILA
Manila
Bay
Nielson & Nichols Fields
CAVITE

CORREGIDOR
28 Feb

Lamon Bay

Laguna de Bay
MAUBAN
10 Apr
DAET

NASUGBU
ATIMONAN
Tagaytay Ridge
TIAONG
LUCENA
SIAIN
CALAUAG
14 Apr

Bicol Peninsula

NAGA
CATANDUANES

Balayan Bay
BATANGAS

LUBANG IS.

XXXX

CALAPAN
24 Jan
BOAC

2 May
Contact

1 April
158 Regt CT

XXXX
LEGASPI

Mindoro
BURIAS
IROSIN

SAN JOSE

Sibuyan
Sea

San Bernardino Str.

Jap defense sectors
Shobo Group
(Yamashita)
152,000 men

Kembu Group
(Tsukada)
30,000 men

Shimbu Group
(Yokoyama)
80,000 men

Luzon
6 Jan

MANILA

Samar

2 Jan
Leyte

US Seventh Fleet
(Oldendorf)
carrying US Sixth Army
200,000 men

Mindanao

OCCUPIED BY US
FORCES, 1 JAN 1945

YAMASHITA'S HEADQUARTERS

HELD BY JAPANESE REMNANTS
UP TO END OF WAR

0   MILES   100
0   KILOMETERS   150

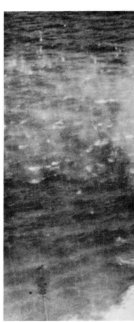

gle lasted two weeks; it cost the Americans 1000 dead but the local Filipino civilians suffered more, with perhaps 100,000 killed as their city was progressively burned and destroyed around them. Before the Americans could use the magnificent Manila harbor, Corregidor had to be captured, and this was done with seaborne and airborne landings, followed by ten days of bloody fighting.

Yamashita fought on. In May, although southern Luzon was in American hands, the Japanese were still strong in the north, in the Sierra Madre and Cordillera Central mountains. How long the Japanese could have held out was never tested, because when Japan made peace in August, Yamashita, still with 50,000 troops at his disposal, surrendered.

MAP above: *The fighting on Luzon.*
Right: *Men of the 145th Infantry move past the badly damaged main post office building in Manila as the fierce fighting for the city continues.*

Left: *A Japanese destroyer is sunk by attacks from B-25 bombers during operations in Philippine waters.*
MAP below: *The fighting for Iwo Jima.*

Iwo Jima and Okinawa

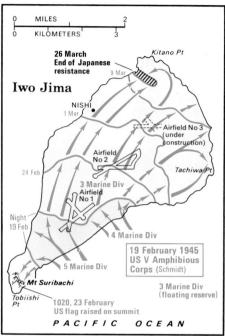

Iwo Jima

26 March
End of Japanese
resistance

Kitano Pt
9 Mar

NISHI
1 Mar

Airfield No 3
(under construction)

Airfield
No 2

Tachiwa Pt

3 Marine Div
Airfield
No 1

24 Feb

Night
19 Feb

4 Marine Div

5 Marine Div

**19 February 1945
US V Amphibious
Corps** (Schmidt)

Mt Suribachi

3 Marine Div
(floating reserve)

*Tobiishi
Pt*

1020, 23 February
US flag raised on summit

P A C I F I C   O C E A N

After their recapture of the Philippines, the Americans visualized three more steps to be taken before the invasion of Japan itself. These were to be the wrecking of Japanese war industries by heavy bombing, the destruction by submarines of what was left of Japanese shipping, and the capture of two islands, Iwo Jima and Okinawa, which lay between the Philippines and Japan.

Iwo Jima was a small island, less than five miles long, but large enough to accommodate vitally important airfields. In Japanese occupation, these airfields could be used to send fighters against US bombers on their outward or inward flights against Japan. In American hands, the airfields would enable fighter escorts to be provided for those bombers over Japan and would serve as emergency landing places for any that were damaged.

Over 20,000 Japanese soldiers and sailors defended Iwo Jima, and they had been building strongpoints, emplacements, and bunkers in prepara-

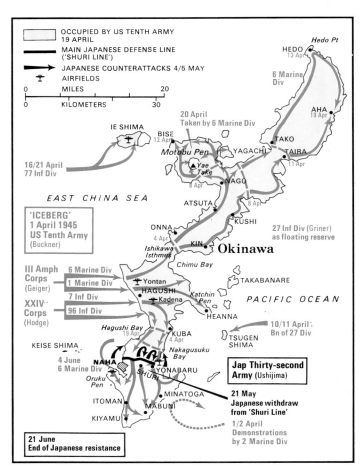

tion for static defensive operations which, it was hoped, would cause the American attackers endless casualties and delay. For this reason, the US Fifth Fleet, using five battleships as well as smaller ships, was sent to subject the island to a three-day bombardment. Two Marine divisions then landed, on 19 February 1945, only to discover that the Japanese had been hardly affected by the bombardment. Nevertheless, in the first day the Marines managed to fight their way across the island, cutting it in two. One division then turned south and assaulted the heights on the southern tip on 23 February. The other division, helped by reserves, went northward very slowly and at high cost against the well-emplaced defenders. It was not until 26 March that the Americans could regard the island as captured.

Just as Japanese resistance on Iwo Jima was coming to an end, the Americans launched their invasion of Okinawa. This was a rather larger island, about 60 miles long, with four airfields. The Japanese had about 130,000 men here, about double the US intelligence estimates.

In preliminary moves, Japanese suicide pilots did considerable damage to the US carriers, although less to the British carriers with their armored decks which had now joined the Fifth Fleet, but the invasion force stayed on course and on 1 April four divisions, aided by a feint attack by a fifth, landed in the southern part of the island. One division turned to take the northern part of the island, while two divisions turned south against the main Japanese strength. These divisions soon found themselves fighting at enormous cost against well-placed and substantially-built defenses, which were hard to locate in advance. However, the Americans' situation was eased when the Japanese launched successive suicidal counterattacks which not only wasted their fighting men but also, often, revealed their positions. It was not until June that Okinawa was securely in US hands. The Americans had lost heavily on land and at sea. The sea casualties resulted from continuing suicide air attacks, but a naval suicide mission, headed by the *Yamato*, was sunk by air attack before it reached the battle area.

MAP left: *The battle for Okinawa.*
Left: *An M-18 tank destroyer of the 77th Division fires on Japanese defensive positions on the so-called Shuri Line, Okinawa, 11 June 1945.*

Below: *TBM Avenger bombers move in to attack Japanese positions on Okinawa.*
Bottom: *The destroyer USS* Aaron Ward, *almost completely wrecked by an attack by a Japanese suicide plane during the Okinawa operations.*

Air Raids on Japan

From June 1944 US bombers made occasional raids on southern Japan but, based in India and using Chinese airfields as jumping-off points, they could not carry heavy bomb-loads. It was not until captured airfields in the Marianas were enlarged that large-scale strategic bombing could begin. The first major raid, by about one hundred Superfortresses of US 21st Bomber Command, was in November, against an aviation factory near Tokyo. After that, bomber missions of about the same strength were despatched every five or six days. Losses from

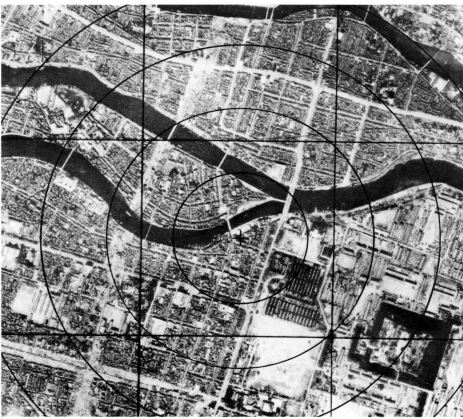

B-29 TARGETS IN JAPAN: FEB/AUGUST 1945

MAIN INCENDIARY (FIRE RAID) TARGETS *

OTHER INCENDIARY TARGETS *

X X X MINE LAYING AREAS

ATOMIC BOMB ATTACK

* FIGURES SHOW PERCENTAGE OF URBAN AREA DESTROYED

0   MILES   150
0   KILOMETRES   200

KOREA

Second atomic bomb dropped on 9 August (over 60,000 casualties)

SHIMONOSEKI

UBE 23

MOJI 27

YAWATA 21 KOKURA

FUKUOKA 22

SASEBO 48

OMUTA 42

OITA 25

KUMAMOTO 20

NAGASAKI

Kyushu

IZUMI

KAGOSHIMA 44

Right: *The B-29 Superfortress* Enola
Gay *which dropped the first atom
bomb on Hiroshima.*
Far left, above: *The nuclear bomb* Fat
Man, *dropped on Nagasaki.*
Far left, below: *Aerial view of
Hiroshima before the attack showing
where the first atom bomb was dropped.*
MAP below: *The bombing campaign
over Japan.*

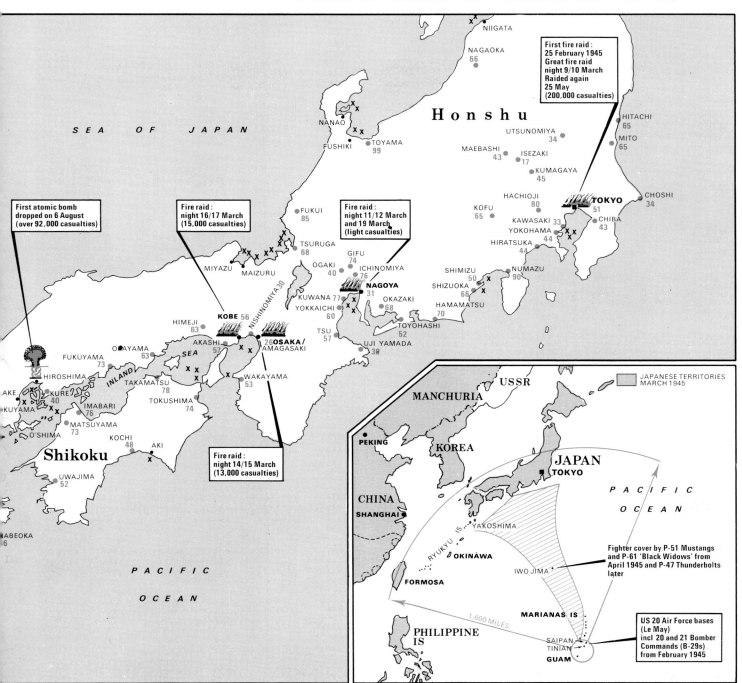

**First fire raid:
25 February 1945
Great fire raid
night 9/10 March
Raided again
25 May
(200,000 casualties)**

SEA OF JAPAN

Honshu

NIIGATA

NAGAOKA
66

HITACHI
65

MITO
65

NANAO

FUSHIKI

TOYAMA
99

UTSUNOMIYA
34

MAEBASHI
43

ISEZAKI
17

KUMAGAYA
45

HACHIOJI
80

CHOSHI
34

**Fire raid:
night 16/17 March
(15,000 casualties)**

FUKUI
85

**Fire raid:
night 11/12 March
and 19 March
(light casualties)**

KOFU
65

TOKYO
51

CHIBA
43

**First atomic bomb
dropped on 6 August
(over 92,000 casualties)**

TSURUGA
68

GIFU
74

KAWASAKI
33

YOKOHAMA
44

MIYAZU

MAIZURU

NISHINOMIYA 30

OGAKI
40

ICHINOMIYA
76

NAGOYA
31

KUWANA 77

HIRATSUKA
44

SHIMIZU
50

NUMAZU
90

HIMEJI
63

KOBE 56

YOKKAICHI
60

TSU
57

OKAZAKI
68

SHIMIZU
50

SHIZUOKA
66

HAMAMATSU
70

AKASHI
57

26 **OSAKA/
AMAGASAKI**

TOYOHASHI
52

FUKUYAMA
73

OKAYAMA
63

INLAND SEA

WAKAYAMA
53

UJI YAMADA
30

HIROSHIMA

TAKAMATSU
78

AKE

KURE
40

IMABARI
76

TOKUSHIMA
74

KUYAMA

MATSUYAMA
73

O'SHIMA

KOCHI
48

AKI

Shikoku

**Fire raid:
night 14/15 March
(13,000 casualties)**

UWAJIMA
52

PACIFIC

OCEAN

ABEOKA

USSR

MANCHURIA

JAPANESE TERRITORIES
MARCH 1945

KOREA

PEKING

JAPAN

TOKYO

PACIFIC

OCEAN

CHINA

SHANGHAI

YAKOSHIMA

RYUKYU IS

OKINAWA

Fighter cover by P-51 Mustangs
and P-61 'Black Widows' from
April 1945 and P-47 Thunderbolts
later

IWO JIMA

FORMOSA

1,600 MILES

MARIANAS IS

**PHILIPPINE
IS**

SAIPAN
TINIAN
GUAM

US 20 Air Force bases
(Le May)
incl 20 and 21 Bomber
Commands (B-29s)
from February 1945

137

Japanese fighters were quite high, around six percent. Moreover, bombing accuracy was poor, thanks to the great heights at which the aircraft flew and the bad weather.

To improve matters, General Curtis LeMay and the US 20th Bomber Command were transferred to the Marianas from India, in order to increase the size and frequency of raids. At the same time, daylight high-level attacks with high explosive bombs were replaced by low-level incendiary attacks on cities at night. The new tactics, which followed the example of the British bombers against Germany, did not require precise bomb-aiming and had the additional advantage that Japanese fighter pilots were not well-trained for night operations. The peak of LeMay's activities came in March, with a massive fire raid on Tokyo, killing at least 80,000 inhabitants and injuring about 100,000 more. American aircraft losses dropped to little

more than one percent.

Daylight raids were resumed when, after the capture of Iwo Jima, US Thunderbolt and Mustang fighters could be provided to escort the bombers over Japan. Japanese fighters were now additionally hampered by fuel shortages, American submarines having taken a stern toll of tankers. Eventually, fighter opposition all but disappeared, at which point the bombers were stripped of most of their guns, enabling a heavier tonnage of bombs to be delivered. In the summer of 1945 not only Tokyo, but the industrial cities of Kobe, Yokohama, Nagoya and Osaka were virtually razed. Thanks more to the high tonnage of bombs dropped than to any accuracy of aim, almost every significant industrial target in these cities was put out of action. Early in August, Superfortresses from the Marianas brought the war to its final week when they dropped atomic bombs on Hiroshima and Nagasaki.

The American Invasion Plan for Japan

When they had won control of Okinawa, the Americans were faced with the task of invading Japan. This had long been envisioned, but because the prospect was now immediate, and because the Japanese had resisted so fiercely on the Pacific islands, the operation seemed daunting even with the crushing superiority which the Americans enjoyed in terms of equipment and trained men. A minimum of one million American casualties seemed unavoidable.

The basis of the plan drawn up for this perilous and undoubtedly costly operation was a pair of major landings. Firstly, Operation OLYMPIC would hit the southernmost island, Kyushu, in November 1945, and be carried out by four corps, one of which would

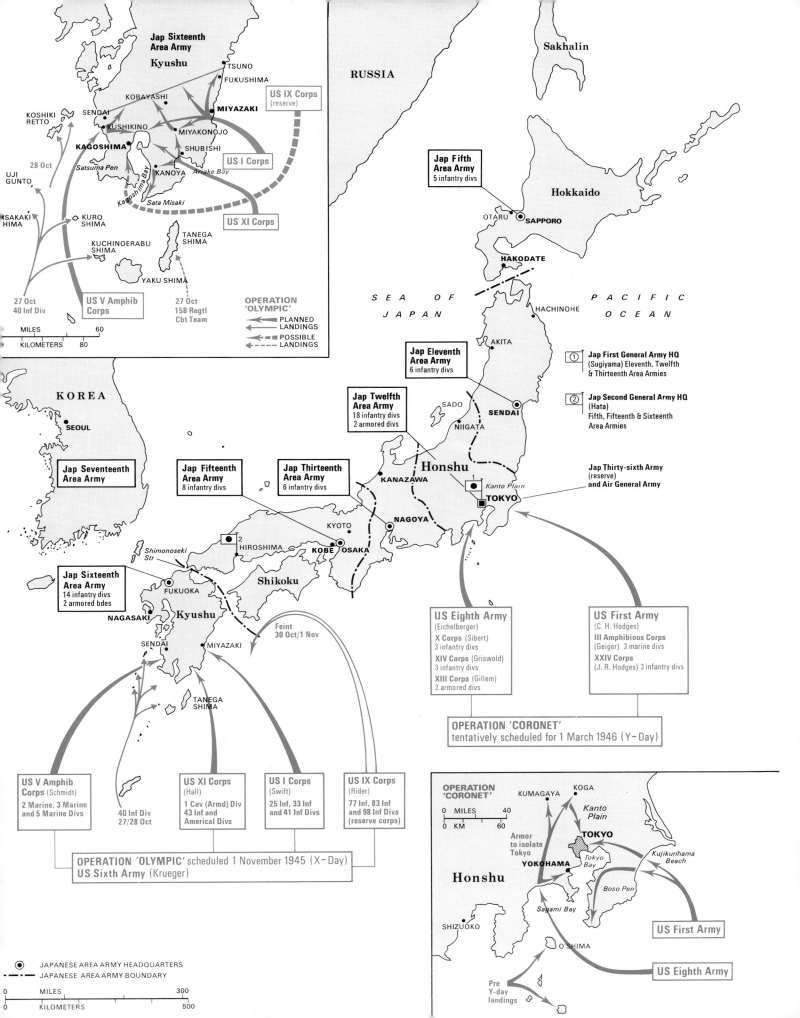

Jap Sixteenth Area Army
Kyushu

TSUNO
FUKUSHIMA
KOBAYASHI
SENDAI
KUSHIKINO
MIYAZAKI
MIYAKONOJO
KAGOSHIMA
SHUBISHI
KANOYA
Satsuma Pen
Arake Bay
KOSHIKI RETTO
UJI GUNTO
28 Oct
SAKAKI SHIMA
KURO SHIMA
Kagoshima Bay
Sata Misaki
KUCHINOERABU SHIMA
TANEGA SHIMA
YAKU SHIMA
27 Oct
40 Inf Div
US V Amphib Corps
27 Oct
158 Regtl Cbt Team

US IX Corps (reserve)
US I Corps
US XI Corps

MILES 60
KILOMETERS 80

OPERATION 'OLYMPIC'
→ PLANNED LANDINGS
→ POSSIBLE LANDINGS
⇢ POSSIBLE LANDINGS

Sakhalin
RUSSIA

Jap Fifth Area Army
5 infantry divs

Hokkaido
OTARU
SAPPORO
HAKODATE

SEA OF JAPAN
PACIFIC OCEAN
HACHINOHE
AKITA

Jap Eleventh Area Army
6 infantry divs

Jap Twelfth Area Army
18 infantry divs
2 armored divs
SADO
NIIGATA
SENDAI

① **Jap First General Army HQ**
(Sugiyama) Eleventh, Twelfth & Thirteenth Area Armies

② **Jap Second General Army HQ**
(Hata) Fifth, Fifteenth & Sixteenth Area Armies

KOREA
SEOUL

Jap Seventeenth Area Army

Jap Fifteenth Area Army
8 infantry divs

Jap Thirteenth Area Army
6 infantry divs

Honshu
KANAZAWA
Kanto Plain
TOKYO

Jap Thirty-sixth Army (reserve)
and Air General Army

Shimonoseki Str
HIROSHIMA
KYOTO
NAGOYA
KOBE **OSAKA**

Jap Sixteenth Area Army
14 infantry divs
2 armored bdes
FUKUOKA
Kyushu
NAGASAKI
SENDAI
MIYAZAKI
TANEGA SHIMA
Shikoku

Feint
30 Oct/1 Nov

US Eighth Army
(Eichelberger)
X Corps (Sibert)
3 infantry divs
XIV Corps (Griswold)
3 infantry divs
XIII Corps (Gillem)
2 armored divs

US First Army
(C. H. Hodges)
III Amphibious Corps
(Geiger) 3 marine divs
XXIV Corps
(J. R. Hodges) 3 infantry divs

OPERATION 'CORONET'
tentatively scheduled for 1 March 1946 (Y–Day)

US V Amphib Corps (Schmidt)
2 Marine, 3 Marine and 5 Marine Divs

40 Inf Div
27/28 Oct

US XI Corps (Hall)
1 Cav (Armd) Div
43 Inf and American Divs

US I Corps (Swift)
25 Inf, 33 Inf and 41 Inf Divs

US IX Corps (Rider)
77 Inf, 83 Inf and 98 Inf Divs (reserve corps)

OPERATION 'OLYMPIC' scheduled 1 November 1945 (X–Day)
US Sixth Army (Krueger)

OPERATION 'CORONET'
KUMAGAYA
KOGA
Kanto Plain
Armor to isolate Tokyo
TOKYO
YOKOHAMA
Tokyo Bay
Kujikurihama Beach
Boso Pen
Sagami Bay
Honshu
SHIZUOKO
O'SHIMA
Pre Y-day landings
US First Army
US Eighth Army

0 MILES 40
0 KM 60

⊙ JAPANESE AREA ARMY HEADQUARTERS
–·– JAPANESE AREA ARMY BOUNDARY

0 MILES 300
0 KILOMETERS 500

Right: *General MacArthur and the Japanese Emperor Hirohito meet in Tokyo after the Japanese surrender.*
Below: *Members of the Japanese surrender commission sign the surrender documents aboard the* Missouri *in Tokyo Bay, 2 September 1945.*

mount a feint operation. The other three corps would each make their own separate landings in the southern-most tip of the island, after which they were expected to make slow progress, against fanatical resistance but enjoying the advantage of air superiority. The second landing would take place four months later, in the spring of 1946, when two US armies, the First and Eighth, would carry out Operation CORONET, consisting of two landings around Tokyo. One of these landings would be just south of Yokohama, which would be captured as other units proceeded to encircle Tokyo from the south. Meanwhile, the second landing, east of Tokyo, would develop into a direct thrust against the capital.

After these initial landings, massive reinforcements were to be sent, but a quick victory was not expected. For this reason the promised entry of Russia into the war against Japan was welcome, since it would lighten the Americans' task. However, with the dropping of the two atomic bombs in August the picture changed completely. Indeed, the justification for dropping these bombs was the belief that they would force Japan out of the war and make an invasion unnecessary. That is what happened. Emperor Hirohito insisted that his government make peace, so the hundreds of thousands of American troops mustered for the invasion had no need to make amphibious assaults. They landed instead as an army of occupation.

THE KOREAN WAR

North Korea Attacks

Although the Allies, including Russia, had agreed during World War II that Korea would become a free and independent state, the postwar tension between Moscow and the West meant that the country became divided into a northern, Communist, state and a southern, western-orientated, republic. The dividing line between North Korea (the Korean Peoples' Republic) and South Korea (the Republic of Korea or ROK) was the 38th Parallel of latitude. The intention, supported by votes in the United Nations, had been that the two halves should be reunited following free elections, but the USA and the USSR differed as to the definition of free elections, and it was this insuperable issue that led to the creation of the ROK and the Peoples' Republic in 1948.

It was not long before short outbursts of fighting occurred along the 38th Parallel, and these continued up to the outbreak of the Korean War. In 1949 US troops were withdrawn from the ROK, on the assumption that the new republic could look after itself. At this period US military planners believed that a future war would be global, and were not greatly interested in countries, like Korea, which they acknowledged to be outside the US defense perimeter.

When North Korea invaded the ROK in June 1950, the attack itself, its timing, and the scale of equipment of the attackers all came as a surprise to the US. Seven infantry divisions, supported by an armored division equipped with Russian-built T-34 tanks, swept over the 38th Parallel

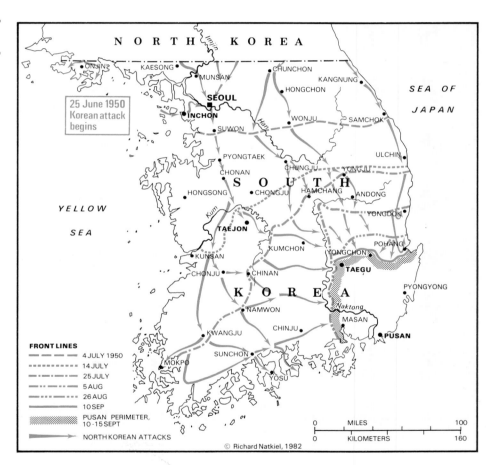

while diversionary amphibious landings were made along the east coast of the ROK. Within three days the ROK capital, Seoul, had been overrun, and by the end of the month North Korean armor was over the Han River, racing toward Taejon.

By that time the first US combat troops were in Korea, having been airlifted in from Japan. On 27 June, profiting from a walk-out on another issue by the Soviet delegate, the UN Security Council recommended UN

MAP above: *The first North Korean offensive and the retreat to the Pusan perimeter.*
MAP top right: *The landing at Inchon.*

members to help the ROK. General Douglas MacArthur became Commander in Chief of the UN Command. The war became a struggle between the Americans and the North Koreans for Pusan, the only remaining good harbor in South Korea.

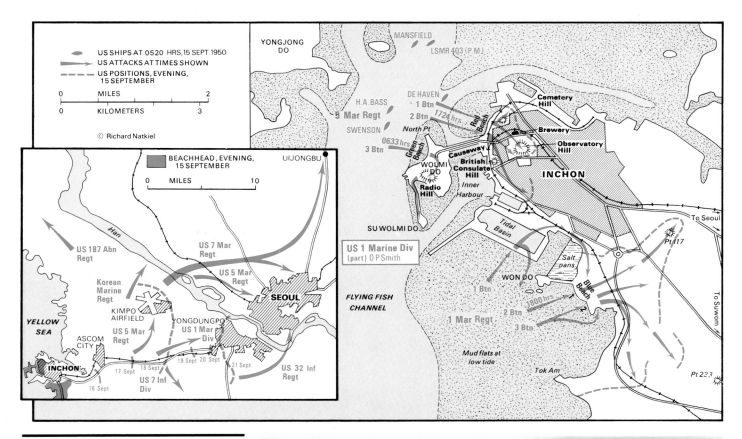

US SHIPS AT 0520 HRS, 15 SEPT 1950
US ATTACKS AT TIMES SHOWN
US POSITIONS, EVENING, 15 SEPTEMBER

MILES 0 — 2
KILOMETERS 0 — 3

© Richard Natkiel

BEACHHEAD, EVENING, 15 SEPTEMBER

MILES 0 — 10

YONGJONG DO
MANSFIELD
LSMR 403 (P.M.)
DE HAVEN
1 Btn
H.A. BASS
5 Mar Regt
2 Btn
1724 hrs.
SWENSON
North Pt
0633 hrs
3 Btn
Red Beach
Cemetery Hill
Brewery
Observatory Hill
INCHON
Green Beach
WOLMI DO
Causeway
British Consulate Hill
Radio Hill
Inner Harbour
SU WOLMI DO

US 1 Marine Div (part) O P Smith

FLYING FISH CHANNEL

Tidal Basin
WON DO
Salt pans
1 Btn
Blue Beach
1800 hrs
To Seoul
Pt 117
2 Btn
1 Mar Regt
3 Btn
To Suwon
Mud flats at low tide
Tok Am
Pt 223

UIJONGBU
Han
US 187 Abn Regt
US 7 Mar Regt
US 5 Mar Regt
Korean Marine Regt
KIMPO AIRFIELD
SEOUL
YELLOW SEA
ASCOM CITY
YONGDUNGPO
US 5 Mar Regt
US 1 Mar Div
INCHON
17 Sept
18 Sept
19 Sept
20 Sept
21 Sept
US 32 Inf Regt
16 Sept
US 7 Inf Div

Inchon

In mid-July North Korean tanks overwhelmed the US forces defending Taejon, and soon General Walton Walker's US Eighth Army was holding back the attackers only 40 miles from Pusan. However, Walker's men held fast long enough for reinforcements to arrive, and by September there was a stalemate, with neither side able to move forward. Against the advice of many of his subordinates, MacArthur decided to break this stalemate with a daring amphibious landing at Inchon, on the northwest coast of the ROK. The US X Corps, rather hurriedly organized, was put aboard ships and on 15 September the landings were made. Three Marine battalions went ashore over the mudflats to the south of Inchon, while three others landed on beaches to the north. Inchon was soon captured, infantry was landed to follow the Marines, and soon the US forces moved on to Seoul, only twenty miles distant.

This landing, over 200 miles in the rear of the North Korean advance units attacking Pusan, was a complete strategic surprise. It coincided with a counteroffensive by the US Eighth

Army out of the Pusan pocket and by the end of September the North Korean army, shattered, had been driven back behind the 38th Parallel.

Above: *Marines storm ashore at Inchon. The ladders on the bow of the landing craft were needed to help the Marines scale the sea wall.*

The Drive to the Yalu

The quick and overwhelming victory of the UN forces after the Inchon landings encouraged the American government, and its allies, to envision setting up the unified, democratic, Korea that had always been the UN aim. MacArthur was therefore allowed to go beyond the 38th Parallel, onto the territory of North Korea. Meanwhile, in October, the General Assembly of the UN voted to arrange for all-Korea elections. Thus the original objective of the UN forces, a return to the 38th Parallel, had been replaced by something more ambitious.

The UN forces, mainly American and South Korean but including contingents from Britain and several other countries, pushed northward on a broad front and on 20 October took Pyongyang, the capital of North Korea. On 26 October an ROK division reached Chosan on the Yalu, the river dividing Korea from China. However, MacArthur did not expect his main forces to reach the Yalu until about the end of December. In October

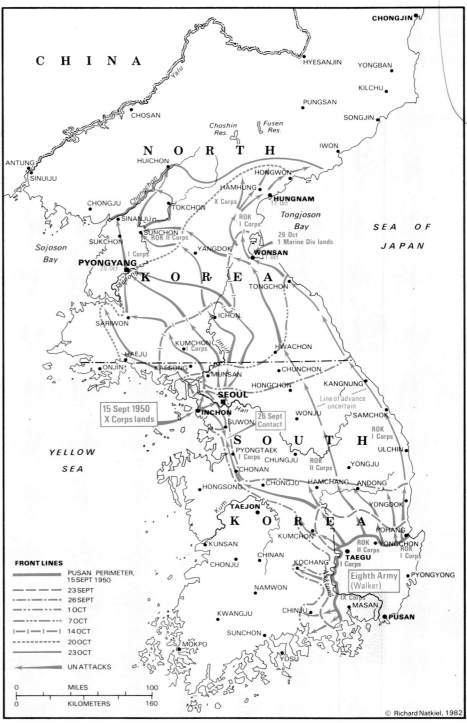

MacArthur and President Truman met on Wake Island to discuss the future of the postwar Korea. The question of possible Chinese intervention was raised, and MacArthur seemed confident that there would be no such move by the Chinese Communists in support of their North Korean neighbors.

On 24 November what was intended to be the last, war-winning, offensive was launched, with the US Eighth Army crossing the Chongchon River and the X Marine Corps, in the north-east, moving up from the Choshin Reservoir. There had already been sporadic clashes with Chinese troops that had infiltrated over the border, and two days after the launch of MacArthur's offensive the UN troops found themselves engaged by massive Chinese concentrations.

MAP left: *The UN offensive September–October 1950.*
Bottom left: *US President-elect General Eisenhower meets with General West commanding the British Commonwealth Division.*

MAP below: *The final stages of the UN advance.*
Bottom: *Scene during the evacuation of the port of Wonsan in the face of the Chinese attacks, 7 December 1950.*

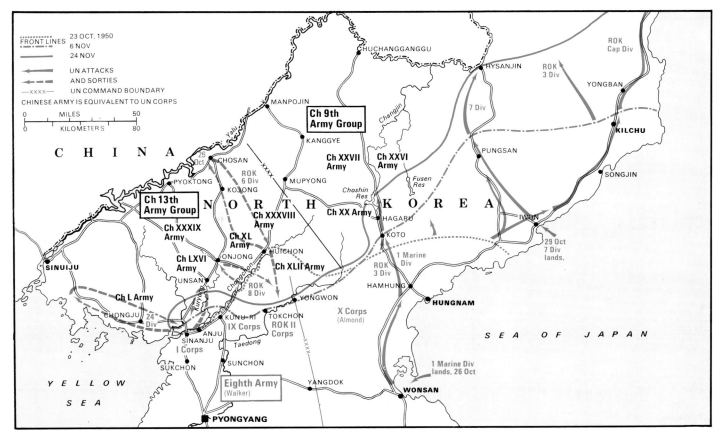

The Chinese Counter-offensive

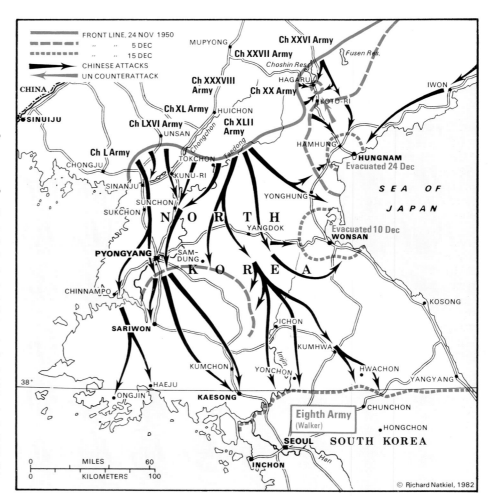

By this time there were about 300,000 Chinese troops in Korea, infiltrated over the Yalu bridges in previous weeks. They were called 'Chinese Peoples' Volunteers,' even though they were regular soldiers, the aim being to avoid giving the impression that the Chinese Peoples' Republic itself had gone to war against the UN forces. The initial Chinese offensives quickly surrounded the US Marines at Choshin, while the US Eighth Army found itself in danger of being outflanked. MacArthur really had only one choice, a helter-skelter withdrawal, which included the evacuation by sea of units cut off by the rapidly advancing Chinese. At the end of the year, instead of standing on the Yalu as had been anticipated, the UN

forces were back on the 38th Parallel. Moreover, the Chinese pushed on to capture Seoul in January. Only supply problems prevented them advancing much farther; they came to a halt about 60 miles south of Seoul.

This gave time for reinforcements to arrive for the Eighth Army which, commanded by General Matthew Ridgway, managed to fight its way back toward the 38th Parallel. Despite this recovery of lost ground, however, the UN situation was grim, for there was now the prospect of a long grinding war against the enormous manpower reserves of China.

MAP left: *The Chinese forces recapture North Korea.*
MAP right: *The final UN gains.*
Below left: *Soldiers of the 25th Infantry Division fire on Chinese positions, April 1951.*
Below: *General MacArthur (center) on a visit to the front line.*

Stabilizing the Front

In the spring of 1951, in an attempt to inflict such heavy losses on the Eighth Army as to weaken UN and US resolve, the Chinese began two great offensives. Advancing in masses against UN forces which were well-situated and well-equipped, they suffered enormous losses. The UN forces, taking advantage of this, then mounted their own offensive, with the demoralized Chinese surrendering in large numbers. This took the UN troops to a good defensive line just north of the 38th Parallel.

On Soviet initiative, armistice talks then began between the two sides. Soon the talks were moved to Panmunjon, where they continued until 1953. During this two-year period of protracted negotiations the war continued along the ceasefire line, but only on a local and sporadic scale, and naval and

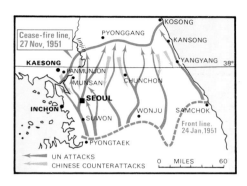

air strikes against North Korea were continued. Eventually, a demarcation line based on the existing front line was agreed, and a settlement reached about prisoners of war. This permitted a general ceasefire to be signed on 27 July 1953. US forces had suffered about 142,000 casualties, South Korean about 300,000, and British Commonwealth about 7000. Chinese and North Korean casualties were estimated two million, while civilian deaths may have exceeded one million.

THE VIETNAM WAR

General Situation

In 1954 the Geneva Conference brought to an end the first stage of the Vietnam War. This had been fought between the colonial power, France, and the Communist-led guerrillas of the Viet Minh independence movement. The latter was headed by the French-educated Communist Ho Chi Minh, and its forces, which toward the end had become regular armies well-equipped with Russian arms by neighboring China, were commanded by General Vo Nguyen Giap. After 1954 the French, finally defeated at Dien Bien Phu, left Indochina, which was divided into four states, Laos, Cambodia, the Democratic Republic of Vietnam, and South Vietnam. The frontier between Ho Chi Minh's North Vietnam and American-supported South Vietnam was the 17th Parallel.

It had been agreed that the two halves of Vietnam would be unified after elections, but South Vietnam refused to hold these on the grounds that they would not be freely conducted in North Vietnam. By the late 1950s, anti-government South Vietnamese, trained in North Vietnam, returned to the south and set up the terrorist group, Viet Cong. At first it concentrated on murdering government officials, but in 1958 it made a

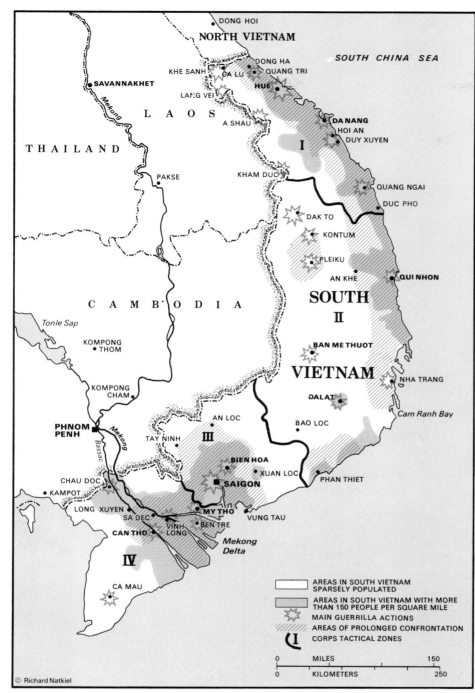

MAP left: *The general situation in Vietnam during the American involvement.*
Below: *A US Marine stands guard over a crowd of Vietnamese refugees.*

Above: *Man of the 173rd Airborne Brigade in a position guarding the Bien Hoa air base. This photograph was taken in May 1965.*
Far left: *A tank of the 11th Cavalry moves into action during fighting in War Zone C in April 1967.*

large-scale attack on an outpost of the Army of the Republic of Vietnam (ARVN), during which an American advisor to the latter was killed. In 1960 the Viet Cong formed the National Liberation Front (NLF) with its regular army, supported by regional and village militias. Much of its strength in men and supplies came from North Vietnam, although this fact was concealed. The Ho Chi Minh Trail, a primitive but resilient line of communication along the Vietnam-Cambodia and Vietnam-Laos fron-tiers, became the lifeline of the NLF. In 1960 the continuing successes of the NLF against the ARVN prompted the US government to send further military advisors, backed up by finan-cial and military aid. The advisors, who often led ARVN units into action, multiplied as the situation worsened, and eventually President Kennedy sanctioned the despatch of US combat troops. There were 16,000 of these in South Vietnam by 1963, and under President Johnson this figure rose to about 500,000 by 1968.

Search and Destroy

By the end of 1966 four regular North Vietnamese infantry divisions, thinly disguised, with about 70,000 NLF troops were operating in South Vietnam, helped by the local and temporary forces supplied by the NLF militias. General William C Westmoreland, directing US and ARVN operations, favored a war of attrition at this stage. While US bombers pounded the Ho Chi Minh Trail, his ground forces tried to destroy Viet Cong base areas. In both lines of attack successes were won, but the enemy, who most often disappeared into the jungle at the first signs of attack, was usually back to normal within a few days. In the summer of 1966, in South Vietnam's northernmost province, the build-up of North Vietnamese regular forces reached a point where large-scale engagements between them and US Marines took place, usually causing heavy casualties to both sides. US search-and-destroy operations also occurred farther south. In the jungles of Tay Ninh Province, near the southern end of the Ho Chi Minh Trail and not far from the South Vietnam capital of Saigon, Operation ATTLEBORO took over 20,000 US troops, of whom nearly one thousand became casualties. In the same area, in February-May 1967, Operation JUNCTION CITY caused about 1800 casualties to US and ARVN forces. Viet Cong and North Vietnamese losses were considerably heavier, although inflated at the time by highly optimistic 'body counts' sent in by the US units. The NLF and North Vietnamese command was quite satisfied with the casualty ratio, believing (rightly as it turned out) the Americans would soon reach the limit of acceptable losses.

MAP above right: *Operation Junction City*.
Right: *Men of the 7th Marines advance across a rice paddy.*
MAP opposite: *The air war in Vietnam.*

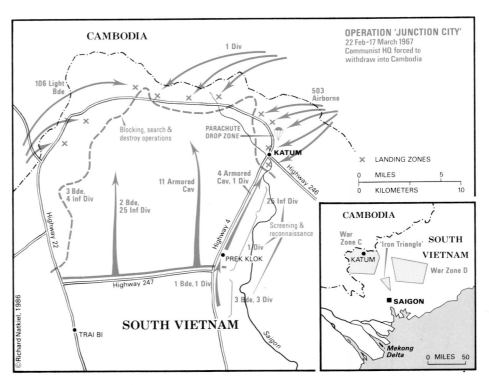

150

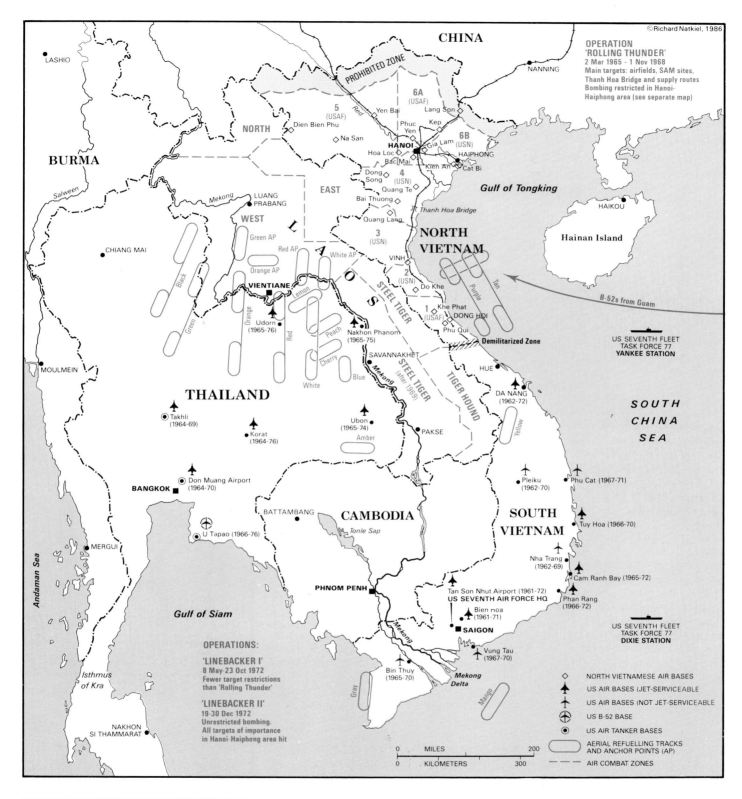

Operation 'Rolling Thunder' and the air war over Vietnam, showing air bases and combat zones.

OPERATION 'ROLLING THUNDER'
2 Mar 1965 – 1 Nov 1968
Main targets: airfields, SAM sites, Thanh Hoa Bridge and supply routes Bombing restricted in Hanoi-Haiphong area (see separate map)

OPERATIONS:

'LINEBACKER I'
8 May-23 Oct 1972
Fewer target restrictions than 'Rolling Thunder'

'LINEBACKER II'
19-30 Dec 1972
Unrestricted bombing. All targets of importance in Hanoi-Haiphong area hit

◇ NORTH VIETNAMESE AIR BASES

✈ US AIR BASES (JET-SERVICEABLE)

✈ US AIR BASES (NOT JET-SERVICEABLE)

⊕ US B-52 BASE

◎ US AIR TANKER BASES

▭ AERIAL REFUELLING TRACKS AND ANCHOR POINTS (AP)

--- AIR COMBAT ZONES

| 0 | MILES | 200 |
| 0 | KILOMETERS | 300 |

The Air War 1965-72

At first it was US aircraft carriers which flew sorties over Vietnam. Then air bases were built and it was to protect one of these, Da Nang, that the US Marines were first put into Viet- nam in 1965. Over the zone of con- flict, South Vietnam, the Americans had total command of the air, which they exploited with savage ground- attack sorties. However, because the Viet Cong presented few large targets, the damage inflicted was not at all equal to the effort expended.

As the involvement of North Viet- namese regular units became more obvious, the idea of bombing North Vietnam itself became attractive, the aim being to show that the Communist effort in South Vietnam might prove very costly in North Vietnam. In February 1965 Operation FLAMING

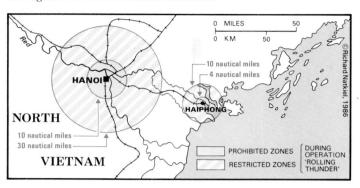

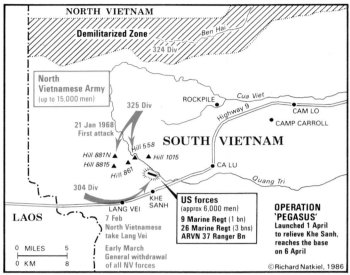

DART undertaken jointly with ARVN aircraft, resulted in strikes against army barracks at Dong Hoi. A year later, faced with a worsening military situation, President Johnson approved a longer bombing operation, ROLLING THUNDER: attacks began with the bombing of the naval base at Quang Khe in March 1965, and the raids continued into 1968, with Washington exercising a strict and sometimes resented control over the local air commanders with the aim of avoiding undue damage to civilian targets. By mid-1965, 900 sorties a week were being flown. However, North Vietnamese morale showed no signs of cracking. In spring 1966 the ban on bombing in the heavily-populated Hanoi/Haiphong area was partially lifted so that oil and railroad installations could be hit. But despite the destruction inflicted (by end-1967 864,000 tons of bombs had been dropped, compared to the 503,000 tons dropped in the Pacific war of 1941–45), the North Vietnamese always seemed able to make good the damage.

In 1972 ground-attack strikes did much to turn back the Easter invasion of South Vietnam, and at the same time renewed bombing of North Vietnam was authorized. Then, later in the year, with a US-China rapprochement on the way and new pressure being needed to improve the US negotiating position in Vietnam, President Nixon authorized Operation LINEBACKER I. This involved the destruction of air-bases, power stations, oil installations and railroad facilities, some of them

quite close to Hanoi. Thanks to more accurate 'smart' bombs, this seven-month campaign inflicted considerable damage and reduced supply movements. Finally, just as an American withdrawal was being negotiated, Nixon inaugurated LINEBACKER 2, twelve days of heavy bombing including Hanoi and Haiphong. The aim was to strengthen the US negotiating position at a critical point, and very heavy damage was caused, although civilian casualties were much lower than was reported at the time. Twenty-six US aircraft were lost, but most of the ground-to-air missiles launched against them failed, many of them exploding in urban areas and adding to the death toll.

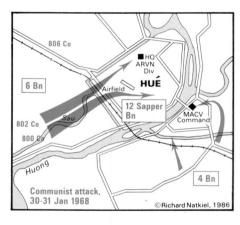

The Tet Offensive

The Viet Cong's Tet Offensive began in late January 1968, preceded by the siege of 3500 US Marines and some ARVN units at Khe Sahn. It took the form of attacks on cities and towns by small units which infiltrated into the urban areas and then launched attacks on vital government buildings. The tactics worked, insofar as in early February 44 provincial capitals, including the former national capital of Hué, were in Communist possession. Some Viet Cong even penetrated inside the compound of the US Embassy in Saigon. But in due course the attackers were ejected with heavy

Above: *Vietnam was the first conflict in which helicopters played a substantial role. This photograph shows troops of the 50th Infantry deploying from their UH-1D near Bong Son during fighting in October 1969.*
Right: *A river assault boat operating in the Mekong Delta area uses its flamethrowers against suspected Viet Cong positions, December 1968.*

losses, usually by ARVN units. The heaviest fighting was in Hué, where it took three weeks to throw out the assailants. The concurrent siege of Khe Sanh also failed, the defenders being relieved by a US Cavalry formation which broke the encirclement.

The Final Communist Offensive

The Tet Offensive was, for the NLF, a failure which had the effect of a victory, for it did much to convince the US public that, despite all the effort and sacrifice, the Communists still held the initiative. American troops, whose morale was deteriorating, were progressively withdrawn. By mid-1972 the ARVN was virtually carrying on alone, for the bulk of US and other foreign ground troops had already left. During 1972 the Communists began a big offensive, with formations crossing the 17th Parallel, and also entering from Cambodia, while uprisings were staged in the Binh and Quang Ngai provinces. In this summer campaign the ARVN units, sometimes deserted by their officers, had usually been routed.

In December 1974 the last Communist offensive began with the capture of Phuoc Long province, at which point the South Vietnamese President decided to abandon all the Highlands and move his troops back to defend Saigon. This retreat turned into a rout. Pleiku and Hué were lost, and then, in March, Da Nang. The remaining battleworthy units of the ARVN made a last stand at Xuan Loc, 40 miles north-east of Saigon, and managed to hold out for nearly a week. Only three divisions were then left to defend Saigon, and by May the war was over.

MAP above right: *The defeat of South Vietnam in 1975.*
Right: *Vietnamese troops move into action in the town of Cholon in 1968.*
Opposite: *Aircraft aboard the nuclear-powered carrier USS* Enterprise *seen while the carrier was helping protect the final evacuation of American personnel from Saigon in April 1975.*

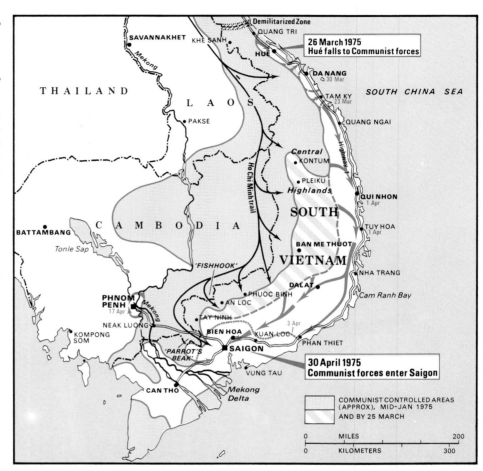

LEBANON

The Marines in Beirut

In the early 1970s Lebanon was an oasis of peace and prosperity in a long-troubled Middle East. The Christian and Moslem segments of its population lived side by side, with mutual suspicion but also with a preference for tolerance over animosity. But from about 1975 other states, especially Syria and Israel, dragged the country into the turmoil of the Arab-Israeli conflict. Members of the Palestine Liberation Organization (PLO) found refuge there, and soon used its capital Beirut and its southern frontier area as bases for attacks on Israel and Israelis.

Although a United Nations force had been installed on the southern frontier, Israel invaded Lebanon in 1982, but an agreement negotiated under US auspices in August provided for an Israeli withdrawal while the USA and a few other countries supplied troops to keep the peace for thirty days. The US Marines who were sent as part of this force were duly withdrawn in September but returned before the end of the month to help stabilize the very disturbed situation which had developed in Beirut following the assassination of the Lebanese President.

The Marines were assigned to protect Beirut Airport, and lived in their own compound. On October 23 a suicide terrorist attack, consisting of a truck laden with explosives being driven into the compound entry, resulted in the death or injury of hundreds of Marines. Although locations beyond Beirut sheltering anti-government militias were attacked by

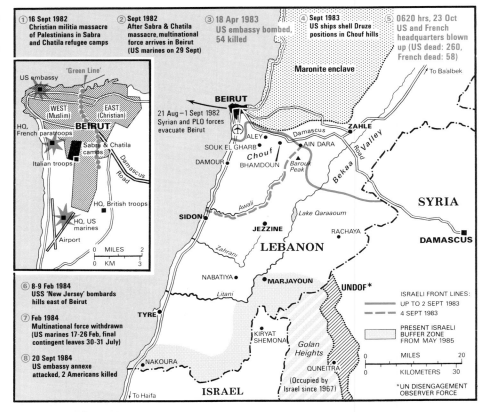

① **16 Sept 1982** Christian militia massacre of Palestinians in Sabra and Chatila refugee camps

② **Sept 1982** After Sabra & Chatila massacre, multinational force arrives in Beirut (US marines on 29 Sept)

③ **18 Apr 1983** US embassy bombed, 54 killed

④ **Sept 1983** US ships shell Druze positions in Chouf hills

⑤ **0620 hrs, 23 Oct** US and French headquarters blown up (US dead: 260, French dead: 58)

⑥ **8-9 Feb 1984** USS 'New Jersey' bombards hills east of Beirut

⑦ **Feb 1984** Multinational force withdrawn (US marines 17-26 Feb, final contingent leaves 30-31 July)

⑧ **20 Sept 1984** US embassy annexe attacked, 2 Americans killed

ISRAELI FRONT LINES:
UP TO 2 SEPT 1983
4 SEPT 1983
PRESENT ISRAELI BUFFER ZONE FROM MAY 1985
*UN DISENGAGEMENT OBSERVER FORCE

US aircraft, and shelled by US warships, American public opinion was unwilling to risk further lives in an intractable sectarian quarrel, and it was not long before US forces were withdrawn. The last elements of the international force left in April 1984.

MAP above: *US involvement in Lebanon.*
Left: *Ruins of the US Embassy, Beirut.*
MAP above right: *The Grenada operation.*
Right: *Cuban prisoners under guard at Point Salines airfield.*

INTERVENTION IN GRENADA

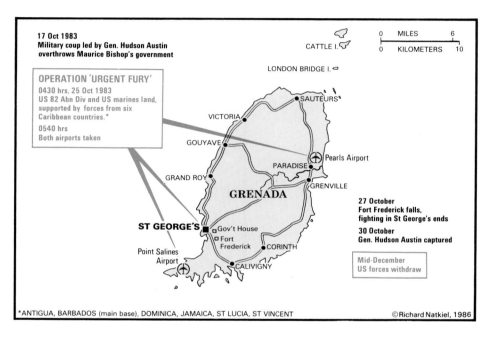

17 Oct 1983
Military coup led by Gen. Hudson Austin overthrows Maurice Bishop's government

OPERATION 'URGENT FURY'
0430 hrs, 25 Oct 1983
US 82 Abn Div and US marines land, supported by forces from six Caribbean countries.*
0540 hrs
Both airports taken

CATTLE I.

0 MILES 6
0 KILOMETERS 10

LONDON BRIDGE I.

SAUTEURS

VICTORIA

GOUYAVE

PARADISE — Pearls Airport

GRAND ROY

GRENVILLE

GRENADA

27 October
Fort Frederick falls, fighting in St George's ends

30 October
Gen. Hudson Austin captured

ST GEORGE'S ■ Gov't House
Fort Frederick

Point Salines Airport

CORINTH

CALIVIGNY

Mid-December
US forces withdraw

*ANTIGUA, BARBADOS (main base), DOMINICA, JAMAICA, ST LUCIA, ST VINCENT

©Richard Natkiel, 1986

The US Invades

After gaining its independence within the British Commonwealth, the former colony of Grenada endured a troubled political situation which by 1983 had resulted in a moderate Marxist government. In October 1983 the more extreme elements in this government launched a coup in which the prime minister was killed and the insurgents took control.

The US government, already troubled by the existence of a leftwing government here, and additionally alarmed by the knowledge that Cuban workers were helping to build a new airport in Grenada, decided to intervene. The first landings were quietly undertaken by special-task naval 'Seals,' and the main assault took place at dawn on 25 October, when US Marines were helicoptered in to take control of Pearls Airport. An hour later, Army Rangers parachuted on to the new airport in the south. Here, at Point Salines, there was considerable resistance, largely from the Cubans, but the airport was under US control by the end of the day. Meanwhile, in the afternoon, Marines came ashore near the capital, St George's, and took Fort Frederick and the prison as a prelude to entering the town. On 26 October the whole island was brought under US control. It had been a short operation, and only 18 Americans were killed. If 400 men contributed by neighboring Caribbean governments are included, the total number of troops used was only about 6500.

LIBYA AND TERRORISM

The Terrorist Threat

Well before 27 December 1985, when five US civilians were killed in terrorist attacks on Rome and Vienna airports, American anger over terrorism had been building up, focusing on Colonel Moamer Qadhafi of Libya, a violent advocate of anti-American terrorism. On 24 March 1986 Libya fired at US aircraft flying legally over the Gulf of Sirte, below Qadhafi's 'line of death' (32° 30′N). The Americans retaliated, destroying at least three Libyan patrol boats.

On 5 April a bomb credited to Libya exploded in a West Berlin nightclub, killing one American and injuring hundreds more. This was seen as the proverbial last straw, and early on 15 April the US launched a two-pronged attack on Libya. Fifteen A-6 aircraft from the carriers *Coral Sea* and *America* struck near Benghazi, while 18 British-based F-111s hit three targets in Tripoli. One F-111 was lost in the raids, and hundreds of Libyans were killed or injured, many of them civilians. Qadhafi offered no immediate reprisals.

MAP: *US attacks Libya, April 1986.*

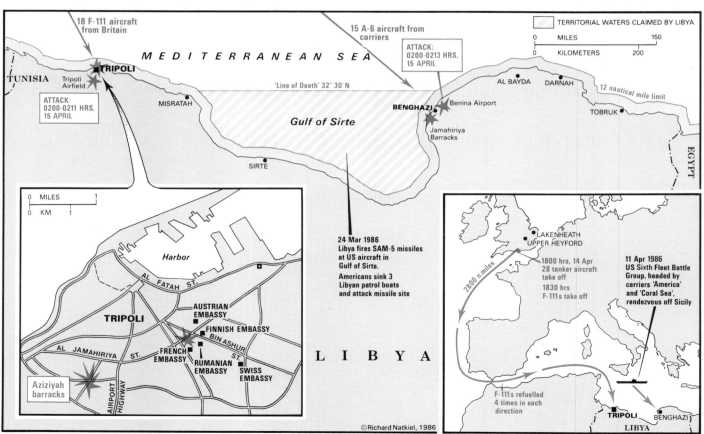

18 F-111 aircraft from Britain

15 A-6 aircraft from carriers

ATTACK: 0200-0213 HRS, 15 APRIL

TERRITORIAL WATERS CLAIMED BY LIBYA

MILES 0 — 150
KILOMETERS 0 — 200

MEDITERRANEAN SEA

TUNISIA

TRIPOLI
Tripoli Airfield

ATTACK: 0200-0211 HRS, 15 APRIL

MISRATAH

'Line of Death' 32° 30′N

Gulf of Sirte

SIRTE

AL BAYDA   DARNAH

12 nautical mile limit

BENGHAZI   Benina Airport

Jamahiriya Barracks

TOBRUK

EGYPT

L I B Y A

24 Mar 1986
Libya fires SAM-5 missiles at US aircraft in Gulf of Sirte.

Americans sink 3 Libyan patrol boats and attack missile site

Tripoli inset

MILES 0 — 1
KM 0 — 1

Harbor

AL FATAH ST.

TRIPOLI

AL JAMAHIRIYA ST.

AUSTRIAN EMBASSY
FINNISH EMBASSY
BIN ASHUR ST.
FRENCH EMBASSY
RUMANIAN EMBASSY
SWISS EMBASSY

Aziziyah barracks

AIRPORT HIGHWAY

Europe/Mediterranean inset

LAKENHEATH
UPPER HEYFORD

2800 n.miles

1800 hrs, 14 Apr
28 tanker aircraft take off

1830 hrs
F-111s take off

11 Apr 1986
US Sixth Fleet Battle Group, headed by carriers 'America' and 'Coral Sea', rendezvous off Sicily

F-111s refuelled 4 times in each direction

TRIPOLI   BENGHAZI
LIBYA

©Richard Natkiel, 1986

Index

Numbers in *italics* refer to illustrations.

Acknowledgments

The publisher would like to thank Adrian Hodgkins who designed the book and Penny Murphy who compiled the index, as well as the following agencies which supplied the illustrations:

Bison Picture Library: pages 2-3, 35, 38, 43, 50, 77, 96-7(bottom), 96, 98-9, 102-3, 110(top), 111, 113(both), 115, 117, 128, 128-9 (top), 132-3(top), 137, 141, 148, 152, 156, 157
Anne SK Brown: pages 13(top), 42, 45
Imperial War Museum, London: pages 85, 108, 144
Library of Congress: pages 7, 13(bottom), 16(bottom), 23, 24, 26-7, 29(bottom), 33, 34, 39(top), 56(bottom), 61, 63
National Army Museum, London: pages 10, 17(both), 19, 25(bottom)
National Maritime Museum, London: page 21(right)
Naval Historical Foundation, Washington DC: page 27(top)
Peter Newark's Western Americana: pages 8(both), 14, 16(top), 27(bottom), 28, 39(bottom)
New Orleans Museum of Art: page 29 (top)
New York Public Library Picture Collection: page 52
Smithsonian Institute, National Anthropological Archives: page 59(left)
Texas State Library, Austin, Texas: page 30
US Air Force: pages 89, 99, 100(both), 125, 132-3(bottom), 136(both), 138
US Army: pages 83(both), 86-7, 88, 110(bottom), 121(bottom), 134, 145, 146, 147, 149(bottom), 153(top), 154
US Marines: pages 135, 140-1, 143, 149(top), 150
US National Archives: pages 1, 9, 18, 32, 56(top), 59(right), 62, 65, 67(both), 68, 69, 71, 73(both), 79, 81, 90, 91, 92-3, 96-7(top), 103, 119, 121(top), 126-7, 128-9(bottom), 130, 134-5
US Naval Historical Center: pages 8(top), 20, 21(left), 25(top)
US Navy: pages 4-5, 153(bottom), 155
Virginia State Library: page 41
VMI Museum: pages 36, 44
Yale University Art Gallery: pages 14-15